194X

Architecture, Landscape, and American Culture Series
Katherine Solomonson and Abigail A. Van Slyck, Series Editors

Medicine by Design The Architect and the Modern Hospital, 1893–1943
Annmarie Adams

194X Architecture, Planning, and Consumer Culture on the American Home Front
Andrew M. Shanken

A Manufactured Wilderness
Summer Camps and the Shaping of American Youth, 1890–1960
Abigail A. Van Slyck

The Architecture of Madness Insane Asylums in the United States
Carla Yanni

194X

Architecture, Planning, and Consumer Culture on the American Home Front

Andrew M. Shanken

Architecture, Landscape, and American Culture Series

UNIVERSITY OF MINNESOTA PRESS
MINNEAPOLIS • LONDON

The University of Minnesota Press gratefully acknowledges the financial assistance
provided for the publication of this book from the Publications Fund,
Department of Art and Archaeology, Princeton University.

Published by the University of Minnesota Press
111 Third Avenue South, Suite 290
Minneapolis, MN 55401-2520
http://www.upress.umn.edu

Printed in the United States of America on acid-free paper

Library of Congress Cataloging-in-Publication Data

Shanken, Andrew Michael, 1968–
194X : architecture, planning, and consumer culture on the American home front /
Andrew M. Shanken.
p.   cm. – (Architecture, Landscape, and American Culture series)
Includes bibliographical references (p.   ) and index.
ISBN 978-0-8166-5365-2 (hc : alk. paper) – ISBN 978-0-8166-5366-9 (pb : alk. paper)
1. Architecture and society–United States–History–20th century.   2. Architecture–United
States–Planning.   3. Architecture–United States–History–20th century.   4. City planning–
United States–History–20th century.   5. United States–Social conditions–1945–
I. Title.   II. Title: Architecture, planning, and consumer culture on the American home front.
NA2543.S6S53   2009
307.1'216097309045–dc22
2008043154

18 17 16 15 14 13 12 11 10 09   10 9 8 7 6 5 4 3 2 1

CONTENTS

Preface

Serendipity launched *194X: Architecture, Planning, and Consumer Culture on the American Home Front* in 1996, but events have overtaken it, dragging it into the twenty-first century. In the process of researching and writing this book, a cultural industry has grown up around World War II that parallels the American interest in the Civil War. Not only has academia lavished attention on the period but newspapers, the History Channel, Hollywood, and nonfiction writing have devoted a staggering amount of attention to the ever-widening moment between the Depression and the Cold War. I began this project by calling World War II a hinge between these two longer and more elaborated eras. Since then, I have observed the fiftieth anniversary of World War II and the Holocaust; encountered the second wave of memory wars in the academy, much of which emanates from the reconsideration of World War II; followed debates over the national memorial to World War II in Washington, D.C.; watched *Saving Private Ryan* and *Pearl Harbor* – just to scratch the surface of this national obsession. The hinge has grown loose, and to stretch this already burdened metaphor, the door will not shut properly anymore on World War II.

In spite of this interest, scholars have missed some of the fundamental experience of the home front. First, 194X, a term the home front invented as the architectural equivalent to V-Day, reflected a spirit of anticipation that powerfully influenced the mood of the moment. When architects and planners offered up visions of what postwar buildings and cities might look like, they took part in a much larger cultural lean toward the future. The war followed an earlier, and arguably darker, era of anticipation in the Depression. One of the most important cultural currents of both the Depression and the war years, anticipation (forecasting, yearning, planning: the name changes with the writer and audience) goes virtually unexamined in the scholarship. This temporal fact of this period deserves its due. Anticipation colored the thought and language of economics, the social sciences, big business, popular culture, and consumer culture, all of which profoundly affected architecture. This book situates architecture in the shared vocabulary of these pursuits and particularly in the shared temporal imagination.

Second, little of the work on World War II takes on architecture or urban planning as its primary subject, in part because much of the architecture on the home front took the form of ephemera and the "unbuilt," a paper architecture buried in archives and magazines, unexecuted urban plans, and pamphlets. In moments when anticipation intensifies—and nonmilitary building declines—the role of images as didactic, instructive, therapeutic, and practical also intensifies. The print media and advertising, even in the midst of paper shortages, experienced creative explosions during the war that coincided with a restless moment for architecture, when the field was undergoing tremendous change. Other scholars have explored the growth of advertising and its role in the war, an amazing story of propaganda and patriotism. But a broader cultural history that frames architecture and planning in its cultural and rhetorical context, including advertising, is still lacking.

In this moment, planning became a kind of cultural mantra, repeated endlessly by architects and captains of industry, in the press and advertisements, by government agencies, and in political and economic circles. Experts from these many fields lumped the various distinct types of planning—urban, regional, social, national, and even individual acts of planning—into one great phenomenon that defies easy explanation but which, I argue, is essential to understanding American culture between the Depression and the Cold War. The home front embraced planning as a panacea in so many contexts and with such force that we must wrestle with it as a cultural phenomenon, not a narrow emission rising from academia, public policy, a particular professional group, or the cracks in mainline American culture. For a brief moment (if fifteen years is brief!) planning became normative, tested out as the bedrock assumption. Although this bid for a planned society failed, should we neglect its failure as inevitable we shall learn nothing from it.

Acknowledgments

I have often felt a strong wind at my back, from supportive mentors and colleagues, both in and outside art history: At Haverford and Bryn Mawr Colleges, Barbara Miller Lane, Ellen Stroud, Roger Lane, Carol Hager, Jeff Cohen, and Dan Gillis. At Princeton, Patricia Brown, Dorothea Dietrich, Ted Champlin, Linda Mahler, Rebecca Graves, Susan Lehre, and Diane Schulte. John Pinto went many centuries out of his way to advise me. His wry sense of humor, support, and guidance repeatedly buoyed both the project and my spirits. Cynthia Field mentored me through research at the Smithsonian. Michael Lewis has served *in loco adviseris,* reading drafts and acting as a one-man postdoctoral continuing-education program.

This book has profited from the tireless and often anonymous work of archivists and librarians: Tony Wrenn and later Nancy Hadley at the American Institute of Architects; Judy Throm, Eva Krider, and others at the Archives of American Art; Bill Hooper at the Time, Inc., Archives; Janet Parks, Curator of Drawings and Archives at the Avery Archives and a trusted counsel and friend; Paul Chénier at the Canadian Centre for Architecture in Montreal; the staff at the Archives Center at the National Museum of American History; Jim Roan at the library of the National Museum of American History; Andreas Nutz at the Vitra Design Museum; the archivists and librarians at the Hagley Museum and Archives; and the archivists and librarians at the Syracuse University Archives, the Cornell University Archives, and the Architectural Archives of the University of Pennsylvania, especially William Whitaker, whose insights have been invaluable.

The project has been supported generously by grants from the Smithsonian Institution, the Center for the Advanced Study of the Visual Arts (CASVA), the Getty Grant Program, the Institute for Advanced Study and the Canadian Centre for Architecture, a Committee on Research Grant at Berkeley, a Regents Junior Faculty Fellowship from the University of California, a National Endowment for the Humanities Summer Stipend, a Grant-in-Aid from Oberlin College, as well as grants from Princeton University.

Many people have weighed in, from Larry Bird and Charles McGovern at the Smithsonian Institution, to John Wilmerding, Esther Da Costa Meyer, Christine Boyer, and Robert Judson Clark at Princeton University. Mary Woods, Gabrielle Esperdy, Jonathan Massey, David Smiley, Annabel Wharton, Carol Krinsky, Sandy Isenstadt, Barry Bergdoll, Jackson Lears, Donald Albrecht, and Alan Brinkley all provided important criticism. Kathleen James read a draft of the first chapter I wrote; as Kathleen James-Chakraborty, she read much more and pointed me to the University of Minnesota Press. Her support has been pivotal, her presence at Berkeley missed. Kathleen Moran and Richard Hutson, Paul Emmons, Barry Bergdoll, Paula Lupkin, and Philip Goad all allowed parts of this book to be tested in public lectures. Kate Solomonson has been an extraordinary reader and editor.

At Oberlin College, Erik Inglis and Heather Galloway, Julie and Ray Davis, John Pearson and Audra Skuodas, Susan Kane, Barb Prior, Michael Henle, Cynthia Comer, Gwendolyn Love, and Joseph Romano all gave of themselves generously, as did William Hood, who provided the icebreaker that allowed me to move from dissertation to book. David Brownlee at the University of Pennsylvania taught me, gave me my first job teaching, and has been a stalwart supporter of this project and me. Susan Solomon shared her knowledge of Louis I. Kahn, her house, and her friendship. At Berkeley, I thank Marc Treib, Paul Groth, Nicholas de Monchaux, Waverly Lowell, Elizabeth Byrne, Maryly Snow, Steven Brooks and the AVRL staff, and my brilliant research assistants Avigail Sachs, Melissa Smith, Cecilia Chu, and Kristina Nugent.

To the people with whom I have been closest these years, who have nurtured the other parts of my life and without whom this book would be impossible: Michael Elowitz, Benjamin Friedman, Stephen Mihm, Jon Castro, Rose Lurie, Laurie Mittenthal, Amy Riesner, Sepideh Ravahi, Christy Gruber, Geneviève Dalpé, my brothers Eddie and Ben, my parents, and my wife, Vika Teicher.

A special thanks to Simon Breines, who at ninety-seven was the oldest person I interviewed. He opened his papers to me and talked for hours with stunning recall, sharing his recollections of the period and personalities, most of whom he knew intimately. Simon died on the day of our last interview and with him went the final living testimony of the architecture of 194X. He embodied its optimism to the end.

Introduction: Planning the Postwar Architect

This is a book about planning, specifically the culture surrounding planning during World War II in the United States and particularly its intersection with architecture and consumer culture. Actual master plans play a negligible role, as do buildings. Rather, it is a cultural history of home front anticipation that takes the intertwined realms of architecture, planning, and consumer culture as its point of departure and views the intersection through the experience of the architectural profession. Almost from the moment the war ended the Depression, Americans began to forecast the world after the war. Buildings and cities provided vivid material for speculation, and architects posed as expert prognosticators. *Architectural Forum,* one of the leading architectural magazines of the day, invented the term 194X to describe this wartime anticipation of postwar architecture and urbanism, a kind of V-Day for the built environment.

Visions of the future proliferated during the war as part of a culture of planning, best understood through an image created by the architects Oscar Stonorov and Louis I. Kahn in 1944 (Figure I.1).[1] Stonorov and Kahn charted planning in its many varieties into a series of concentric rings, growing from house planning to national planning. They represent one grand historical force, organically connected through resources and the social, economic, and political energies that link the local with the national. The diagram expresses what one architect during the war called "total planning," the home front analogue to total war.[2] Stonorov and Kahn's use of planning transcended narrow professional or technical definitions. Geography and the city were essential but insufficient elements of their vision, as were land use, resources management, politics, economics, recreation, social factors, regionalism, and local activism. From the family, "healthy, secure and busy," to the nation, a single swelling movement, almost mystical in nature, takes hold and gives shape to American culture, growing out of the people at the base of the image.

That force, I argue, was Stonorov and Kahn's attempt to distill the culture of planning into a diagram that could be understood by anyone. For if such a collectivist vision were to take root in the United States, the architects believed, it would do so through the

Figure I.1. Louis I. Kahn, diagram of planning, 1944–45. Reprinted with permission of the Louis I. Kahn Collection, University of Pennsylvania, and the Pennsylvania Historical and Museum Commission.

people, acting to develop an inchoate form of democratic planning. This vision took on both national and international meaning. As an intensely planned activity, war generalized and naturalized planning, putting the essentially specialist term, associated with city and regional planning, into wider circulation. Total war (and its equivalent in resources management) made planning universal, linking individual acts of restraint with national and wartime planning. The stakes, amid the rise of fascism in Europe and the growing power of Soviet Communism, both of which relied on famous three- and five-year plans, can scarcely be overstated. Individual acts of planning were thus implicitly linked with changes of world-historical importance.

With these international models of planning as the backdrop, Americans rooted around for answers to similar social and economic problems. The United States had suffered through a decade of depression in the 1930s, which some critics considered a permanent plateau of the business cycle, if not the more ominous end to corporate capitalism.

Only through collective action, many architects and planners came to believe, would the nation right itself. Stonorov and Kahn thus charted more than a gestalt vision of planning; they created a structure for responsible collective action in a world looking beyond capitalism.

The Architect-Planner

Stonorov and Kahn were not alone. Their confreres happily jettisoned many of the traditional roles of architects, including as form-givers and designers of those discrete art objects called buildings, and repositioned themselves as architect-planners, world-makers, and organizers of vast activities, materials, and geographical regions. As William Lescaze, the important Swiss-trained modernist who practiced in the United States after 1920, wrote: "If we are not the 'Master Builders' of old, let us be sure that we are the *master planners*."[3] Unexpectedly, this proposed transformation would be partly negotiated through alliances with big business. Why did architects shift turf during the war and stake claims on planning? And why did many of the most compelling visions of 194X emerge out of advertising and promotion? In part, they turned to planning and advertising as a way of saving a profession that had been beaten down by a decade of depression and war. These conditions not only softened up the profession to reconsider its identity but also awakened it to the necessity of public relations, overturning long-standing prohibitions against certain forms of architectural advertising.

In the 1930s and 1940s, architects groused over the many threats to their profession, including old enemies, such as builders, contractors, and engineers, and new ones, especially government and corporate design bureaus. Industrial engineers posed a special threat, as their work branding and streamlining products for major corporations spilled over into high-profile architectural commissions. Industrial designers like Walter Dorwin Teague and Norman Bel Geddes dominated the expositions of the 1930s. Hal Burnett, a trained architect who went on to become a publicist—most prominently at the 1934–35 Century of Progress Exposition in Chicago—likened the architectural profession to the conquered nations of Europe, "totally unprepared to meet and master the various streamlined, panzer-like movements that have rolled in to capture the cream of building profits."[4]

The New Deal presented a threat of a different sort. Agencies like the Public Works Administration, the Works Progress Administration, and the Resettlement Administration brought in waves of architects as draftsmen and site planners, but they also altered the terms of practice. The Supervising Architect's Office of the United States quickly became the largest architectural office in the world, promising architects some relief from Depression conditions. According to American Institute of Architects (AIA) President R. H. Shreve, architects, having lost as much as 90 percent of their building opportunities because of the Depression, hungrily accepted this government work.[5] The evolving arrangement, however, came with new conditions and restrictions.[6] Architects repeatedly cried foul over the office's hiring practices. More importantly, their largest employer had become a federal bureaucracy run by politicians and economists or by the local governments that carried out much of the New Deal work. Moreover, they were thrown into large-scale projects with "experts" from a range of fields, a forced collaboration from on high that threatened their creative and professional autonomy.

As the approach of World War II brought the moribund economy to life, sparking production, circulating capital, and melting unemployment lines, it also brought the economy under increasingly tight control. Rationing and restrictions on nonmilitary building came in waves, as did conversion to war production. By the time the United States entered the war, architects had enjoyed an all-too-brief window of activity, a short burst of private building in those months before Pearl Harbor when American neutrality slowly eroded and the economy found its legs again in supplying the Allies. While full employment all but ended the Depression for the average American, for architects, war meant a return to privation. *Pencil Points* critic Talbot Hamlin referred to the "rude shock" of the priorities order of late 1941, which began restricting use of vital materials and curtailed all nonmilitary building. He gloomily added: "Draftsmen and architects who have been busy and hopeful are suddenly workless and perturbed."[7] New York architect Eugene Raskin painted an even bleaker picture of the postwar era. If the Allies were to win, he predicted, the government would be the primary patron of architecture: "The private citizen, as is already becoming evident, will stand little chance of building for purely private purposes. You will do well to get into some field where activity is likely — defense housing, factories, camps, fortifications, etc. . . . You can forget about private practice," a forecast he extended indefinitely into the postwar future.[8] Even ambitious and talented architects like Oscar Stonorov struggled during the war. In spite of taking in some important emergency war housing in Pennsylvania, Stonorov repeatedly tried to enlist because work was so slow.[9]

War jolted an already vulnerable profession into a state of crisis. The initial infusion of war-related work tapered off quickly. By 1944, "total building construction had been curtailed to a third of the 1941 rate, a level matched only by the bleakest years of the Great Depression."[10] Thirty percent of all architects served in the armed forces, but only 39 percent of them, according to a survey of the AIA, performed some duty related to architecture. Of the remaining 70 percent left on the home front, only 29 percent found work in architecture.[11] War darkened the mood considerably. Charles Maginnis, president of the AIA from 1937 to 1940, wrote in 1944: "Things are disturbing the leisure of the professional mind. The architect is not happy. . . . Swarms of disembodied engineers move across his dreams, bearing awful implication of his submergence in the impending scheme of things."[12] Architect J. Woolson Brooks wrote: "By its own admission, the Profession of Architecture is sick, so sick that its members see imaginary vultures hovering over the body even before the undertaker has been called."[13] Brooks observed that architects were bound together "by a persecution mania instead of by zeal to fulfill their destiny of creating a better world."[14] Howard Myers, the publisher of *Architectural Forum*, wrote that architects had been fending off threats on their "professional monopoly" for years. First it was the engineer, then the contractor, then the "brotherhood of streamliners, the industrial engineers. . . . And now a fourth threat appears in those mystical gentlemen known as city planners."[15]

Architects fared poorly at placing themselves in key wartime design and building positions. The war, as an immensely complex orchestration of shuttling human beings around the globe, housing and training them, erecting defenses, and supplying troops with the material and shelter they needed in order to fight, was an architectural and planning exercise of unprecedented magnitude. Yet architects struggled to convince the armed forces of their utility, while engineers or builders received the lion's share of this work. The dilemma centered on the architect's reputation for being too artistic and individualistic, both liabilities in war. By contrast, the engineer was seen as practical, technical, and able to follow orders, the perfect foot soldier for building projects strained by the exigencies of war.

To advocate for the profession, the AIA sent D. K. Este Fisher, a Baltimore architect and planner, to Washington in 1942. At the annual AIA convention in 1943, Fisher delivered news that architects already knew well: "To put the matter very bluntly, observation in Washington seems to indicate that the architect is not a person in great demand in these times. We are being classed with bond salesmen and aesthetic dancers as of little conceivable use in the War effort, except perhaps as draftsmen."[16] "Architecture," he continued, "is looked on as a refuge of dilettantes, any of whom do not require their professional income for their living, and are generally not anxious to get their shoes muddy."[17] Trying to stir up his fellow designers, he wrote: "Too many 'employers' in Washington, and perhaps in the industrial centers, think we are half-baked engineers—artistic, impractical, unreliable, not a little bull-headed and over-bearing: even 'sissy' in comparison with the 'tough' engineer."[18]

Kenneth Reid, the editor of *Pencil Points*, had already voiced similar concerns shortly after the war began: "*[T]he profession must have leaders*—leaders who are not victims of the disease of appeasement, leaders who are not hamstrung by diffidence, leaders *of undeniable maleness* who are bold and forthright and stoutly aggressive."[19] He called for the emergence of "Architectural Man," a new professional type who traded in the soft sensibility of the artist for the muscle of the planner. The readership cheered Reid on with letters to the editor, including a cartoon of "architectural man" drawn by Royal Barry Wills, the popularizer of the Cape Cod house (Figure I.2).[20] Wills's cartoon gave a martial cast to the idea when he urged the architect-planner to take up a hammerlike t-square, cast aside the "silk hat and gardenia" of his foppish past "and beat hell out of everybody." At the same time, Ayn Rand novelized a similar image of "architectural man" in the character Howard Roark, whose taut, muscled body and relentlessly rational cast of mind cut the figure of an architect-warrior who had sloughed off the sentimental trappings of architectural practice—which paralleled his molting of architectural ornament.[21]

Figure I.2. Royal Barry Wills, cartoon in *Pencil Points* 23 (June 1942): 8. Courtesy of Penton Media.

Toward a Modern Profession

Warranted or not, this reputation reflected something in the structure of the profession. Even in the 1940s, architects were caught between paradigms of professionalization that were defined on the one hand by its more successful and mature cousins, law and medicine, and on the other hand by shifts in consumer culture that challenged much of the foundation of the disinterested authority of expertise in architecture.[22] The common refrain that architecture operates as an "old boys' network" is really a comment about the structure of authority in the profession. Such networks of prerogative emerged out of the conditions of nineteenth-century urban culture, in particular the associations, historical societies, library companies, and clubs that fostered mutual exchange between learned gentlemen.[23] A more formal institutional framework began to mature in the twentieth century, based in the university and in professional associations—as opposed to intellectual associations. The AIA took root during the reign of the first paradigm, as a club, and, essentially, a men's club. The character of the early AIA lay somewhere between an association of mechanics, like the Philadelphia Carpenters Company, and a learned society with vague professional ambitions, but before professional ideals in architecture were clear or had the institutional support of universities and a system of national accreditation.[24] Over the next century, architects would build much of this institutional infrastructure. Yet even in the 1940s, the AIA floated in the still water between tides. The romance of the old gentleman's club enjoyed by a nineteenth-century urban cultural elite marked the culture of American architects deep into the twentieth century, long after mature models of professionalization had been richly articulated.

One of the major cultural dilemmas for architecture going back to the mid-nineteenth century, when the AIA formed, was straightforward, if nettlesome – it was also one of the central questions for cultural elites in the same period: How does a group find cohesion in a society of strangers?[25] The professional dilemma added a wrinkle to the question: How does a group of strangers bound by a common practice establish its authority in a quickly nationalizing economy of consumers and impersonal corporations? Even in the mid-twentieth century, architecture had still not found a persuasive and abiding answer to that question, nor had it created the internal means to assert, regulate, and publicize that authority. Of course, within most cities, architects cultivated clients in their own community or social group. The anonymity of mass society in cities spawned what Thomas Bender has referred to as "closed social cells," and for architects these could be tremendously important circles for commissions and for building a reputation.[26] But beyond these groups, architecture had not secured for itself the authority of medicine or law because it had failed to construct the national institutional framework out of which an anonymous authority could grow. For doctors, this entailed a tight nexus between universities, hospitals, and credentialing, with the American Medical Association presiding over it and acting as the font of public relations. The legislation that brought doctors a monopoly over medical practice, abolishing mountebanks and other health providers, gave that nexus a national profile and granted it the external authority of the government.

By contrast, architects established their academic perch relatively late, and the nexus surrounding it proved comparatively fragile. The architectural firm, for instance, pales before the role of the hospital, and the AIA shrank from its bureaucratic role of power broker, lobby group, and proselytizer until the postwar decades. Instead of the AIA, other commercial forces stepped in to assume some of these roles. *Sweet's Catalog* and *Dodge Reports* came to supply important information on new products, building codes, and forecasting, at the same time taming and regulating the flow of architectural and building information and knowledge.[27] Instead of a forceful journal as the mouthpiece of the profession, architecture had a shifting number of commercial architectural magazines, the *Octagon*, a glorified newsletter until it became the *Journal of the AIA* in 1944, least among them. Instead of a single professional body that could pull the influence and dues of all architects and harmonize them into one voice as a lobby group and supply concerted public relations, architects splintered into state and local societies, while the AIA struggled until after World War II to consolidate its membership on a national scale. In 1940, only 3,100 of the nearly 20,000 architects that show up in the U.S. Census belonged to the AIA.[28] Some of this failure has to do with the nature of architectural practice itself, with its double life in art and technique, in affairs cultural and matters practical; but some of it stems from a simple inability to perceive or respond to the changing social structure and the place of architecture within it—the partial blindness caused by an old paradigm blocking the new one from full view.

American planners, by contrast, had an even later start and, owing to the diversity of their education, training, and professional accreditation in architecture, landscape architecture, engineering, economics, and law, had an even more tenuous purchase on professional organization. The profession arose as part of the Progressive Era's response to the urban conditions that accompanied industrialization in the nineteenth century.[29] The National Conference on City Planning (NCCP) formed in 1910, a year after the first conference of its kind in the United States. The first journal, *The City Plan,* appeared in 1915. By any measure, the planning profession in this period was tiny. A small group of planners such as John Nolen, Frederick Law Olmsted Jr., and Harland Bartholomew dominated the field through the mid-1920s, when regional planning and a host of new planning organizations began to alter the professional landscape.[30] The American City Planning Institute (ACPI), the counterpart to the AIA, had a mere twenty-one members in 1917 when it formed. By 1940, it had grown to eighty-nine members, seventeen associates, and forty-three junior members *in the entire country.*[31] With the war, the ACPI suspended its main organ, *The Planners' Journal,* and all but ceased operation.[32]

From Architecture Culture to a Culture of Planning

Architects opportunistically thrust themselves into this vacuum. D. K. Este Fisher pitched planning as the natural domain of the architect and made it the centerpiece of his lobbying campaign in Washington, D.C. In 1943, the AIA's annual convention in Cincinnati took up planning as its theme, and the organization set up local committees to ready plans for postwar cities and towns under the auspices of Walter R. MacCornack's Committee on Postwar Reconstruction. In early 1944, the AIA encouraged the use of a new wartime emblem, a striped stamp with three horizontal bands, evocative of the American flag (Figure I.3).[33] The old seal of the AIA, a heraldic eagle fanning its wings in front of a Doric column, centered the design, but "PLAN NOW" ran across the bottom band, urging the profession toward its new identity. While some of this amounted to little more than posturing or desperation, many architects did not distinguish between architecture and planning and believed that architecture deserved some special place at the table.[34] The École des Beaux-Arts and the Bauhaus alike emphasized the importance of rational planning, and both extended the value from the microcosm of the individual building to the macrocosm of the city. Planning, in other words, offered common ground in a moment of clashing modes of pedagogy, practice, and taste.

Editors of architectural magazines altered copy, invented new formats, and in one case, even attempted to change a magazine's name to resonate with the culture of planning. Kenneth Reid set out to transform *Pencil Points* into a forum for his new "Architectural Man." Realizing that "the magazine of the drafting room," the magazine's subtitle, no

Figure I.3. Plan Now, American Institute of Architects seal from World War II, from cover of *A.I.A. Bulletin: Official Notice to Members* 2 (April 1944). Courtesy of Syracuse University Archives.

longer fit the times, Reid announced a competition in June 1942 for a new name, offering a $500 U.S. war bond to the winner. Twenty-six of the 344 entries chose the name "Plan," overwhelming evidence that the readership understood and supported the new editorial direction of the magazine and of its advertising. A Columbus, Ohio, architect named Harry J. Nichols won the prize for his explanation of why "Plan" best suited the magazine. In addition to being "modern, terse, active, alive and prophetic," "the word 'PLAN,' alone," he reasoned, "will be one of the most important words in American usage during the remainder of the war period—and even more important in the postwar period."[35] "Plan" was not merely a cultural ethos in the making, "It was an architect's word—the one most important word in his vocabulary—the word he uses most—the word that most completely describes his place in America's social, cultural and economic patterns."[36] To Nichols, the architect had become a planner, and *Pencil Points* represented the new calling best.

"Plan," however appropriate, did not stick because another publication had the name copyrighted. In fact, in 1943 there were at least four other English-language publications with the name "Plan," and another four in Russian, Bulgarian, German, and Spanish. But Reid would not be deterred from his mission. He wrote: "'PLAN' as a guiding spirit for our editorial course, however, is very much a reality. We see it as the key word—or rather the key idea—of the future, both before the end of the War and after."[37] The editor strategically deployed this keyword to attract advertising at a moment when *Pencil Points* teetered on the edge of bankruptcy.[38] *Architectural Forum* and *Architectural Record* experienced similar conversions to planning in 1942 and 1943. As corporations began to pitch their products in terms of postwar planning, using visionary images of architects and cities, these magazines remade themselves into appropriate visual and ideological landscapes for these ads. Editorial policy reinforced advertising copy, and editors now curried to the architect-planner.

The conversion to planning in the press was part of their continuing sponsorship of architectural modernism.[39] Many of the seminal ideas of the Modern Movement in architecture were carried on in the context of urbanism and in the name of planning. As such, the planning urge adapted the work of the International Congress of Modern Architecture (CIAM) and European modernists to the significantly different context of the American city. The emergence of what one might call violently ambitious plans for the city was of one piece with the emergence in the United States of the Modern Movement itself. For the sake of argument, let me state the case as boldly as possible: World War II made the Modern Movement in America. It suckled its young, organized its minions, and gave it an honorary seat in the boardrooms of corporations that would rule the "American Century." The war also humbled the profession, providing exactly the sort of moment of self-reflection that is necessary for change to take place. But whereas, in the same moment, "New York stole the idea of modern art" from Paris, nothing so concentrated occurred in architecture.[40]

Planning elaborated the Modern Movement's emphasis on the social responsibility of architecture in the 1920s and 1930s. Architects who were stuck on the home front, with few opportunities for service and fewer for design, attempted to reorganize themselves as planners. Louis Kahn, Hugh Stubbins Jr., Carl Koch, Marcel Breuer, and Serge Chermayeff gathered around Joseph Hudnut to form the American Society of Planners and Architects.[41] The ASPA, the first significant attempt to create a professional organization for what Hudnut called the progressive wing of the profession in the United States, took the form of a planning organization. Other more regional groups formed as well: Task in Boston, Telesis in California, and the Commandos (later called Action Group) also in California.[42] All of them attempted to create models for local planning efforts by publishing, creating exhibitions, or researching local conditions. Their devotion to planning demonstrates a level of commitment going beyond the sort of superficial vogue created by the high emotion of war or the opportunism of the building boom. To the contrary, it grew naturally out of long-standing modernist ideals and the experience of the Depression and New Deal.

In architectural writing alone, the war stimulated a small library on planning by leading architects and critics. Books by progressive architects include William Lescaze's *On Being an Architect* (1942) and José Luis Sert's *Can Our Cities Survive? An ABC of Urban Problems, Their Analysis, Their Solutions* (1942), the CIAM contribution to wartime debates on planning; Eliel Saarinen's *The City, Its Growth, Its Decay, Its Future* (1943); Ludwig Hilberseimer's *The New City: Principles of Planning* (1945); and Walter Gropius and László Moholy-Nagy's *Rebuilding Our Communities* (1945). Gropius also contributed to *The Problem of the Cities and Towns* (1942), the proceedings of a conference on urbanism at Harvard. Aesthetic and physical interests in planning mingled with social and economic perspectives: Camillo Sitte's *The Art of Building Cities: City Building According to Its Artistic Fundamentals* was first translated into English during the war, and Lewis Mumford's *City Development: Studies in Disintegration and Renewal* (1945) brought in insights from demography, economics, and other social sciences.[43] Paul Zucker's *The New Architecture and City Planning: A Symposium* (1944) contained articles by many of the brightest lights in architecture and planning. Henry Churchill's *The City Is the People* (1945) made perhaps the most articulate case for urban planning as the foundation of a permanent program of deficit or compensatory spending that would forever modify capitalism.[44] Sigfried Giedion's *Space, Time and Architecture: The Growth of a New Tradition* (1941), while clearly a revisionist history of architecture, devoted its final chapters to urban planning, positioning a mystical form of planning as the culmination of his space-time theory. Paul Goodman and Percival Goodman capped the planning moment with *Communitas,* a book written by a utopian thinker and his architect brother, published in 1946 but a quintessential product of the home front.

This incomplete list doesn't even touch on the mountains of literature published under the aegis of government agencies, private institutions, nonprofits, and business groups, such as the National Resources Planning Board, the Carnegie Foundation, the Twentieth Century Fund, the Chamber of Commerce, the Producers' Council, the AIA, or the hundreds of plans created during the war or soon after that were based on these books and pamphlets. George B. Galloway compiled some of these sources in *Postwar Planning in the United States,* a multivolume series published between 1942 and 1944 that listed organizations involved in planning *of any sort.* Galloway's ecumenical compendium restated Stonorov and Kahn's diagram in list form. Add to these the more strictly political and economic accounts of planning, such as Friedrich A. von Hayek's *The Road to Serfdom* (1944) and Herman Finer's retort, *The Road to Reaction* (1945); Barbara Wootton's *Freedom under Planning* (1945); Ferdynand Zweig's *The Planning of Free Societies* (1942); and Harold Laski's *Will Planning Restrict Freedom?* (1944).[45] These books only begin to demonstrate how ubiquitous the word *planning* became during the war.[46]

All of this ferment would have been significant in and of itself, but it happened within a much wider cultural interest in planning. Big business, bruised from the Great Depression and, in spite of its contributions to the war, not yet redeemed in the public eye, joined architects in seeing urban planning in terms of social responsibility. Dozens of companies concerned themselves with urban planning, either advocating projects in their literature or underwriting specific projects for 194X. The list of companies includes Zurn Plumbing, Janitrol Plumbing, Revere Copper and Brass, Stran-Steel, United States Gypsum, and Alcoa. If we count those companies that conscripted planning for use in their advertising, the list would multiply several times over. The corporate world faced enormous stakes. With predictions that the United States would return to depression after the war and the government preparing to regulate the building industry – the nation's largest – it behooved big business to influence the nature of postwar reconstruction. The threat that the government would shift from war production into public projects, indefinitely extending the New Deal, gravely challenged the laissez-faire basis on which corporate America depended. Corporate interest in sponsoring urban reconstruction emerged out of complex urges, on the one hand driven by a sense of social responsibility in a time of great patriotic fervor, and on the other hand motivated by self-interest and an attempt to preempt public planning projects. As all of these contexts make clear, planning is not just part of culture but a form of culture unto itself, a mode of behavior and a conceptual framework embedded in history. In these roles, planning became one of the keywords of the home front.

Lost Horizons

The Depression and the war, however, turn out to be aberrations in American history. Taken together, they present an extended moment in which an ideal of vast, centralized planning was taken seriously and pursued programmatically. Urban reconstruction on a scale previously unimagined (one never achieved by the piecemeal planning of the postwar decades) rested on a sophisticated and deeply considered base of social and economic planning. Collectivist assumptions naturally colored the planning urge, but one did not need to be a fellow traveler to support epochal changes in social structure and urban form in either period. In the context of what to many seemed to be the collapse of industrial capitalism, and the challenge of foreign "isms," Americans contemplated their own version of a planned society. Charts like Stonorov and Kahn's made it more palatable — linking individual planning to larger national programs — and democratic, rooted in the people. However, outside of economic history and a sparse literature in the history of cities, the anticipatory planning of the home front has been almost elided from the histories of the period.[47] Even David Kennedy's magisterial *Freedom from Fear* (1999) steers clear of reading the war in terms of planning.[48]

We may blame the brevity of the period. Sandwiched between the more sustained periods of the Great Depression and Cold War, two eras with strong rhetorical personalities, the home front has seemed like a time of rhetorical suspension. With the exception of Paul Fussell's accounts of the creative neologisms of the war and, to a lesser extent, the home front, 194X has remained curiously mute, especially in architecture and planning.[49] Consequently, postwar historians, writing through the lens of the Cold War, wove fittingly epic narratives of these two eras while suppressing or ignoring one of its most epic tales: the battle over planning, a contest over the future of democracy and capitalism. To put this in plain terms, Americans and their institutions have tended to choose the self-interest and individualism of the free market over the nationalized model more prevalent in postwar Europe. The faith once put in planning now seems so remote, even obscure, that its historical retrieval faces decades of cavalier indifference or ideological antagonism, a form of silencing fueled by Cold War anxiety, bull market profits, as well as the failures of American attempts at creating a public safety net.

In architecture and planning, these issues ran a similar course. The anticipatory architecture of 194X, the forgotten oeuvre of the war years, remains little known, yet it fills in the blank between the growth of interest in the Modern Movement in the 1930s and its wholesale acceptance in the 1950s. More astonishing, the larger frame of planning and consumer culture in which it rested is virtually forgotten. This frame forces a reconsideration of the hackneyed claims that modernists "sold out" to corporations after the war. This wrongheaded view of modernism misses the very nature of architecture, a promiscuous profession because of its relationship to the market, and perhaps never more so than in the 1930s and 1940s, when professional survival depended on alliances with corporations and government agencies.

Following the lead of many artists in the period, architects eagerly sought commissions in advertising. And why not? The dream was to make the world modern, and ads were often the first place a modernist aesthetic found a popular perch. War, moreover, altered the public's perception of big business. Corporations fought the war with ads and materiel. The conditions of war, in fact, forged bonds between architects and the corporate world through the admen who represented the latter. Corporations had the power to change the world, and many expressed both a sense of social responsibility and a faith in the power of the material world to change society—two ideas that translated well into progressive architecture. The roots of the Modern Movement in architecture, particularly at the Werkbund, had tapped into similar links between industry and design. The ads of World War II recalled the earlier moment, giving architects relatively free reign to express ideas on a broader platform than they had on their own—and this in the context of war, when the profession felt neglected. The ads made architects relevant, positioning them as experts in the context of patriotic pitches for postwar social responsibility. In short, the social mission of the Modern Movement remained very much alive during the war, but the legacy of the Depression and the war itself encouraged a shift in emphasis from social housing to the sort of comprehensive planning of Stonorov and Kahn's diagram.

Since failure often leads to forgetting, the commitments to a planned society in the United States have slipped out of historical consciousness. The following chapters aim in part to resurrect the cultural meaning of planning in the early 1940s, when many Americans had bought into the collectivist ideals on which planning is predicated. The home front waged war, or more accurately, it waged the postwar through a temporal construct of paper architecture, master plans, advertising, and words as two-dimensional representations of what could be after the war. Part of the effort here is to reconstruct the mood of the moment. Chapter 1, "The Culture of Planning: The Rhetoric and Imagery of Home Front Anticipation," examines the rhetoric and imagery around planning in the 1930s and 1940s. A wide range of sources and images gave planning new meaning, including the National Resources Planning Board, and building on this agency's work, Henry Luce's advocacy of planning in *Fortune* magazine. Planning found its way into unexpected domains, including advertising and promotional literature from the building industry, academic writing in psychology and sociology, and family planning. Taken together, they demonstrate the dissemination and changing resonance of planning during the war, when it became a social paradigm, akin to engineering in the nineteenth century, providing a model for thought and behavior as well as for national identity.

Chapter 2, "Old Cities, New Frontiers: Mature Economy Theory and the Language of Renewal," plumbs the economic rhetoric at the base of the culture of planning. Keynesian economics armed architects and planners with a language to discuss urban rehabilitation after the war. Mature economy theory, based on earlier fears of the end of the frontier, proposed that the Depression, rather than being a severe downturn in the business cycle, was a permanent condition, one interrupted temporarily by war. The idea aroused fears that American culture was mature, meant in the pejorative sense of being senescent, having lost its vigor. Rejuvenation necessitated massive socioeconomic and physical restructuring. This chapter explores the cultural meaning of the mature economy theory and shows how it leached into the culture of planning, informing the plans and thinking of Walter Gropius, José Luis Sert, and other architects, as well as influencing the visions of 194X in advertising, the architectural press, and the famous postwar plans for Pittsburgh, now known as Renaissance One.

While the mature economy theory gave planning the authority of the social sciences and created a conceptual tabula rasa for the postwar city, advertising filled it in with visionary images of buildings and cities in 194X. Chapter 3, "Advertising Nothing, Anticipating Nowhere: Architects and Consumer Culture," elaborates the relationship among architecture, planning, and consumer culture through the wartime advertising campaigns of Revere Copper and Brass, U.S. Gypsum, General Electric, and other companies. These campaigns used splendid, original designs by the leading progressive architects of the day, designs in which the architects anticipated the architecture and urban form of 194X. The ads form a discrete and neglected body of work in American architecture, one that fleshes out the moment between the tentative emergence of modernism in the United States in the 1930s and the mainstreaming of modernism in the 1950s.

Chapter 4, "The End of Planning: The Building Boom and the Invention of Normalcy," details the collapse of the culture of planning. The fall of the National Resources Planning Board in 1943 and a strong reaction against planning in Congress and among classical economists undermined the possibility of radical and truly comprehensive planning in the postwar period. The anticipatory advertising of the war came under attack, and a number of new ad campaigns by *Time* magazine, National Gypsum, and other companies arose to discredit first the dream house and then the culture of planning. Even some architect-planners criticized the more visionary strands of postwar planning. By the end of the war, little of the ethos of 194X remained.

Less a linear narrative of events or a storyline with a discernible plot, these chapters create a tale of interwoven short stories. There is no obvious temporal or historical introduction; the plotline does not build through event and action; and the crescendo, if one exists, is more anticlimax. It is a story of failure rather than resolution. What gives this moment coherence is a mode of inquiry and practice that vividly imagined architecture within the larger culture in a vital and integrated way. In turn, this mode of operation created a mood at once fitful and strident, and romantically in search of totality in the midst of fracture. The mood is obvious in the images and keywords of the home front: its creation and its dissipation by the end of 1945 *is* the story.

1 The Culture of Planning

The Rhetoric and Imagery of Home Front Anticipation

Architects embraced planning in the cultural context of the home front, when New Deal, wartime, and postwar planning overlapped. These three forms of planning gave the moment its rhetorical and visual character, filtering widely into American culture and tilting Americans toward the future. The culture of planning emerged out of these specific historical conditions. It reflected a response to the coming of age of urban planning, but it also grew out of the larger crisis of industrial capitalism. The entire western world seemed to be in the throes of a systemic shift marked by, among other things, a move toward centralized planning. The rise of the Soviet Union and of fascism offered up two models of state planning parallel to the New Deal, which presented itself as a middle route out of the crisis. In the United States, many economists and political scientists explained the Depression as a corrective to an intemperate laissez-faire economy. Some form of planning seemed inevitable. Architects turned to planning, in other words, not merely as part of a narrow professional pursuit: they had thrown in their lot with a cultural force of national and international dimensions.

The war, itself the most immediate model of planning for the home front, also seemed to result from the imbalances of modern industrial capitalism. Authors as disparate as Karl Polanyi, Johan Huizinga, and Sigfried Giedion—a political scientist, historian, and art historian—sounded dark notes about the structural causes of the war, linking it to the capitalist order or, much like T. S. Eliot, taking it as evidence of a more profound decline in civilization.[1] These authors and others made an almost mythic pessimism pervasive, tethering the war to capitalism and capitalism to the end of civilization. The experience of the American home front offered a route out of this pessimism, if not an economic model for revising capitalism. Through sacrifice to the greater good, and through one of the most massive planning efforts in history, the United States created an unparalleled war machine and manufactured an unusual sense of social cohesion. Centrally controlled, if by military necessity, wartime planning quickly righted the American economy. It created full employment, distributed vital materials around the world, erected new housing developments and, in some cases, whole cities. Carrying these efforts and attitudes into peacetime America became a common refrain during the war, and planning, a key agent of wartime success and harmony on the home front, became a generalized way of thinking about community and a way out of the crisis itself.

As Americans lived through the transformation from New Deal to wartime to postwar planning, the city served as a site, both literally and abstractly, for thinking through potential socioeconomic, political, and physical changes. The great planning projects of the New Deal, designed as "make work," to boost morale, and to prime the pump of the economy, gave way to a home front flush with work and money and obsessed with planning the postwar world. Wartime writing popularized planning, not merely as a strictly professional or technical pursuit but as a cultural phenomenon. This was, after all, similar to Stonorov and Kahn's goal: to communicate with a broad public about the exigencies of planning everything from a single house to the nation's largest projects, and to demonstrate their interconnectedness (see Figure I.1 in the Introduction). The word *planning* became one of the keywords of the American home front, written endlessly in architectural and governmental literature but also found in less expected places: Henry Luce celebrated planning in the pages of *Fortune* magazine; Erik Erikson imported it for psychology; the newly named Planned Parenthood recast birth control in terms of planning; and advertisements and corporate public relations campaigns put the word before the eyes of millions of Americans. All of these sources inherited their ideas of planning from the New Deal, especially from the work of the National Resources Planning Board (NRPB), a lesser-known New Deal agency that set the rhetorical tone for planning in the 1930s and early 1940s. A centralized clearinghouse of planning ideas, the NRPB willfully played with the word in its literature in the 1930s and 1940s. NRPB planners set up models for urban planning that would have a wide influence in architecture, the media, the social sciences, and advertising, the subjects of this chapter. By the time the war began, the NRPB's campaign, and New Deal planning in general, had been melded into an increasingly broad, complex, and sometimes frivolous culture of planning.

Planning as Culture

As a keyword, planning exhibited figurative qualities, standing in for other ideas, such as the future, better living, comfort, order, and most emphatically, the potential for a radical change in the social structure. As a metaphor, planning implied the coalescence of what George Lakoff and Mark Johnson have called a conceptual framework, a way of understanding the world, much as engineering gave a metaphorical structure to an earlier period.[2] Images and actual plans bolstered the word, spatializing the future, at least in two-dimensional images. Increasingly diffuse usage made planning a cliché, one, to be sure, with many of the drawbacks of a hackneyed term, but also with the density of assumptions of overuse. To put this another way, in addition to being a technical pursuit and a profession, planning is also a figurative activity, a form of representation in which one object or idea stands in for another, but with a temporal twist or lag. This is not to say that plans themselves are not also literal objects. Scholars have attended to them as a visual medium, although they tend to focus on the grand plans of Daniel Burnham, Frank Lloyd Wright, or Le Corbusier at the expense of more generic ones. As a result, the visual conventions used in urban plans remain understudied, the metaphorical quality of the word and idea downplayed in favor of its social, political, architectural, or theoretical content, all important and necessary fields of inquiry. Where a traditional painting represents through visual means, and architecture through visual and spatial means, planning represents its object, the city, through a complex omnibus of images, maps, charts, texts, and publicity (which may itself represent the plan, becoming a representation of a representation of an intended object, the city, or of a process). Much of this material may not be art, but it is a form of representation, a figment of the future aroused in response to actual conditions. Planning in this sense is analogous to historical fiction, but unlike the backward-looking literary genre, its clipped narrative creates an anticipatory endpoint. It romances the nostalgic future, a potential urban reality that seduces with sentiment drawn from a modified or improved present or past.

This unusual status makes planning the great temporal art form, even more than science fiction, which is literature set in the future, as opposed to a genre developed solely to represent the potential nonfictional future. This status frees scholars to examine planning in its broadest sense as a form of culture, or, put differently, as a cultural form. It allows the study of all manner of planning at once, regardless of the specific medium or intention. A formal master plan and family planning, social and economic planning, as well as the uses to which consumer culture put planning are all part of the same phenomenon, a culture of planning.

To one degree or another, planning has always existed. New Deal planners made this point when they rooted their form of planning, as will be shown, in the Homestead Act, the provisions made for public education in the nineteenth century, the conservation of public lands, and antitrust legislation. Their possible disingenuousness should not spoil the point. Indeed, planning may be a fundamental impulse of humanity, a social function almost indistinguishable from consciousness. Yet such a universalizing view misses the point, even if it rings true on some level. All times do not plan equally. It goes without saying that planning is contingent, culturally and historically. The distance to the future waxes and wanes with the stresses and strains of the present. One would be hard pressed to find a more immediate future than 194X, or one more planned. Only revolutions offer up spontaneous futures like 194X, and usually at the cost of great memory loss—heads must roll in order to usher in *Vendémiaire*, the first month of the French Revolutionary calendar. The planning of 194X arose out of a culture of deferment intensified by the economics of the Depression, politicized by the ideological contests in the United States and abroad, and yoked to consumer culture in anticipation of the postwar building boom.

Plan for Planning: The National Resources Planning Board

The New Deal powerfully shaped the home front's understanding of planning. Most Americans have at least a passing familiarity with the "Alphabet Soup" agencies of the New Deal, chief among them the United States Housing Authority (USHA), the Federal Housing Administration (FHA), the Home Owners Loan Corporation (HOLC), the Resettlement Administration, the Civilian Conservation Corps (CCC), the Bureau of Reclamation, the Public Works Administration (PWA), the Works Progress Administration (WPA), and the Tennessee Valley Authority (TVA). As improvised as these agencies were, they were essentially planning organizations, attempts to take stock of the material and human resources of the nation and to reorganize them in order to move beyond the crisis of industrial capitalism.[3]

While the PWA was certainly the largest material contributor in terms of building, and consequently in employing architects, the NRPB set the moral and rhetorical tone of planning in the 1930s.[4] Because of its short existence and the fact that the NRPB never acted beyond its publications, its achievements are easily overlooked.[5] At a crucial moment for the formal profession of planning, when state and city planning boards were beginning to proliferate, the NRPB further stimulated their formation, provided a model for their operation, the guiding principles for their work, and furnished the literature and professional connections that would serve them in their early years. It also brought together planners from many different backgrounds and regions, creating a de facto forum for a field still undergoing rapid change.[6] The NRPB provided an especially broad understanding of planning. This legacy deserves more attention, from the practical and ideological content of its literature to its strategies for publicizing planning and the visual culture surrounding its work. Its influence can be gauged in part by how many of its central concerns remain with us today. The agency emphasized local participation and organization (a legacy that would reemerge strongly in the 1960s), coordinated planning on all levels, and gave planning an accessible image. It furthered the role of both the social sciences and hard sciences in planning and propagandized tirelessly to give planning the national profile it lacked and needed in order to be effective. And of great importance, the NRPB conflated all kinds of planning into one great national effort, playing on ambiguities of meaning to create a planning ethos that saturated the larger culture. It also reconditioned the word planning for American consumption. Architects looked to the bureau as the best hope for centralized planning in the United States, one that would coordinate comprehensive urban planning efforts in the context of economic, social, and national planning.

The NRPB grew out of the National Industrial Recovery Act (NIRA, 1933), changing its name several times in the 1930s, from the National Planning Board (1933–1934) to the National Resources Board (NRB, 1934–1935), National Resources Committee (NRC, 1935–1939), and finally the NRPB (1939–1943).[7] The driving personalities behind the board remained constant throughout its nine-year history, including Charles E. Merriam, a professor of political science from the University of Chicago, and Wesley C.

Mitchell, a Columbia University economist and an expert on business cycles who headed the National Bureau of Economic Research. Roosevelt's uncle, the architect and planner Frederic A. Delano, headed the organization. Delano had been a member of the Regional Planning Association of America, took part in the Regional Plan of New York of 1929, and was an important planner in the nation's capital. Merriam, Mitchell, and Delano sought to bring city planning together with "sociological planning" and regional and national planning—the basis of Stonorov and Kahn's later chart. Their initial work, mostly technical in nature, focused on the assessment of public works projects, surveying and research on population, land use, industry, housing, and natural resources; and the prevention of wasteful duplication of effort and resources among departments, bureaus, and agencies of the local, state, and federal governments. With no authority to make specific urban or regional plans, the agency turned into a propaganda campaign for the sort of planning that Kahn and others would later champion.

By 1934, the NRB had crafted a coherent mission for comprehensive urban planning based in social, economic, and national planning that went considerably beyond the slum clearance of the 1920s. The *Final Report* of that year blurred the divisions between different kinds of planning, rooting them all in important episodes in American history.[8] The report, the first major opportunity for the board to state its aims, consisted mostly of a long essay called "Plan for Planning," which rooted planning in home economics and ordinary business, an attempt to translate the abstruse techniques of planning into familiar terms. "Planning goes on continuously," the report offered, "in every well-directed home, in every business, in every labor or agricultural group, in every forward-looking organization."[9] The essay thus dissolved the distinct fields into which planning had been slowly crystallizing during the previous half-century in an attempt to make it accessible to the public. The ambiguity of the word *planning* itself, its ability to mean many things to different constituencies, endowed it with an abstract quality over and above any technical or professional definitions. The NRB used this ambiguity to refashion planning into a cultural condition, a state of mind with a particularly American cast. Already in 1934, with the first New Deal projects going up, planning was awash in social significance.[10]

In an effort to establish planning as a normative and "American" activity, the report set out to debunk the view that planning implied regimentation, offering in its place a sufficiently abstract definition with rich links to great American traditions. The essay first took up definition by negation. Defending itself against American antagonisms toward social and economic planning, the bureau adamantly objected to centralization: "The centralization of all planning in Washington is not contemplated, and even if possible would not be desirable, since *planning is an attitude* and practice."[11] More than anything, the NRB realized that planning was an alien concept to most Americans, whose deeply rooted individualism ran counter to the common misperception of planning as "the wholesale regimentation of private life," commonly associated with totalitarianism.[12] Planning did not involve "a comprehensive blue print of human activity to be clamped down like a steel frame on the soft flesh of the community" by the government. "The national life is like a moving wave," the *Report* asserted, "in which a new equilibrium must

constantly be found as it sweeps forward." Contrary to the claims of critics, "sound planning . . . brings about a fresh release of opportunities rather than a narrowing of
choice."[13] Turning the tables on laissez-faire capitalism, the report argued that
monopolies and trusts were a form of

> private regimentation, often of an oppressive character, unless the community sense
> of social justice brings about governmental defense against tyrannical exercise of
> private power. Over and over again in the United States, as elsewhere, the commu-
> nity has been obliged to intervene to protect the weaker against the insolence and
> oppression of private citizens, who took by the throat serfs, slaves, dependents,
> employees, crying "pay me what thou owest," in terms of injustice and outrage.[14]

Planning, as they defined it, was by nature less oppressive: "Even martial law tends to
become civil; and over-centralized planning must soon begin to plan its own decentralization."[15] Planning, the report implied, followed some unstated natural law akin to the
self-regulation that classical economists attributed to capitalism.

The *Report* thus cleverly reversed the associations of capitalism with freedom and
planning with tyranny. The first, beset with collusion and excess, had a long history of
threatening freedom, and the second, when pursued with zeal, possessed a regulating
automatism, like that ascribed to the market but driven by the mechanism of planning
itself. In other words, good planning guarded against the potential excesses of planning
that could lead to totalitarianism. Ergo, plan for planning, a redundancy that created two
forms of planning out of one. Planning, the technical and physical process, now took on
another layer. What at first seems nonsensical or tautological turns out to be an important splicing of definitions. Two overlapping forms of planning came into play, both rife
with ambiguities. The planning that leads to overcentralization belonged to the established technical fields of industrial, social, and economic planning, bound together
by national planning. The planning that "plans its own decentralization," by contrast,
expressed a social attitude, or perhaps something more: an élan vital at the heart of
democracy's social justice – the idealistic creed of liberal government.[16]

History, the authors argued, bore out the NRB's claims that Americans were planners. "Private initiative always presupposes the existence of a planned system of public
order within which it may operate."[17] While this system had been unstated, Americans
had been planning under a different name since the nation's beginnings. The *Report*
called planning "an American tradition that is as old as the Constitution and as widespread as business enterprise."[18] It likened the Constitutional Convention to a "large-
scale planning board" and Hamilton's "Report on Manufactures" of 1791 to the bureau's
own work in coordinating national resources. Jefferson's Secretary of the Treasury,
Albert Gallatin, articulated a policy of public education and "internal improvements which
anticipated some of the land planning of today."[19] The board argued, furthermore, that the
Homestead Act of 1862 was really a prescient form of land-use planning, an organized
federal effort to deal with the nation's resources. The public education system, the Federal Trade Commission and the Sherman Antitrust Act of 1890, conservation under the

first Roosevelt, and mobilization for the Great War were all part of a great American tradition of planning. Even trade unions, farmers' societies, and employers' associations, the authors argued, prefigured the sort of planning the NRB hoped to coordinate.[20]

This propaganda for planning was more than posture. The stakes in 1934, at a low point in the Depression, were grave: "Not passive acceptance but violent explosion is the alternative if we fail to develop security and progress by rational and evolutionary methods."[21] The tone recalls Le Corbusier's rhetorical question at the end of *Toward a New Architecture:* "Architecture or Revolution?" Only now, planning has taken the place of architecture. Strong meat for a government report! The authors offered planning as the method through which Democracy could save itself from the "unbalance, insecurity, and suffering" of the Depression and the system that caused it: ". . . no system, political or economic, unless it faces frankly the grave realities of modern economics and governmental life and boldly takes the initiative in broad plans for a better day, can be protected against explosion that wrecks and twists while social discontent struggles to build some new structure promising more to the body and soul of those who feel themselves disinherited by the existing order of things."[22] The NRB's tacit, though thinly veiled, assumption was that laissez-faire capitalism had failed and only a planned society could save it.

The NRPB Plans for 194X

In 1939, however, the mandate shifted decisively. That year, the Supreme Court abolished the National Industrial Recovery Act, under whose authority the bureau operated. With its existence in jeopardy, Roosevelt, who was partial to the organization, re-created it as the National Resources Planning Board, exercising his power under executive emergency, and placed it directly under his authority as an independent cabinet in the executive branch.[23] It still depended on Congress for its budget, and so lived a year-to-year existence, but from then on the NRPB acted with the confidence of its newly acquired independence from congressional approval and of its direct support of the president.[24] For the next four years, the NRPB pressed an agenda that drew urban planning more closely into the planning gestalt.[25]

With the approach of war, and depression conditions waning, the NRPB intensified its focus on urban planning, leading to a number of specific forays. Between 1940 and 1942, planning slowly shifted from a palliative for economic disorder to a proposal for postwar reconstruction. The NRPB set up an "Urban Section" devoted to issues of urban planning and commissioned Louis Wirth, an NRPB consultant, to elaborate his earlier work for the bureau.[26] Wirth, a leading urban sociologist from the famed Chicago School, believed that urban planning should be approached as a form of community building rather than merely as an expedient to create full employment after the war, an idea then in vogue among some economists and administrators associated with the New Deal.[27] He also encouraged the NRPB to find ways to stimulate greater citizen participation in local planning efforts, something reflected strongly in its wartime literature. Under his influence and the leadership of Robert B. Mitchell, the Urban Section set out to create demonstrations of urban planning as models for the rest of the country and to distill their experience into a simple pamphlet on progressive planning for the lay public. Mitchell, a planner who had worked for the Federal Home Loan Bank Board and the Chicago City Planning Commission, and Edmund Bacon, both of whom would soon come into contact with Louis I. Kahn through the American Society of Planners and Architects (ASPA), and later as important planners in Philadelphia, drafted a plan in 1941 for experimental projects in nine different cities.[28] These projects were to serve as regional models for comprehensive planning in which local organizations worked with NRPB agents to fashion long-term master plans for their town. The NRPB cut it down to three demonstrations when Congress reduced the bureau's appropriation for 1942. After much wrangling over selection criteria and under great pressure to get something done before the end of the war, the Urban Section settled on Corpus Christi, Salt Lake City, and Tacoma.[29] The NRPB made a serious effort to root these three projects in local action, using local universities and planning bodies for research; asking local engineers, schools, and police departments for input; and publicizing their efforts in local newspapers and through citizens groups.[30] These publicity campaigns modeled local planning and engaged whole communities in the effort.

One of the important results of the experiments was the publication of the planning pamphlet *Action for Cities: A Guide for Community Planning* (1943), which became a key document for planning efforts during and after the war.[31] It provided communities with a step-by-step guide to planning, disseminated the idea of comprehensive planning, and did so with an idealism that betrayed nothing of the precariousness of the NRPB: " . . . [new techniques] make possible the realization of plans which would have been Utopian a decade ago" – hardly the tone of a cautious group.[32] The first step, a quick "reconnaissance" of the town or city, cleverly deployed war rhetoric in the service of planning, implicating it in the larger struggles of the day. Next, citizens had to be mobilized, participation being the basis of democratic planning. Farming out research to local organizations sped up the process and gave authority to the plan, something that plans foisted on cities by outside planners often lacked.[33] Local universities, chambers of commerce, women's groups, church groups, doctors, public utilities, and recreation departments would do the research, studying the population, economy, social patterns, and physical infrastructure. This sort of mobilization of local resources, planning's version of total war, applied the rhetoric and spirit of the war to what by 1943 had come to be called postwar planning. The local citizen-planners, with the help of the NRPB and local authorities, would orchestrate a plan based on the future desires of the community. *Action for Cities* also touted a number of ideas that had become stock features of urban planning, including full employment; community services for housing, education, and cultural facilities; connections to regional planning; and the idea of neighborhood units. Planners had been working with these ideas for some time, but the pamphlet combined them in a manual for the lay public, making them popular, practical, and canonical.

The most important contribution of *Action for Cities* was rhetorical. Still guarding against popular and official distrust of planning, the pamphlet called for "programs of planning action" and a "campaign of economic action." Action emphasized doing, offsetting the negative view of planning as a form of fantasy, at times replacing the tainted word entirely. Critics derogated planning as totalitarian or as an impractical activity for theorists and "long-hairs," as Robert Moses called planners.[34] "Action," another word with a military resonance, girded planning against such attacks. "A Plan for Planning," the language of the 1934 *Final Report*, had become a plan for action. The "Tools for Planning Action," however, were hardly as vigorous as the rhetoric, beginning with legislation to bring redevelopment corporations into existence, to make land acquisition and assembly easier, to access federal aid for slum clearance, and to enable collaboration on many levels. New administrative arrangements would bring different levels of planning together, and tax and revenue devices would produce the capital necessary to plan on a grand scale. They wove all the mechanisms of land use and urban planning from the 1930s into a kind of "how-to" guide. Zoning, subdivision, codes, and public land reserves would aid in the control of land use, and incentives to "private action" would foster public support for the planning process. While the guide focused on what could be done as soon as the war ended, it also instructed towns to make six- and twenty-year plans. A much less immediate goal lay behind the call to action. "During the war period," the authors conceded, "probably the most profitable and feasible program of action that can be planned for is the continuance of planning itself."[35] The greatest chance for action lay not in planning but in convincing the public of the value of planning. The contrast with the actual war could not have been starker. In place of action, we find a retreat into a plan for planning. As an embattled organization, which derived its very character from the constant threat of dissolution, the NRPB created a literature of persuasion. The authors made publicity a centerpiece of bringing "Plans into Action," as they called one section, including the use of newspapers and radio, town meetings, and planning classes in the local school system. Propaganda and education would transform planning into a cultural force that emanated from the public will and a patriotic duty on which the future of community rested.

Abstraction and Persuasion

Action for Cities tapped into an emerging *visual* language architects and planners were then creating to communicate their agenda to the public, including maps, demographic charts, bubble diagrams, photographs, contour models, and other more abstract experiments of their own invention.[36] A general land-use diagram for the demonstration in Tacoma, which the NRPB called a "diagram of general functional relationships," sketched out the findings of the reconnaissance free of topography and the urban reality on the ground (Figure 1.1). Far from a literal mapping exercise, the abstract drawing helped the planners "dramatize in 'graphic language' the essential relationships of areas and uses."[37] In the spirit of Stonorov and Kahn's contemporaneous diagram, *Action for Cities* explained: "Such diagrams are useful for reducing problems of relationships to essentials. They are not plans, but guides to use in working out plans."[38] Like the concentric rings

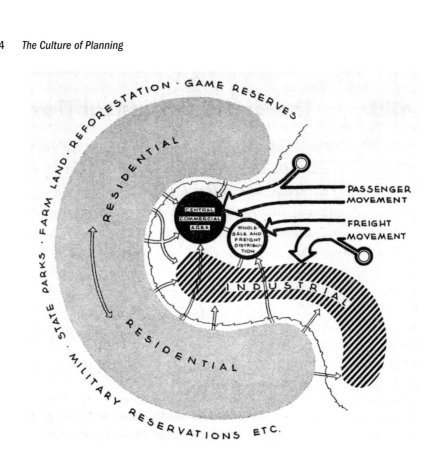

Figure 1.1. National Resources Planning Board (NRPB), diagram of urban planning for Tacoma, Washington. Reprinted with permission from *Action for Cities: A Guide for Community Planning*, copyright 1945, Public Administration Service No. 86 report.

in Stonorov and Kahn's chart, a textual halo around the residential amoeba elaborates the relationship of Tacoma to the larger realm of regional planning: state parks, farmland, reforestation, game reserves, and military reservations, the last reminding people of the integral relationship between military and urban planning.

The diagram for Tacoma was intended as an accessible and schematic visual language for planning, a field that had typically produced mountains of inscrutable charts and diagrams, maps and plans, many of which resisted public participation. Joseph Hudnut, the dean of Harvard's Graduate School of Design, condemned these more technical publications for being "bound in bourgeois cloth and fattened with statistics . . . like *amorini* above a rococo altar."[39] In other words, to Hudnut, this morgue of master plans that collected dust in libraries was as unconvincing as the overwrought architectural styles of the eighteenth century had become for modernists. By contrast, the NRPB's demonstrations reached for a contemporary visual language that would enhance popular support by distilling planning down to a few broad strokes. This sort of abstraction gained power through the implicit contrast to the stock photographs of slums in New Deal literature and elsewhere (Figure 1.2).[40] Such close-up "mug shots" of failing buildings endowed the slum with the picturesque morbidity of social realism and found its complement in the organic purism of the NRPB's abstract diagrams, which represent the whole city.

Figure 1.2. Slum versus public housing. *What the Housing Act Can Do for Your City,* 1938.

By the time the war began, these sorts of graphic experiments were becoming common in urban planning (see Plate 5 and Plate 8). In the 1930s and 1940s, architects and planners worked extensively with images that one is tempted to call *un*architectural: graphs, charts, diagrams, and the promotional material put out by city planning organizations, materials that described neither the architectonic nor the spatial qualities of buildings. Charts and diagrams of one sort or another have probably always played a role in architecture and planning, if only as preparatory lines in the sand. But their use changed and intensified in the 1930s with the rise of the government as the largest client, the emergence of the social sciences and a society of experts, and the increasing complexity of bureaucracy in the period.[41] Additionally, architects had to contend with the maturation of corporate culture and the advertising and public relations campaigns that went with it. In order to assert authority in this changing milieu, architects and planners reached beyond the prevailing forms of architectural representation — plan, section, and elevation — for an abstract, popular, resolutely modern, and purportedly universal language in which to engage the public in thinking about planning.[42]

This quest for a popular language for planning had roots going back at least to Ebenezer Howard's diagrams in *Garden Cities of To-Morrow* (1902). The subsequent rise of Otto Neurath's ISOTYPE (International System of Typographic Picture Education) after World War I, the aestheticized charts of the Bauhaus, and the proliferation of organization charts in the 1920s and 1930s reflect a growing interest in finding a universally accessible, quasi-technical, and persuasive visual language for communicating ideas about the built environment to the public.[43] Neurath, a Vienna School philosopher, sociologist, and activist, invented the isotype in the aftermath of World War I precisely in order to engage the common person in social and urban reconstruction.[44] Neurath, who had strong connections with the Bauhaus, believed that conventional charts were inaccessible to the public and attempted to overcome their shortcomings by creating universal, self-explanatory icons. An isotype-based chart following the so-called Vienna Method expressed quantitative information by repeating equal-sized figures, each of which represented the same amount, rather than by changing scale to represent quantity. New Deal agencies rapidly adopted his system. For instance, in this chart published by the United States Housing Authority, the icons demonstrate quantity by multiplication, not magnification, each one representing a fixed amount of families or housing units (Figure 1.3).[45] They create a pictorial equivalent to a numerical chart. In the same way that the cathedral was the bible of the illiterate in the middle ages, Neurath believed that his visual system would allow common people to grasp statistical data, making them more informed and better citizens.

The icons spread throughout the United States in the 1930s, including conspicuously into American architecture, which immediately took liberties with the system.[46] As early as 1937, Neurath himself published an article on their use in planning in *Architectural Record* (see Plate 1).[47] *Pencil Points,* another leading architectural magazine of the day, used isotypes as a purely aesthetic device on its cover in 1945 (see Plate 3).[48] For an issue on new factories and office buildings, the designer, architect Stamo Papadaki, stacked seven stories of isotypes of workers, and superimposed them over an office building. The floating horizontals of the building and the rows of icons sprang from similar sources, endowing the pages of the magazine with the same modernist aesthetic as the architecture within. The statistical icons were absorbed into organization charts and became common fare in urban planning literature during the war, especially in Britain, and soon they filtered into advertising and promotion.[49] This is to say that by the begin-

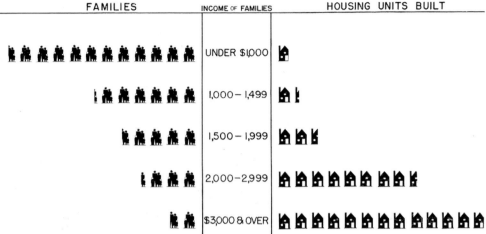

Figure 1.3. Isotype. *What the Housing Act Can Do for Your City,* 1938.

ning of the war, the NRPB could choose from a range of emerging representational strategies that were entering planning through a wide range of literature.

A diagram published in the NRPB's Corpus Christi demonstration, while cruder than the Tacoma diagram, reveals the sort of visual experimentation of the period (see Plate 2).[50] A distant kin of the isotype appears in crude form in the top register, giving pictorial form to the productive activities that fell under the aegis of the plan. Construction, manufacturing, retail, finance, transportation, services, and government all find expression in icons, each of which is tagged to a percentage of the overall economy of the city. What could have been a dry chart of numbers in columns becomes an image, but without losing the empirical feel of a chart. Below, a homespun version of the Tacoma diagram maps out the zones of the city as imagined in 1950, a satisfyingly round number that lay one temporal beat beyond 194X but which in 1943 was still imminent. Other populist gestures fill the image. The bright colors and simplicity of the silkscreen process suggest a craft activity, something any layperson could do at home, rather than the rocaille of statistics that Hudnut dismissed. Instead of a literal mapping exercise, which would require an ability to "read" a site plan or map, an orange grid spreads informally until held at bay by a corrugated brown line presumably representing retail services. The thwarted grid then reaches out picturesquely in multiple directions, prevented from fulfilling its orthogonal monotony, or what Le Corbusier might have called its rational destiny.[51] A thick red line bounds the city like a medieval wall, trying to rein in the frayed edges that were the reality in most American cities as they decentralized their way through the twentieth century. Neither highway nor literal armature of any kind, the line forms the imagined moral boundary that the unplanned city of industrial capitalism and the automobile had neglected.

The image subtly links New Deal, wartime, and postwar planning in ways that would be cumbersome with words alone. Where one might expect the label "Corpus Christi 1950," instead the most prominent text reads "Employment 1950," an appeal to continued fears of a return to depression (and unemployment) after the war. This would have resonated strongly with Americans scarcely four years removed from the Great Depression. The call for full employment, moreover, had just entered home front discussions, as economists and politicians debated the merits of the British Beveridge Plan for the United States—a topic explored more fully in chapter 3.[52] Government-induced full employment, some economists theorized, would forestall a postwar depression much in the way that the war ended the Depression by putting every able-bodied person to work. The connection to city planning was implicit: after the war, publicly sponsored urban reconstruction would offer intensive and sustained employment. One more visual cue reinforced this reading: the planners placed the word "training" in the exit corner, where the eye leaves the page, another appeal to the labor dislocations of depression and war and an important part of reconversion and the assimilation of returning veterans. It is the only word not directly tied to the chart or the abstract plan.

Beyond the visual fact of abstraction in the NRPB diagrams lay the more holistic and profound search for a new kind of planning and a new kind of planner. In *Space, Time and Architecture,* Sigfried Giedion wrote that the modern planner required a new feeling: "When he is seeking, for instance, the proper location of a cemetery or a market hall, he must be able to go over his plan with almost tactile perceptiveness, sensing the contrasting character of its districts as plainly as though they were velvet or emery beneath his fingers."[53] The image recalls Wassily Kandinsky's claim that "man has developed a new faculty which permits him to go beneath the skin of nature and touch its essence, its content."[54] Giedion, who argued that cubism and other early twentieth-century movements in painting were evidence of the "invention of a new approach, of a new spatial representation," applied the idea to shaping the city.[55] The NRPB's diagrams seem to be attempting the same thing.

Abstraction in planning, as in painting and architecture, had come to signify more than a break with tradition.[56] Abstraction was the *cri de guerre* of modernism in the 1930s—or at least one of the cries of this very vocal collection of movements.[57] In other words, artists and architects brandished abstraction. Far from an inert visual mode, or fashion, abstraction seemed to possess force in and of itself, to be endowed with the power of erasure, the ability to sweep out the old and usher in new modes of communication and behavior. In some sense, this is the nature of any new paradigm. As Meyer Schapiro claimed in his seminal essay, "Nature of Abstract Art," written contemporaneously with the advent of the isotype into American architecture and New Deal literature, abstract art had "the value of a practical demonstration," the very word the NRPB's

Action for Cities used to describe its three experiments.[58] It unmasked image-making of the "extraneous content" of figurative painting, revealing what he believed to be "pure form."[59] The promise of abstraction for planning would have been seductive, especially where the clutter of slums and the intractable problem of weak eminent domain laws made pure form, and therefore pure design, virtually impossible.

Schapiro takes us further: "The art of the whole world," he claimed triumphantly, "was now available on a single unhistorical and universal plane as a panorama of the formalizing energies of man."[60] Abstraction, as a form of image-making with the nature of a "practical demonstration," yet bubbling over with the "formalizing energies of man," offered a parallel to the presumed tabula rasa of urban planning that lies beneath many of the schemes in this period, from the NRPB diagrams to Stonorov and Kahn's chart. These abstractions aimed at the universal at the same time that they reveled in the ahistorical, in the possibility of liberation from the drag of history—and from the obstacle of pre-existing buildings, even if they played a role in the technical part of the plan. A similar spirit emanates from Neurath's isotype, which creates abstract figures as universal signs with the ultimate goal of putting them to practical use. Armed with the incredibly rich and varied language of abstraction, NRPB planners painted over Le Corbusier's brazen and far more literal plans to destroy the heart of Paris in *The City of To-Morrow and Its Planning*, which, since its publication in 1925, had become one of the leading paradigms of urban planning.[61]

As the lingua franca of modernists, abstraction was seen as ameliorative, instrumental, and revelatory. Its claim to universality offered an ideal mode for planning, whose very nature remained, even at this late date, an abstraction, and which, in its most radical form, aimed to liberate the masses. Abstraction conveniently hid planning's most violent aspect, namely, its assertive destruction of the city of the present, which many architects believed was stuck in the straitjacket of the past.[62] Planning, the social abstraction that would rid the world of slums, create equality, reconstruct cities into ideal urban fabrics, and, as the NRPB's diagram shows, extend the city's organization to region and nation, called on visual abstraction as its mouthpiece, as its promoter. Here was the visual equivalent of "plan for planning."

Fortune Magazine and Planning

What made a *culture* of planning out of what otherwise would have been isolated attempts to frame the debate about postwar cities was the free exchange between the NRPB and other realms of culture. *Architectural Forum*'s wartime pamphlet, *Planning with You*, echoed the ideas of *Action for Cities*. So did Stonorov and Kahn in two pamphlets they created for Revere Copper and Brass (see chapter 3) and the Allegheny Conference on Community Development's "Civic Clinic for Better Living" (treated in chapter 2). *Fortune* magazine became the least expected route of dissemination, when Henry Luce, the owner of Time, Inc., which published *Fortune, Time,* and *Architectural Forum*, became interested in planning. Between 1943 and 1945, the pages of *Fortune*—to that point an unabashed celebration of laissez-faire capitalism—aired radical planning ideas, including those of Harvard and NRPB economist Alvin Hansen and planning activist Guy Greer. The latter peppered the magazine with articles on planning and helped *Fortune* and the *Forum* stage their own "demonstration" in Syracuse, New York.

Hansen and Greer, who also play an important role in the next chapter, were central figures in postwar planning and had close ties to progressive architects like Walter Gropius and Eliel and Eero Saarinen. Hansen, a former president of the American Economics Association, coined the term *secular stagnation* to refer to the demographic basis of the economic depression. At Harvard, he trained a generation of economists in the uses of deficit or compensatory spending as a tool for leveling off the vicissitudes of the business cycle, which remains the basis of fiscal policy today. Greer, a banker who had written on economics for *Harper's* monthly magazine in the 1930s, worked under Hansen in the late 1930s for the Board of Governors of the Federal Reserve System and wrote widely on economics and planning during the war, sometimes as Hansen's ghostwriter.[63] At the core of their economic policy lay the idea of decommissioning soldiers into jobs in urban reconstruction, thereby absorbing the flood of returning troops after the war to avert postwar depression.

Just before the United States entered the war, as economic advisors to the NRPB, they produced a controversial pamphlet on planning called *Urban Redevelopment and Housing*, often referred to as the Hansen-Greer plan.[64] Architects knew the plan well because Hansen presented it at the 1942 meeting of the AIA in Detroit. The report laid out a program for urban planning as the keystone in a larger national planning effort. Trading on an honest fear of a return to depression after the war, Hansen and Greer saw local planning efforts as major sops for excess labor. In theory, full employment would not only boost morale, it would maximize the circulation of capital, producing a high level of consumption and, in turn, stimulating production. As the most important American interpreter of the ideas of British economist John Maynard Keynes, Hansen stimulated the vogue for such Keynesian solutions in the late 1930s, when the belief in consumption displaced production as the primary index of economic health. Under the desperate conditions of the Depression, many New Dealers turned to deficit spending as a means of increasing employment and consumption. During the war, a similar logic prevailed in the NRPB, although official reports downplayed Hansen's ideas for fear that they would meet a negative reception in Congress and among business leaders.[65]

Before urban planning could be used to create full employment, planners had to confront the nettlesome problem of assembling enough land to plan on a grand scale. The Hansen-Greer plan pressed for the administrative courage to assemble land on a scale hitherto impossible, even unthinkable, within the bounds of American capitalism. The two economists believed that an antiquated urban fabric trapped modern society, preventing its full economic and social realization. Technology and society changed faster than cities, which they believed had to be rebuilt almost wholesale according to well-considered plans developed from the conditions of the present and those anticipated for the future. *Urban Redevelopment and Housing* insisted on liberal legislation and federal aid that would allow local agencies to assemble enough land in order to carry out comprehensive plans, calling for "square-mile" planning. Such aid not only seemed possible but, by the end of the war, seemed probable.[66] The pitch would have played well among progressive architects, many of whom had been arguing a similar cause since the 1920s, Le Corbusier being the most famous example. The indefatigable Greer took the message on tour in 1942 and 1943, campaigning for the Hansen-Greer plan with bankers, architects, engineers, academics, realtors, housing officials, and in *American City* magazine.[67] Both authors understood the importance of finding allies in industry and the planning professions and in creating a swell of public support.

Cheered by liberal New Dealers, architects, and many planners, the Hansen-Greer plan met a chillier response among many business leaders and in Congress, which balked at the broad powers the plan granted local municipalities to assemble land. Critics took this as a threat to the basic Constitutional right to own private property. In fact, the authors remained purposefully vague on the issue of radical eminent domain, proposing a more moderate plan to allow local municipalities to assemble land through democratic processes and then to offset their costs by renting or selling the large tracts to developers. This overstepped the bounds of the NRPB, shackled as it was by congressional funding and limited by its lack of power to enact its plans. If Hansen and Greer wished to see their ideas fully disseminated, they would need to work through different channels. *Fortune* gave them that opportunity.

Contrary to what Michael Augspurger sees as *Fortune*'s move away from cooperative capitalism and a designed society, the war temporarily intensified Henry Luce's interest in planning.[68] In January 1942, the magazine established a "Post-War Department" and published anticipatory studies of America in a new section called "America and the Future." When *Architectural Forum*, another Luce publication, invented 194X, *Fortune* adopted "194Q," as in the article "Transition to Peace: Business in A.D. 194Q."[69] The magazine began airing Hansen and Greer's views on the economy in November 1942 in an article in which the two economists forthrightly advanced the idea of urban redevelopment through compensatory fiscal policy, a recapitulation of their NRPB report.[70] Nothing could cut more radically against the grain of the magazine. *Fortune* had begun as an unbridled celebration of free market capitalism, but Luce had experienced a change of heart in the late 1930s, when the media mogul adopted an ideology of the social responsibility of business and the mass media.[71] During the war, *Fortune,* which aestheticized capitalism for captains of industry, applied its ample rhetorical and visual strategies to sponsor an ideology of planning that openly challenged the philosophy behind the magazine.[72]

In December 1942, *Fortune* joined forces with its Time, Inc., mate, *Architectural Forum,* to explore postwar planning through the new "Fortune-Forum Experimental Department." Led by the architect George Nelson, then a young associate editor at the *Forum,* the new department started the "Syracuse Project," a venture in city planning based on the NRPB demonstrations.[73] The magazines hired the well-known planners Russell Van Nest Black and Hugh Pomeroy, both NRPB consultants.[74] Hansen and Greer also served as consultants, along with planner Jacob Crane of the National Housing Agency, architects Henry Churchill, Richard Neutra, Walter H. Blucher, and others.[75] Working with local planning groups in the spirit of the NRPB "actions," they created a plan for Syracuse. In defense of this sort of planning, *Fortune* argued: "Our economy must find a peace production program that approaches the war program," a reference to Hansen and Greer's idea of compensatory spending on large public urban planning projects as a means of creating full employment.[76] Only the rehabilitation of American cities came close to the magnificent scale of the war as an experiment in planning and deficit spending.[77] Consequently, the article called for expanded local power and autonomy to acquire and hold title to land, to make zoning ordinances retroactive, and to enact legislation that would create a national policy of city rehabilitation and create federal funding for local efforts. In these ways, the Syracuse Project emulated both *Action for Cities* and the Hansen-Greer plan. Luce essentially carried out privately what the NRPB had set into motion.

What business readers encountered in *Fortune*, architects found in *Architectural Forum*, which commissioned twenty-three architectural firms to design a range of hypothetical buildings for Syracuse and published the results in May 1943 in its "New Buildings for 194X" issue. The range of projects and architectural talent was stunning, often presaging the shape of postwar design: Stonorov and Kahn designed a hotel; Mies van der Rohe, a museum; Charles Eames, a city hall; Victor Gruenbaum (soon to shorten his name to Gruen) and Elsie Krummeck, a shopping center; Pietro Belluschi, an office building; Carl Koch and John Johansen, a movie theater; the firm of Perkins, Wheeler and Will, a school; Antonin Raymond, an airport; William Lescaze, a service station; and Hugh Stubbins Jr., a hospital (Figure 1.4 and Figure 1.5). All of these buildings fit into a preordained site plan for a "hypothetical town of 70,000" people, but which the editors linked directly to Syracuse, making clear the basis for their demonstration by inserting a description of the Syracuse project beneath the plan (Figure 1.6).[78] The great individual efforts all had to submit to the overall plan, which proposed to create a pedestrian zone on main street, a surfeit of off-street parking, and a host of coordinated improvements to the institutional infrastructure of the city much like what many towns sought after the war. The editors wrote that the plan showed how a single building "designed to meet a progressive and farsighted program, can become a potent force toward better over-all planning."[79]

While the *Forum* focused on the physical demonstration, the *Fortune* article on Syracuse confronted its ideological basis. The magazine faithfully backed even the most controversial parts of the Hansen-Greer plan about land acquisition, something attributable to the fact that the unsigned article was almost certainly written by Guy Greer, who at that very moment was tirelessly publicizing his proposal with Hansen for postwar planning.[80] In fact, Luce hired Greer away from his job helping Hansen at the Federal Reserve and placed him on the Board of Editors of *Fortune*, where he followed up the Syracuse article with a series of five more articles on planning that appeared over the next eighteen months.[81] Greer's work had prepared him well for the assignment. In 1942, he

Figure 1.4. Hotel by Stonorov and Kahn. "New Buildings for 194X," *Architectural Forum* 78 (May 1943): 71.

helped Hansen and Walter Gropius organize a conference on urbanism at Harvard, for which he edited the proceedings as *The Problem of the Cities and Towns*.[82] Between his work for the NRPB, his ties to Hansen, his lecturing, and his experience at Harvard, he had intimate knowledge of the state of planning and knew most of the key planners of the day. Greer made little effort at objectivity, pressing an apology for progressive planning.

In his next article for *Fortune*, he began with an attack on the piecemeal effort of New York planner Robert Moses, which he called tactical—as opposed to strategic—planning, going so far as to call Moses an "anti-planner" who "attack[s] the sorest spots at dawn, without presuming to try to plan in terms of the whole community."[83] Continuing with the sort of war metaphors then ubiquitous in the United States, Greer spoke of fitting every tactical decision in urban planning into a larger strategic battle plan, or "there will be slight chance of winning the war."[84] Growing bolder than in his first tentative foray into Luce's media world, Greer stated that public control of urban land was necessary, but insufficient: "This means all the land without as well as within the city limits," reaching beyond the "negative control" of zoning to empower local government to purchase and hold land.[85] In other words, Greer's planning depended on the confiscation of private land, and not merely by local municipalities but rather on a *regional* scale because few cities were equipped to assemble land so broadly: "for it does such violence to the

CITY HALL   CHARLES EAMES, LOS ANGELES, CALIF.

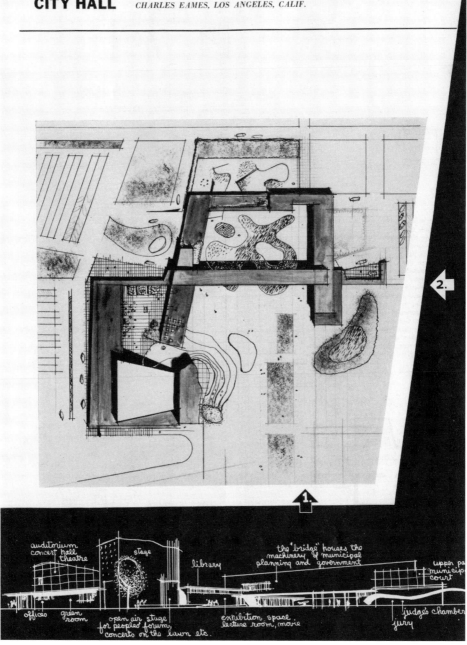

Figure 1.5. City hall by Charles Eames. "New Buildings for 194X," *Architectural Forum* 78 (May 1943): 88.

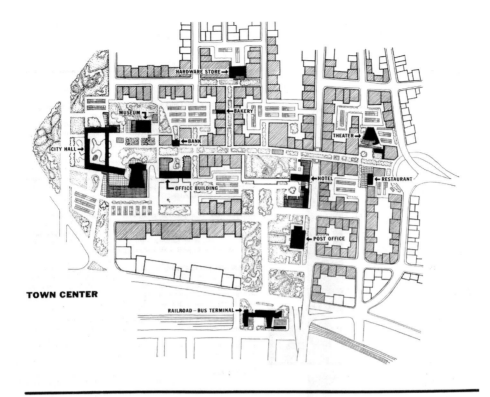

TOWN CENTER

SYRACUSE, N. Y. At the beginning of this year, the editors of FORTUNE and THE ARCHITECTURAL FORUM discussed a venture of impressive proportions with representatives of the city of Syracuse, New York. It involved the preparation of plans for the complete redevelopment of the city after the war.

Syracuse was chosen for this cooperative effort for a variety of reasons. A busy industrial community of 200,000, it has many of the characteristics and the problems of a thriving city of medium size. It has a highly diversified industry, an excellent university, no real slums. Like other typical communities it is still trying to force motor traffic through horse-and-buggy streets, it has too much noise, too little sun, too few parks and too many commuters who waste years of their lives in a daily escape to the fringes and open country. Most important, it has a citizenry which is progressive and interested in improving the community.

At this writing the planning program is under way. There are a number of groups, working under official sponsorship, which are gathering data on the city's needs and problems, studying ways and means of implementing accepted proposals. Plans are being developed under Sergei Grimm, head of the City Planning Commission, with the active assistance of outside consultants. Russell Van Nest Black is chief city-planning consultant; Hugh Pomeroy, President of the American Institute of Planners, has been retained as special consultant. Chief of the economic advisers is Ernest Fisher of the American Bankers Association. Other specialists will be made available to the city as they are needed.

The importance of a project of this scope needs no emphasis at this time. Progress of the studies will be watched by communities all over the U. S. For the citizens of Syracuse there exists a unique opportunity, not only to give the development of their city direction toward new goals of livability and human efficiency, but to take the leadership in a movement which may well capture the imagination of the entire country.

It will be the joint privilege and responsibility of FORTUNE and THE ARCHITECTURAL FORUM to report the story of the new Syracuse.

Figure 1.6. Site plan. "New Buildings for 194X," *Architectural Forum* 78 (May 1943): 71.

laissez-faire tradition that few people can bring themselves to bow to its necessity."[86] Greer let history discredit the laissez-faire tradition, launching into a crash course on the history of planning from Ebenezer Howard's Garden Cities (the "most important single contribution . . . to a solution of the modern urban problem"), the City Beautiful Movement, Patrick Geddes and Lewis Mumford, Radburn, New Jersey, the growth of suburbs, slum clearance, and the PWA, to the contemporary work of the NRPB, José Luis Sert, Eliel Saarinen, the Regional Plan Association of New York, and the trend toward decentralization.[87] He used history to Americanize planning, representing it as a tradition threatened by laissez-faire capitalism and the poverty of imagination of "realistic" planners like Moses. Greer thus condensed a history of modern planning, capped by the work of the NRPB, into a pithy essay for *Fortune* readers.

In January 1944, Greer called the very idea of private property into question:

> If the cities are to solve their problems within a period of years rather than generations, they will be obliged to re-examine some time-honored notions of property rights and privileges. In many instances the means will have to be found for the redevelopment of very large interior areas, in single coordinated operations, probably in conjunction with new developments in the suburbs. This cannot be done piecemeal under the laissez-faire traditions of the past.[88]

The NRPB had suggested as much, partly in following the Hansen-Greer plan. But Greer now moved beyond the NRPB with his visual argument, illustrating his article with the work of architect J. Davidson Stephen, a fellow in city planning at Cranbrook during the war (see Plate 4).[89] Stephen worked alongside Eliel Saarinen, who led a workshop on urban planning for Detroit architects.[90] The younger Stephen, building on Saarinen's ideas on "organic decentralization," devised a visual system of representation that, like the isotypes, was intended to be accessible to the lay public.[91] Stephen's vibrant diagrams projected the flow of decentralization in 1990 with symbols and bubble charts composed of colored construction paper that he cut into a variety of shapes and sizes keyed to population and glued onto a map. He propagandized his system with unusual vigor during the war, exhibiting the work in Cincinnati, Toledo, New York City, Louisville, St. Louis, and Minneapolis in 1943 and 1944, and lecturing widely on Detroit and Plymouth, a small town to the west of Detroit.[92] The content is almost inscrutable from the plans, but, as with the NRPB diagrams, this hardly seems to be the point. Stephen aestheticized planning, turning it into art. Eminent domain, stroked by the legerdemain of his bubbles, which trail a gray wash like incendiary comets crossing a crepuscular sky, becomes something more like a constellation than forcible eviction. For Plymouth, Stephen crossed the biomorphic stage of early abstract expressionism, then in vogue, with the population charts or isomorphs used in planning (see Plate 5).[93]

Like the NRPB diagrams, these images reached beyond literal description to touch people on the plane of aesthetics, providing an image for anticipation and for planning. In using the plan, Greer clearly sought a visual language for planning that could compete with the lavish visual experience of the rest of *Fortune*. Luce made the article the cover story that month, for which Peter Vardo created an abstract collage with the simple caption "City Planning" (see Plate 6). Vardo explored the tension between the preexisting city, represented in the undercoat of the schematic gray site plan, and the imposition of urban planning, represented in an overlay of colorful shards and force lines, most of which ignore the gray pattern beneath. As the shards hover above the city, awaiting 194X, we are left to wonder who would win the "battle of the approach" of Greer's title. In the end, Vardo further aestheticized Stephen's method, turning his colorful schemes into cover art.[94] Normalizing the strangeness of the juxtaposition of the words "fortune" and "city planning," the cover and Stephen's graphics made planning visual, hot, and modern, a world away from the conflict between laissez-faire capitalism and public spending as a permanent peacetime policy.

In July 1944, with the Allies building out from their beachhead in Normandy and the prospect of postwar planning and of the building boom sharpening, Greer turned to the London County Council's (LCC) County of London Plan of 1943, which he used as evidence of a new spirit in planning (see Plate 8).[95] It is worth pausing on this exceptional plan, which may be the most important urban plan to come out of the war years, if not the most important master plan for Americans since the Regional Plan of New York of 1929. Since the turn of the century, the LCC, London's principal planning agency, had erected dozens of successful housing blocks and formulated plans for parts of London. Its plan of 1943 by planning pioneer Patrick Abercrombie and architect J. H. Forshaw was a watershed, assimilating the neighborhood planning principles borrowed from American planners into a comprehensive plan that respected the historical fabric of the town while taking radical action to remedy overcrowding, the dearth of parks and open space, and wartime destruction. It cut a middle path between the radical surgery of Le Corbusier, which strongly implied a nearly omnipotent central planning agency, and laissez-faire, which implied its opposite.

The LCC plan gave Greer an alluring image to chaperone some alarming ideas into the public sphere. The *Fortune* plan derived from an image in the LCC's plan called the "Social and Functional Analysis," which divided London into discrete neighborhood units, seductively illustrated as amoebic organisms swimming within the larger and looser organism of London (see Plate 7). The Thames, as economic, cultural, and aesthetic spine, ties them together. While it had much less Corbusian bravado than the 1937 MARS Group's plan for London, which superimposed a herringbone of arterial highways over the city, it nonetheless represented a radical plan for comprehensive decentralization and forced migration without sacrificing the local autonomy and character of London's neighborhoods.[96] If London, a city of fantastically entangled administrative bodies, could plan a coherent urban body, Greer argued, any American city could do the same, but not without removing the fiscal and legal obstacles in the way of the comprehensive physical overhaul of the city.

In spite of its name, the "Social and Functional Analysis," which, like the NRPB's "diagram of general functional relationships," scarcely communicates any technical information, came laden with meaning beyond its organic appearance. By the time Greer published it, the original image was already in play in American planning circles. In a lecture during the war at the Art Institute of Chicago, for example, Gropius compared it to Pieter Breughel's "Battle Between Carnival and Lent" (1559), a reference that at first seems purely visual (see Plate 9).[97] The sublimely colorful street life of the Dutch painting provided a visual parallel to the vibrant biomorphism of the LCC plan.[98] Gropius also couched the comparison in the romantic medievalism that often lay beneath the surface of the Modern Movement. Seemingly ignoring the religious theme of the painting, Gropius wrote of the organic community of the medieval European town, finding a similar ideal in the cellular approach of the LCC. London had grown out of the agglomeration of many smaller towns; the LCC plan simply restored their coherence, their physical and social integrity.

Given the context of war, however, the reference to the "Battle between Carnival and Lent" cannot be innocent. The moralism of the Breughel, based on visual puns and vignettes, explores the contest between overindulgence and sobriety, the bacchanalian surrender to lust and greed of Carnival, and its flipside, the call for social order and discipline of Lent. One would be hard pressed to find a better demonstration of the contest between laissez-faire ideology and planning. The analogy hinges on the sense of suspension shared by winter and war. The "battle" between Carnival and Lent is enjoined in March after Ash Wednesday on the barren fields of late winter, a time of fasting and penitence commemorating the fasting of Christ in the wilderness. With the abundance of spring around the corner, the social control of denial, of foregoing pleasure in the face of plenty, serves as a reminder of the fragile balance struck in any society between its resources and consumption. Without stretching Gropius's intentions too far, we might see the rationing and restrictions of war as a form of Lent. The comparison to the Breughel, then, sent a moralistic warning to the American home front—then producing at full capacity and, as Gropius wrote in 1944, flush and eagerly anticipating the spring of 194X—to remember the wartime lessons of social order, to remember the long view of planning after the rigors of the war economy slackened. Gropius, who fought in World War I, would have recalled the harsh aftermath of the Great War and used the essay to impart a lesson.[99]

This is to say that urban plans like these were charged with meaning, especially in 1944, as it became more apparent that the Allies would win the war in Europe, drawing the home front closer to its already mythified postwar. Such plans used image-making, abstraction, and visual analogy to rehearse ideas on the stage of a home front *primed rhetorically* to receive them. It seems unlikely that the readership of *Fortune* encountered them with the same rich interpretive talents of Gropius or Greer, but they brought their own interpretive matrix, drawn from business, economics, and increasingly from the culture of planning itself, to the encounter. This was ample equipment to read J. Davidson Stephen's and the LCC's abstractions as radical revisions. Where images failed to communicate, Greer's text more than compensated. He favored the most radical British proposals, including the nationalization of all land and the central control of local planning, proposals made from the ruins of England in the midst of the blitzkrieg that proved much more provocative on unscathed American soil.[100]

The themes that Greer's *Fortune* articles adopted—the use of urban planning as a tool to stave off postwar depression, the need for comprehensive planning driven by local participation, and the necessity for a vast federal role in planning—were common threads running through post–New Deal discussions. More importantly, the magazine's sponsorship of planning threw into question the nature of American society and demanded faith in a greatly modified system. A shift to a new economic system implied shifts in belief, and this called for new rhetoric and a conceptual framework that enabled the possibility of transformation. The social sciences supplied such a framework.

Planning Families, Planning Minds

As a metaphor for the future, planning embraced seemingly unrelated fields, linking the most intimate aspects of family life with community and nation, tethering urban planning to sociology, demography, and psychology. Virtually every field, especially in the predictive social sciences, came under its rhetorical spell or could reposition itself using the term. The demographic basis of the NRPB's demonstrations, which can be found in pictorial form at the base of Kahn's chart (see Figure I.1 in the Introduction), runs through wartime literature in many fields. In one of the most telling examples, the American Birth Control League renamed itself Planned Parenthood during the war. Originally a Progressive Era movement started in Brooklyn in 1916 by Margaret Sanger, the American Birth Control League (named in 1923) worked to legalize birth control and to provide safe abortions for women. Sanger and the League embraced eugenics as a tool for controlling population growth rates in immigrant and poor populations. This was far from unusual in the period.[101] The League merged with the Clinical Research Bureau in 1939, reflecting the growing importance of standards and statistical data, and again changed its name, this time to the Birth Control Federation of America.[102] In 1942, the membership voted to change the name to Planned Parenthood Federation of America.[103] In one of the new organization's early publications, *Planned Parenthood: Its Contribution to Family, Community, and Nation,* a family, visually a cross between a Norman Rockwell poster and social realism, stands proudly awaiting the effulgent future under the new name, Planned Parenthood (Figure 1.7).[104] Images like this belied the realities of the moment. War brought on a rising divorce rate, and migration and wartime service caused immense social and marital upheaval. Like everything else in wartime, the family needed planning.

The word *planning* modernized the organization. Leagues and federations sounded like Progressive Era efforts. It erased the association between birth control and social control through eugenics, a connection no longer tenable, especially with the emergence of Nazi eugenics. Planned Parenthood thereby distanced itself from its earlier incarnation by adopting the metaphorical framework of planning. In lieu of the moral force eugenics once supplied, planning lent it the authority of New Deal, wartime, national

Figure 1.7. Planned Parenthood, *Planned Parenthood: Its Contribution to Family, Community, and Nation* (New York, 1944). Reprinted with permission of the Sophia Smith Collection, Smith College.

and social planning, establishing a parallel between personal and national planning. The change also reflected a changing agenda. With the high tide of immigration over, the mission shifted from providing safe methods of birth control and abortion to immigrants to a more comprehensive agenda of educating families. It was resources planning for the family unit, an NRPB for the home, or the social equivalent to Kahn's house planning. Giving family planning a patriotic gloss, the subtitle directly yoked family planning to larger realms of planning. The shift had socioeconomic underpinnings, as well. Part of the instability of the Depression, according to Keynesian economists in the United States, grew out of a leveling of the population growth rate.[105] A static population made for static consumption and a flat market with little chance of intensive development. Birth control, instead of being a progressive measure, was tinged with the negativity of the Depression, something the image on the 1944 pamphlet subtly responded to by showing a family with three children, one above zero-population growth.

We have lived so long with the idea of family planning that it is difficult to recreate how strange it may have been in 1942 to pair the words *parenthood* and *planning*. Of all the levels of planning, surely the family, as the bastion of privacy and individualism, resists centralized control. Even the rhetoric of the culture of planning seems ill suited to the family, especially in the 1930s when the population growth rate declined. Yet the conditions of the home front normalized the pairing in the context of the domestic conservation of materials. Victory gardens, salvaging scrap metal, conserving rubber and gasoline: these gave national importance to simple acts done in and around the house. Family planning fits into this list, if not seamlessly then well enough that the name and idea met general acceptance and remain with us today.

Similar appeals to planning can be found in the small but compelling literature on the psychology of planning produced during the war.[106] In "Sex Roles in Postwar Planning," for example, the author began: "Before we can plan an intelligent program of reconstruction of sex roles, there is need for an extensive investigation of the attitudes of young people of both sexes concerning the kind of postwar they want."[107] Physical reconstruction lent the author a model for how to think about changing gender roles, which she extended with another war metaphor: "Isolationism between the sexes, like isolationism between nations, must give way to cooperation."[108]

In another pairing of planning with psychology, hospital expert Isadore Rosenfield wrote an article in *Architectural Forum* on an Oscar Stonorov and Louis I. Kahn design for the Philadelphia Psychiatric Hospital, using the title "Planning for Shock Treatment" (Figure 1.8).[109] Rosenfield, who consulted on the project, believed that a quasi-social scientific process of understanding shock treatment would shape a new architecture, sweeping aside outdated hospital typologies. Rosenfield and others had written of hospital planning in the 1930s, but the meaning here takes on a subtly different hue, especially in light of Kahn's deep involvement in planning, which Rosenfield would have known from moving in similar circles. Planning buffered the idea of shell-shocked veterans returning as mental patients by providing a sense of control over something quite out of control.

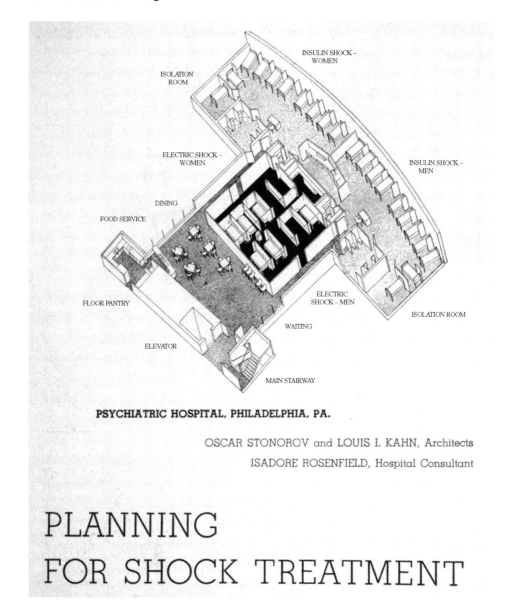

Figure 1.8. From "Planning for Shock Treatment," *Progressive Architecture* (November 1946): 88. Reprinted with permission of Penton Media; the Louis I. Kahn Collection, University of Pennsylvania; and the Pennsylvania Historical and Museum Commission.

What held for the family or the individual could be stretched to cover national psychology, and in fact, with the disaster of national socialism and the replanning of Europe looming, psychologists saw in reconstruction a new challenge for psychology. In 1945, psychologist Erik Erikson wrote "A Memorandum to the Joint Committee on Post War Planning," in which he borrowed planning for psychology, and conversely, lent psychology to planning.[110] The American Association on Mental Deficiency set up the Committee in 1944 to consider the problem of German mass psychology after the war. Meeting at Columbia University in the spring of that year—more than a year before the war would end—the group debated the "nature of this German character and its probable reaction to defeat and post-war settlements."[111]

In his brief to the conference, Erikson skirted issues of urban reconstruction and the economic and political reconfiguration his title suggests and delved into the psychic and social reprogramming of the totalitarian mind. "He who wants to reeducate another nation or 'change' another nation's 'basic character structure,'" he wrote, "has to be a part of an unequivocal historical force. This committee, a professional group within one nation, endeavors not only to play a useful part delegated to it by the usual executives of national history but also expressly wishes to suggest or to determine a scientifically planned history, based on a psychiatric master plan."[112] Without a figurative trace, Erikson applied the language of urban planning—the master plan, but also the rhetoric of planning—to psychology in order to cleanse the "German mind," which he believed was "trained to think totalitarian, and suggestible to paranoid historical concepts."[113] The new "mental hygiene" imposed by the master plan would effect sweeping historical changes. In fact, the very history of Germany would be planned as an essential part of its mental cleansing. The psychiatric master plan sounds ominously like a mass brainwashing, a cultural or psychological application of total war, or a Marshall Plan for the mind.[114] Few Americans would have protested such a "plan" in 1945, no matter how close to the plans of their vanquished enemy their own plans came.

Reversing the order of influence typically held up by architects and planners, Erikson's proposal rendered any type of national, economic, or urban planning as mere superstructure; at the base, psychiatric planning anchored all of the other forms of planning. Erikson's planning, antipodal as it may seem to the urban planner's faith in the salubrious effects of a well-constructed built environment, would have intervened in a more extreme way than the rebuilding of a hundred German cities according to American plans. It reflected his belief, in contrast to Freudian theory, that each stage in a person's life cycle presented specific psychological struggles that were fundamental to the shaping of personality. Ergo his optimism that psychology could intervene in the reshaping of the "German mind." The curious matter, however, is why Erikson used the term planning at all when he could have made the same arguments without it. His usage may have been an unconscious borrowing from a ubiquitous word. More likely, he made a self-conscious appeal to the language of the moment as a means of making an otherwise difficult argument accessible or permissible.[115]

Erikson's psychic master plan was not, in fact, so far from the deterministic faith modern architects placed in architecture to transform society. Walter Gropius and Sigfried Giedion, for instance, wrote of psychic or psychological elements as central features of the mission of modern architecture. Erikson may even have borrowed the idea from Lewis Mumford, who wrote in a piece for the "Re-Building Britain" series: "the task of our age is to decentralize power in all its manifestations and to build up balanced personalities."[116] Mumford believed that society waited until "neurosis" appeared before acting, "whereas in a well-balanced life [there] are ways of guarding against a breakdown.

All these needs must be expressed in our designs and embodied in our structures."[117] Erikson inverted Mumford's idea, asserting a well-balanced life as the way to guard against the breakdown of cities and civilization, a psychological determinism.

In the 1930s, psychology, and the social sciences in general, had become increasingly involved in issues of architecture and design, entering them in part through social planning. Architects imported the social sciences for their authority, and psychologists, sociologists, and political scientists applied them to other fields. Roosevelt's "brain trust" and New Deal agencies such as the NRPB predicated their collaboration on the free flow of ideas across disciplinary boundaries, which, at least in spirit, provides a close parallel both to the ways in which different forms of planning coalesced and to the collaborative approach of progressive architects.[118]

Ties between the social sciences and architecture grew stronger throughout the period, stimulated in part by the development of sociometry, the quantitative study of the psychology of groups. Pioneered in the early 1930s by Italian-born psychiatrist Jacob Levy Moreno, the method of interviewing and using measurement techniques to assess and predict behavior in groups quickly penetrated into social and community planning in the late 1930s, including one of the Resettlement Administration communities. On the Resettlement Administration project, Moreno explicitly wrote of the "Sociometric planning of society."[119] Sociometry may have contributed to the holistic approach to planning of architect-planners like Louis Kahn, who had worked for the Resettlement Administration in New Jersey.

Planning and Ballyhoo

As this wide dissemination of planning shows, by 1942 it had become socially available, a word that could bolster an activity or idea previously not understood in terms of planning, like the family, sex roles, psychology, or national mentalities. New wartime advertising campaigns would do what the NRPB, Luce, Erikson, and Planned Parenthood could not: put planning before the public. Literally millions of readers would encounter planning in their weekly or monthly thumb through *Saturday Evening Post, Ladies' Home Journal,* and even the major news magazines like *Time* and *Newsweek.* It is well known that Madison Avenue relieved the government of the onus of propagandizing the war, a story told in more detail in chapter 2.[120] Suffice it to say here that war let loose a stunning array of ads, many part of the deliberate propaganda campaigns of the War Advertising Council. The new advertising campaigns embraced Henry Luce's call for corporate social responsibility by supporting the war or a vision of the postwar world, making the ads complex cultural products: at once both self-serving and patriotic, socially engaged and propagandistic, promotions of war and anticipations of the postwar period. The Revere Copper and Brass ads and pamphlets came out of this context, as did new advertising campaigns by Pittsburgh Plate Glass, General Electric, United States Gypsum, Celotex, and scores of other companies that began preparing for the building boom. Planning, a word by 1942 associated with family, house, community, region, the end of the Depression, the war, anticipation, and patriotism, also entered consumer culture forcefully.

One of the earliest planning ads played on the tightening of the economy as Americans felt the conservation orders begin to take effect in early 1942. An ad for Brasco Modern Store Fronts in March ran the headline "Planned Economy," a double entendre that linked aesthetic economy and fiscal economy in business with the larger wartime idea of a national planned economy (Figure 1.9).[121] With materials rapidly being taken off the market, the individual storeowner, in modernizing a storefront, or planning to do so, would be part of the larger planned economy. Some of the resonance both of Depression-era main-street modernization programs and New Deal planning still linger in the phrase, but by late 1942, the Depression had given way to the home front economy. In October 1942, a Revere Copper and Brass ad claimed to be "Helping to Strike the Spark of Planning," while the more ominous copy read: "After total war . . . total living" (see Figure 3.14).[122] Long before the outcome of the war was in hand, war had become the conceptual framework for the postwar, linked through planning.

With the beginning of the war, ads played on the ambiguity between individual acts of planning and much larger planning efforts, especially linking domesticity to the war effort. Swans Down Cake Flour treated the readers of the *Ladies' Home Journal* to a recipe using the copy "Lunch-box Planners Look!" to promote its "victory lunch-box cakes" (Figure 1.10).[123] While women planned symbolic victory lunches for their children, their husbands drank the drink of planners. A May 1943 Seagram's V.O. Canadian advertisement claimed: "Men who plan beyond tomorrow prefer the world's lightest highball!"[124] Some publicity linked home and war directly. In a Revere Copper and Brass pamphlet of February 1943, housing expert Carl Boester declared: "We are told that the home is the 'shrine of civilization' and that we are fighting this war to protect it. That is a needed and basic reason; but it isn't the whole truth. The fact is that for millions of Americans, the present effort is an all-out fight to get a home."[125] Another Revere pamphlet proclaimed: "The only answer to total war is total planning for peace," which it conceived through the design of a community center.[126] The planning (and mobilization) of war opened up new ways of conceptualizing domestic life.

The point is less about any single appearance of the word *planning* than about the layering of meanings and the building of a context—and ultimately, the creation of a cliché. Contrary to the usual dismissal of clichés as trite or conceptually impoverished, overuse made the keyword more powerful, for this is what clichés do: they labor over meaning and then cover the conscious traces of their work, transforming ideas under the cover of rhetorical banality. They appear innocent, idle, but they contain a density of assumptions, emotions, and personal identifications that, when ripe, displace dominant modes of thought through absorption, exclusion, or overbearing abundance. In packing assumptions into tidy semantic bundles, clichés enter the collective consciousness, supplying the means for communal discourse to emerge. This makes them potent because they go unnoticed, unstudied, unchallenged. They serve as a form of shorthand, the linguistic

Figure 1.9. Advertisement for Brasco Modern Store Fronts, *Architectural Forum* 76 (March 1942): 49.

Figure 1.10. Advertisement for Swans Down Cake Flour, *Ladies' Home Journal* (March 1943): 78.

trace of popular reception and assent. They seem to emerge effortlessly out of the public will (although this is surely misleading) and this gives them the air of something organic and universal, a product of common sense and folk wisdom rather than of cultural construction and artifice. Advertisers helped fashion planning into such a cliché in the 1940s.

As a potent cliché, planning served the coming peace as well as the war. General Electric published an advertisement in December 1944 featuring an interior design by architect G. McStay Jackson along with the copy: "Lighting . . . Planned to Serve" (see Plate 10).[127] General Electric's wartime ad played on the proliferation of the word *planning*, endowing the product with a patriotic aura by likening it to the national planning of the war effort. The ad played on the multiple meanings of service (patriotic, domestic, and military) just as these ideas were blending on a home front primed for the end of the war. It used this ambiguity to transform an act of consumption—or, really, of planned consumption—into a dutiful act of citizenship. Jackson, who peers at the living room from his indentation in the text, becomes the agent of this service and its translation into picture form, something reinforced by the curly bracket subtly formed by the meeting of text and image. At the crux of the bracket sits a copy of a General Electric pamphlet that expands on Jackson's ideas, which directs the eye toward the section and then the image on the left page. The architect, working through the corporation, would be an agent of postwar transformation. By conflating personal planning on the home front and war planning, the ad played desires for personal comfort off of obligations to public service.[128] In doing so, the company joined corporate efforts to stimulate planning on the home front as a contribution to the war effort. But it took liberties with the word, building on changing conventions of use catalyzed by the war.

By the time the war began to turn in favor of the Allies in Europe in 1944, and the home front allowed itself to gaze more intently at 194X, ads relied on planning to try to heat up anticipation and to prepare Americans for reconversion. Ads echoed the Hansen-Greer plan for deficit spending on large public projects to forestall postwar depression. One Alcoa Aluminum advertisement of January 1944 asserted: "Push Civic Planning To Take Up Postwar Slack," a public service advertisement aimed at the building industry in the spirit of the NRPB or of Luce's planning crusade (Figure 1.11).[129] The ad, which promoted aluminum as "the window of the future," takes the form of a double-hung window, with image and text filling the upper and lower registers. The bird's-eye view of the city plays into a tradition of idealized views. In using an aerial photograph, it inserts the gritty reality of the generic city poised on becoming a slum in place of what readers would have come to expect to be a visionary image of the future city. The words "civic planning," splashed like a stroke of paint between the two registers, as if it were a separate reality between word and image, would stave off urban decline.

Civic plans would absorb returning troops and the labor force uprooted by reconversion, enlisting them in the effort to eradicate slums. The Alcoa ad linked the physical conversion of industry from war to peace and the effort to achieve full employment after the war, ideas usually associated with national, economic, and social planning, with the urban transformation of civic planning. The ad argued for urban planning as a form of

Push Civic Planning
To Take Up Postwar Slack

Does your town have slums and blighted areas, houses over fifty years old, not enough modern schools or hospital facilities, an antiquated sewage disposal or water treatment plant? Correcting such conditions is an excellent way of readjusting employment after the war.

Why not start your civic planning right away, so the end of the war won't catch your city unprepared? And while you're putting plans on paper, figure on using Alcoa Aluminum wherever possible.

Architects were including aluminum windows, sills and other aluminum building products in municipal housing projects, before war industries started taking all the metal we could make. Engineers designing water works, sewage treatment plants and other municipal structures used aluminum doors, windows, sills, skylights, spandrels, coping, grating, ducts, conduit and the like.

The superior performance of all of these Alcoa products is an excellent reason for including aluminum in your designs.

We'll gladly tell you how you can include Alcoa Aluminum products in your designs. Write ALUMINUM COMPANY OF AMERICA, 2198 Gulf Building, Pittsburgh, Pennsylvania.

The Window of the Future is Aluminum

ALCOA ALUMINUM

ALCOA
Reg. U.S. Pat. Off.

Figure 1.11. Advertisement for Alcoa Aluminum, *Pencil Points* (January 1944): 93.

civic duty on which the stability of the period depended. In addition to fears that the nation would return to depression or that the end of war would bring on a new depression, as it had after World War I, government experts and critics in the press worried over how the epic forces that turned American industry into such a devastating war machine would be transformed back into a peacetime economy.

Americans who neither read *Fortune* nor kept abreast of the plans of the NRPB could have learned similar lessons from the Alcoa ad.[130] Another ad produced for the Associated General Contractors of America (AGCA) hinted at the same idea, promoting industry's social responsibility for planning (Figure 1.12).[131] A soldier, just off the train, greets the job prospects of the world, which the ad suggests are the home front's wartime responsibility: "This is the time to plan! — to call in architects and engineers and general contractors and discuss your building needs. . . . This step taken now not only helps you but it also helps the nation. The construction industry has no change-over problem, it can start immediately on new construction and modernization . . . but planning and making specifications take time and much of it can be done now thus saving valuable time when peace is declared."

Also in 1944, the J. A. Zurn Manufacturing Company, a plumbing company based in Erie, Pennsylvania, published *A New Era for Building Is Only Marking Time*, a primer on planning that used the 194X slogan to prophesy "a bold break with the present" after the war and encouraged local participation in planning campaigns (Figure 1.13).[132] The pamphlet listed the states and cities that had conducted planning surveys, the names and addresses of important planning organizations, and included bibliographic references to both business and governmental planning literature. According to Zurn, communities would clear slums, decentralize housing and industry, and plan around the growth of air transportation (Figure 1.14).[133] Zurn followed the work of Russell Van Nest Black, one of the NRPB consultants on the *Fortune–Forum* Syracuse Project, and the NRPB's *Action for Cities*, advocating local control, a regional planning approach, and comprehensive planning. The pamphlet also argued that the welfare of the economy depended on urban planning spurring the building industry to productivity in the period of reconversion, the economic argument for planning that forged a consensus between business and more radical planners. Of course, the pamphlet concluded by offering the planning skills of Zurn engineers and the company's files on planning, implicitly providing an alternative to the NRPB as a clearinghouse for planning information. There is no reason to doubt the good intentions of some businesses in promoting planning. In the spirit of the War Advertising Council, business leaders embraced planning earnestly, even if their literature drew a fuzzy line between contributing to the war effort and self-promotion.[134]

What began as public service and wartime propaganda, ads quickly manipulated for promotion, especially in 1944 and 1945, as advertisers ramped up their efforts to position themselves for the building boom. An ad for Duraglas in *The American Perfumer* called for "Practical pre-postwar planning for YOU."[135] "Wish to do some practical pre-war planning, or preparation, whichever you wish to call it?" the ad asked. The

A job can be waiting for him
BUT WE MUST PLAN NOW

These days one hears much about plans for post-war and many of us are wondering what we can do about it—how to proceed to be in a favorable competitive position, how to assure plenty of **jobs** for **returning soldiers,** and how to be sure that private enterprise will meet the new conditions.

What the construction industry has done and is doing for the emergency of **war** is a matter of **record.** Its part in the era to come will be none the less brilliant and helpful to the nation, but plans and specifications must be made well in advance of victory.

This is the time to plan!—to call in architects and engineers and the general contractor and discuss your building needs for the day that may come sooner than we anticipate. This step taken now not only helps you but it also helps the nation. The **construction industry** has no change-over problem, it **can start immediately** on new construction and modernization whenever plans and specifications are approved, but planning and making specifications take time and much of it can be done now thus saving valuable time when peace is declared. **This is blueprint time!**

 # THE ASSOCIATED GENERAL CONTRACTORS OF AMERICA, INC.

NINETY CHAPTERS AND BRANCHES THROUGHOUT THE COUNTRY
NATIONAL HEADQUARTERS—MUNSEY BLDG., WASHINGTON, D. C.

SKILL, INTEGRITY AND RESPONSIBILITY IN THE CONSTRUCTION OF BUILDINGS, HIGHWAYS, RAILROADS AND PUBLIC WORKS

Figure 1.12. Advertisement for the Associated General Contractors of America, *Architectural Forum* (April 1944): 182.

Figure 1.13. Zurn plumbing pamphlet, *A New Era of Building Is Only Marking Time* (Erie, Penn.: J. A. Zurn Manufacturing Company, 1944).

language both plays on the absurd proliferation of prefixes during the war and acknowledges the way in which planning displaced other common words, such as preparation. "Pre-postwar planning, we call it, because you begin to benefit now instead of having to wait until the war ends." The ad conjured the illusion that *planning was doing*, a consumerist version of "Plan for Planning," suggesting that planning brought some tangible gain, when in fact it merely allowed Duraglas to maintain a relationship with the consumer. Ads like this played on the sense of national obligation with only the slimmest pretense to support the war effort or reconversion.

The anticipatory images and rhetoric of the more sincere corporate efforts to stimulate thinking about the postwar world could be easily banalized. In the fall of 1944, shortly after the Allies liberated Paris, Coyne and Delany, a plumbing company, associated its product with "Tomorrow's Planning" (Figure 1.15).[136] "There is a bright future coming for community life in America," the ad exhorted: "The pattern is in the weaving, the plans are on the boards, the funds in the committees' hands awaiting the return of peace." Based on this statement, one expects a normative urban or economic plan. However, the next paragraph asserts that "the acceptance of the FLUSH VALVE in private homes is but one of the foreshadowing changes now accepted as a fact." In other words, the "modern community improvement" promised by the ad, complete with the radiant, shining city in the image, would be attained in part by hooking up the monumental flush valve in one's powder room. The stakes in these ads were always more personal than national. Mueller Climatrol, a "heating and winter air conditioning" company, called for "Planning for

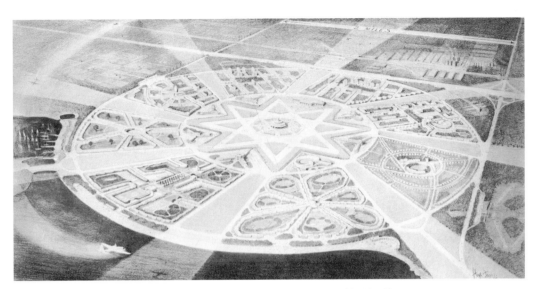

Figure 1.14. Zurn plumbing pamphlet, *A New Era of Building Is Only Marking Time.*

Indoor Comfort," distancing planning from its normative association with a blueprint, as with the AGCA ad (Figure 1.16).[137] Instead, Mueller made planning personal and domestic, almost sensual, a reading the image reinforces by showing a young girl playing ping-pong in a basement warmed by a gas furnace.[138] The failure to plan for reconversion meant a return to depression (and discomfort), a threat Mueller backed up with a strain of the Protestant work ethic and conspicuous consumption: "Planning for indoor comfort" was "an important part of [one's] postwar success," a means perhaps of avoiding social ostracism as well as unemployment. This rather overzealous interpretation makes sense in the climate of the delayed consumption of the home front. As war bonds came to represent the postwar reaping of wartime investment, Carl Boester's argument that the war was a fight for a better home may have come to seem less gratuitous.

In this spirit, the F. L. Bruce Company, a manufacturer of hardwood floors, invented a new human type, the "plan-aheader," the perfect American couple who seem to reenact the nuptial proposal every time they buy—or rather plan to buy—a new product: "Plan-aheaders are planning now for Bruce Streamline Floors" (Figure 1.17).[139] Relatives of the Joneses, the patriotic plan-aheaders were precisely the type to engage in pre-postwar planning, planning their indoor comfort and their flush valve, if not their lunch-boxes and highballs. On the ground, plan-aheaders did not really exist. If we take the oral testimony of World War II from Studs Terkel's *The Good War,* or virtually any other source, the home front did not mirror the ads. Advertising scarcely determines behavior, nor should we expect it to offer a true reflection of people's attitudes on the home front. Ad agencies and the corporate elites who hired them believed in the efficacy of this rhetoric and used it to urge people to plan things that before the war were built, designed, produced, managed, installed, packed, poured, contemplated, and discussed.

TOMORROW'S PLANNING

There is a bright future coming for community life in America. The pattern is in the weaving, the plans are on the boards, the funds in committees' hands awaiting the return of peace.

The acceptance of the FLUSH VALVE in private homes is but one of the foreshadowing changes now accepted as fact. War building has proved this. The water economy, efficiency of purpose, and freedom from fault and common maintenance of the DELANY FLUSH VALVES, over past accepted methods of domestic sanitation, earns them a place in your plans for modern community improvement.

DELANY FLUSH VALVE equipped with NO. 50 VACUUM BREAKER, a device that prevents water contamination, telltales back syphonage. DELANY VALVES are noted for their simplicity and freedom from breakdown.

SINCE 1879
Coyne & Delany Co.
BROOKLYN **N.Y.**

Figure 1.15. Advertisement for Coyne and Delany Plumbing, *Architectural Forum* (September 1944): 191.

Figure 1.16. Advertisement for Mueller Climatrol, *Architectural Forum* (August 1944): opposite 16.

Figure 1.17. Advertisement for Bruce Streamline Floors, *Architectural Forum* (February 1945): 64–65.

Conclusions

We plan to do, but no matter how often we mistake the one for the other, planning is the prologue to action. It is the shadow cast before an anticipated object comes to light. When we reverse these expectations, literalizing planning as the act rather than using it as a metaphor or as preparation, we invest planning unduly with the power to control events. World War II elevated planning in this way. And yet, the urge to plan, even in a nation with a history of resistance to planning, is self-evident. After the cruelest depression in American history, deferred dreams found an expansive outlet in planning, especially as war produced an economy of abundance in a climate of restriction, pushing these dreams still further into the future. Planning operated on many levels at once. It gave form to fantasy. It also acted as a psychological mechanism, working the temporal ambiguity of 194X as a valve for home front anxiety. Admen dressed up this fantasy – playing on what T. J. Jackson Lears calls the "fables of abundance" – in political, economic, and social garb.[140] Planning for postwar consumption rarely sated personal desires without proposing to contribute to greater causes: full employment, urban rehabilitation, or simply the patriotic spirit of the times. This sort of material anticipation depended on the immediacy of 194X for its power. Having a future loom "just around the corner" sharpened the indefinitely deferred dreams of the 1930s.

Americans paired war and planning explicitly. A culture habituated to war and depression, which organized the New Deal around the metaphorical construct of war only to find itself in World War II, turned to planning as the organizing metaphor of the war. But war is a feckless metaphor to wage a war by, while planning—one part forecasting and one part pragmatism—pandered to the fantasy and forecasting nurtured by Western society since Thomas More's *Utopia*, adding to it the research of experts and the authority of statistics, charts, and maps. Planning was prediction with a false sense of agency, a perfect rhetorical cast for the cataclysm of total war.

The home front embraced planning for deep cultural reasons as well as for the strategic reason that all wars require resources planning. The home front abounded with war metaphors; postwar planning frequently absorbed them, and many people hoped that the postwar period would carry home front harmonies and order into peacetime. Much of this carried over a similar approach from the Depression. Much of the New Deal built its rhetoric around military terms, as William Leuchtenburg has persuasively shown.[141] Agencies went to battle for social causes. The Depression became a war against poverty, emulating the control of resources established during World War I. The whole reflects a tight dialogue between war and American identity in the first half of the twentieth century. The United States, in spite of a brief flirtation with isolationism, was quite simply a martial society mentally.

While we tend to think of war as a violent breaking of bonds, it also requires a formidable level of cultural contact: Americans learned daily lessons about Europe and Asia in the late 1930s and 1940s, even if much of it was misinformation. The media painted a picture of Japan, Germany, and the Soviet Union, the three discernible models of the modern "Other," as highly organized societies. These three nations had taken different paths out of the crisis of industrial capitalism of the 1930s. Their decisiveness separated them from the United States. The tentative way Americans approached the world stage and its own affairs between the wars helps explain the confusion in the United States over the cause of the Depression. One of the troubling facts about living through the Depression was that the United States never fully understood it. Experts, in an age of experts, disagreed on its causes and on potential solutions, in part because of an unwillingness to see its international dimensions. Scholars continue to contest the efficacy of the New Deal, a domestic program aimed to solve an international problem.

Everyone seems to agree, however, that war ended the Depression. In other words, an international conflict solved the international economic slump, at least in the United States. Along with that, war temporarily pushed aside the crisis of industrial capitalism in the United States, sublimating it into the fervor for planning. This is why so many ordinary activities came under the spell of planning, in particular those states of being or states of mind that have nothing to do with planning, like comfort. Comfort, in the sense of the Mueller advertisement, cannot be planned. One can only purchase or plan to purchase a heating system. Comfort, in a nation one-third ill housed, rife with slums, and under the rationing of wartime controls, came pregnant with meaning. So did psychological planning, with its pretense to power over the future state of mind of the individual or collective. The many forms of planning, each one serving as another float in a temporal and conceptual pontoon bridge spanning the war, carried valuable ideas and otherwise untransportable fears across the Depression and war, delivering them to the fantasy of "the other side." People imbued that other side, 194X, with near chiliastic meaning, seeing in it the resolution of the crisis of the system, a lifting of the darkness of the Depression, a return to community of a mythic past, as Gropius's medieval reference attests. The postwar, in the hands of the better fantasists, became a kind of afterlife, at very least the promise of something better, something worth fighting for.[142]

2 Old Cities, New Frontiers
Mature Economy Theory and the Language of Renewal

The culture of planning prepared Americans in word and image for what seemed like an inevitable national venture into urban reconstruction after the war. Partisans of planning saw the renewal of cities in far-reaching terms as a transformation of culture and identity in light of the social, economic, psychological, and material dilemmas of the day. The home front posed the city as savior. The problem was, after more than a decade of neglect, cities lay broken and in disarray. Ill planned from the start and formed to serve antiquated functions, most cities faced major social and economic problems that experts routinely connected to their physical forms and infrastructure. Broken cities reflected a broken culture. It followed, then, that a better society required better cities, and the most extreme visions of urban transformation in 194X—for instance, the National Resources Planning Board's (NRPB) square-mile rehabilitation—required unprecedented dislocations of population, the acquisition of private property, and finally, destruction. Clearly planners needed a powerful, seductive argument.

For this they turned to economics, and specifically to an Americanized version of the ideas of British economist John Maynard Keynes. Keynesian economics favored priming the economic pump with public spending projects to smooth the imbalances of capitalism. "The American Keynes," Alvin Hansen, whom we last encountered as an adviser to the NRPB and as an influence on *Fortune* magazine's initiatives in planning, went one step farther. Hansen called the United States a "mature economy," meaning it had stalled at a permanent plateau of development. He favored using urban rehabilitation projects as a fixture of fiscal policy. The rebuilding of cities and regions, the largest possible scale of public intervention in the built environment, would put people to work, stimulate the circulation of capital, spur consumption, and, in turn, drive new production. Cities became the great hope for stemming social and economic decline, a slide backwards that Hansen and others dated to the end of the frontier.

The metaphor of maturity sounded a note of crisis and opened the city up to the most ambitious and destructive planning ideas while at the same time cloaking them in the creative metaphor of the frontier. The mature economy theory focused the agenda of the culture of planning, endowing it with the authority of economics and Americanizing it through the myth of the frontier, which had special currency during the Depression and war. This chapter explores the cultural meaning of the mature economy theory and shows how it influenced the culture of planning and informed the plans and thinking of Walter Gropius, José Luis Sert, and other architects, as well as how it influenced the visions of 194X in advertising, the architectural press, and the famous postwar plans for Pittsburgh, Pennsylvania, now known as Renaissance One.

Walter Gropius, Alvin Hansen, and the Mature Economy

In March 1942, Walter Gropius excitedly wrote to Sigfried Giedion that the very nature of planning in the United States was radically shifting. "The change is so fundamental," he wrote, "that one has to attack all the problems from a new angle."[1] The German architect, just five years into his new life in the United States, was reconsidering the role of architecture in shaping society. "The economical and administrative aspect [of] our problem," he told Giedion, "is of outstanding importance and cannot be separated from the social and technical points of view which we have been interested about so far mostly."[2] "We" referred to the Modern Movement in architecture, and especially to the International Congresses of Modern Architecture (CIAM), which Giedion served as secretary and which had just published José Luis Sert's *Can Our Cities Survive?* (a title that evoked both the war and maturity). That month, Gropius, in addition to working on a project with Martin Wagner for the replanning of Boston, had attended the Harvard Conference on Urbanism, which he helped organize with his Harvard colleague in economics, Alvin Hansen.[3] In fact, the pretext of the conference was to discuss the 1941 Hansen-Greer plan for urban rehabilitation, discussed in chapter 1.

The Harvard conference, as an interdisciplinary gathering of scholars and professionals, brought Hansen and Greer into direct contact with influential architects and planners. Keynesian economists interacted with planners like Earle Draper, Jacob Crane, Walter Blucher, Frederick J. Adams, Gilmore Clark, Carl Feiss, and Alfred Bettman. These were some of the leading planners in the United States.[4] Joining them were NRPB planners Charles Merriam, Charles Ascher, and Charles Eliot, and architects Clarence Stein, Albert Mayer, Joseph Hudnut, Walter Curt Behrendt, and, of course, Walter Gropius and Martin Wagner. Hansen and Greer set the rhetorical tone, extending ideas Hansen had formulated in the late 1930s. In his paper, Hansen claimed that American cities suffered from inadequate planning, simultaneously growing and stagnating: "Like trees decaying at the core but spreading branches wider and wider, they have long been sick . . . and we have at last come to realize that unless they are cured many of them will undergo something analogous to disintegration if not to death."[5] Echoing Le Corbusier's famous metaphor, he likened the solution to "a vast surgical operation . . . not a mere 'beauty treatment' but an all-out attack upon the internal conditions responsible for their external shortcomings."[6] What seems like overstatement was standard rhetoric in 1942, completely consistent with other advocates of the mature economy—and progressive architects.

Gropius and Wagner, in their contribution to the proceedings, echoed Hansen: re-constructing our cities "calls for first relieving the sick bodies of our cities from their high blood-pressure and congestion, in order to improve their damaged circulation."[7] The rhetoric owed a debt to Le Corbusier, who extended the nineteenth-century metaphors of Eugène Emmanuel Viollet-le-Duc. The language dates to an even earlier era, by way of Darwin, Spencer, Comte, and others, to the Early Modern tradition of applying bio-logical metaphors to the social body and to concepts of change.[8] After the Harvard Conference on Urbanism, Gropius now tied these biological metaphors to the powerful overarching metaphor of the mature economy, writing that reconstruction "calls for trans-ferring endangered production as well as purchasing power from a sore spot of the old city area to a sound new city by resettling there those inhabitants of the old city who can no longer be gainfully employed and who have hence become such a serious cause of blight and congestion."[9] The gist of the matter is clear. Gropius had come to believe, fol-lowing the economists at the conference, that most planning problems originated with the issue of private ownership of land, which prevented large-scale planning efforts. In frank admiration of the "strong mentality" of the economists and administrators who composed the majority at the conference, Gropius explained to Giedion:

> It was quite revealing that some responsible persons even brought up the question whether at the end of this war all the land wouldn't have to be declared as public. I gather that the National [Resources] Planning Board went even so far as to suggest this as the only hopeful solution for the future, so the mentality has become ripe for a radical change.[10]

Here we have direct evidence of the NRPB's ideas filtering into architectural thought.

Gropius and Wagner bought into the bureau's call for public ownership of land and reenvisioned the first necessary step in the creation of an urban tabula rasa: the displace-ment of populations on a grand scale as part of the master plan. They stepped beyond a mere physical blueprint for the form of the city, as some magical glyph with the power to transform society, to focus on the intransigence of people rather than on the fixedness of buildings. In the process, they transfigured flexibility, that shibboleth of the Modern Movement, from a problem of walls to a problem of bodies.[11] These bodies, moreover, were themselves pathogens, endogenous sources of the city's sickness rather than symp-toms, or victims, of the sick city.

This fraught line of thinking implied amassing vast central power, something anath-ema to American capitalism, and using it to confiscate property, the sine qua non of capi-talism and protected by the Constitution as free speech. However, the authors cleverly skirted these considerations. Economic rhetoric allowed them to transmogrify people into "endangered production" and "purchasing power," central elements in rejuvenating a mature economy. People, when reduced to economic factors, can be displaced as easily as a line in a ledger book can be erased. Reducing them to "economic factors" thus neutralized them as pathogens, at least rhetorically.[12] With the "endangered production" (read: illness) removed from an area, planners would be able to abandon the "spot rehabilitation" method for the NRPB's "square-mile" method of planning, "generating additional purchasing power within the new cells of the old city body."[13] The mature economy theory simultaneously legitimated Gropius's planning ideals with economics and quieted Le Corbusier's harsher rhetoric with democratic planning. Le Corbusier's surgery "at the city's center," previously the work of planners backed by autocratic power such as Sixtus V or Haussmann, now issued from a democratic body supported by the congressional budget.[14] And the NRPB demonstrations, firmly committed to participation, placed local citizens at the center of this democratic body. Hansen's theory lent Gropius the rhetorical means to call for a comprehensive urban transformation in a period wary of anything totalizing. More importantly, it helped reconstitute planning as nothing less than a natural evolution of the American system.

The conference clearly had a profound effect on the German architect. Gropius immediately went to work reshaping the curriculum of Harvard's School of Architecture. In January 1943, he wrote Maxwell Fry, with whom he had been associated in London, that he was "busy with post-war planning" and that he had "made planning also the backbone for the school as I see this field as the future for the architect who has lost the field of individual tailor-made houses which become more and more out of date."[15] From the earliest days of the Bauhaus, Gropius had been interested in comprehensive planning. Indeed, the history of the Modern Movement in architecture, as much as it is a history of monuments, is also a history of planning.[16] Many European modernists in the 1920s and 1930s had sought nothing short of a total social transformation through architecture. What makes his interest in 1942 remarkable is his renewed faith in this possibility in America. Maturity provided the metaphorical frame for this renewal of faith.

The Mature Economy Theory

We often forget the context Gropius encountered when he first arrived in the United States and joined Harvard's faculty in 1937. That year, the United States stumbled into what has been called the Roosevelt recession, a convulsive reversal of the slow gains of the mid-1930s after Roosevelt, believing that New Deal programs had sufficiently "primed the pump," withdrew federal backing from the banks only to watch them collapse. The faith in American capitalism reached its nadir. Out of the tumult rose a stronger commitment to Keynesian economics. Broadly speaking, Keynesians advocated the use of public spending in moments of recession as a means of jump-starting the economy. Public projects put the unemployed to work, which stimulated consumption. In turn, increased demand for goods and services stimulated production. The theory flew in the face of classical economics, subverting the relationship of production and consumption. Hitherto, classical economists adhered to "Say's Law of Markets," which held that a free market was self-regulating, constantly correcting the relationship between supply and demand. In short, classical economists believed that production drove the economy and that consumption rose to meet the level of production. Keynesians turned this upside down, arguing that consumption drove production and thus held the key to a capitalist economy; in fact, in their view, the survival of capitalism hinged on this relationship.

In the wake of the Roosevelt recession, Alvin Hansen, who arrived at Harvard the same year as Gropius, named the American brand of this theory secular stagnation and coined the phrase "mature economy."[17] The Harvard economist argued that the American economy had slowly lost its vigor since the end of the frontier in the late nineteenth century. Economic expansion had been predicated on the Industrial Revolution and the open frontier that had given the United States its particular character. By 1929, these stimuli had dried up. The condition of maturity, understood as a loss of potency, left more or less two options. The committed industrialist or capitalist could search for new industries to take the place, for instance, of the flagging automobile industry. In the 1930s and 1940s, in fact, articles often cited the personal helicopter and the prefabricated house as future growth industries. Advertisements in particular seized on the idea of the helicopter as an anticipatory tease for 194X, and helicopters, personal fliers, and whirligigs became common in ads and architectural anticipations (see Figure 2.13, Figures 3.30 and 3.32, and Figure 4.4). Such new industries would replace the extensive development of the frontier, exhausted after the 1890s, with a technological frontier, based on the creation of new products. In a mature, consumer-based economy, new "necessities" would emerge out of old luxuries (a matter partly of advertising), new inventions would spark new desires, or planned obsolescence, either by way of shoddily made products or rapid changes in fashion, would create new demands. Hansen and other proponents of secular stagnation were not so sanguine. Without any obvious new industries on the horizon, they believed the only solution lay in reconfiguring the economic system. This meant restructuring industry and public spending to accommodate a relatively unchanging population: in short, to move from a classical laissez-faire system to a planned economy.

These ideas grew out of a theory of world-historical change. Hansen and his followers viewed the Depression as much more than another temporary downturn in the business cycle: they saw it as a harbinger of an entirely new era characterized by the expiration of the peculiar and spectacular forces that drove nineteenth-century expansion, in particular the Industrial Revolution, free or cheap land, and surplus population to develop it. These "exogenous" forces, as Hansen called them, had disappeared, drying up opportunities for private investment. The dilemma, he believed, reached beyond the ordinary problem of business cycles and pointed to much more expansive and long-lasting economic trends. The United States had entered an era "no less basic and profound in character than the Industrial Revolution."[18] With such epochal claims, Hansen took issue with the Keynesian palliative of "pump priming" because he believed they were insufficient stimulants to recovery. Reactive public spending left all the causal imbalances unchanged: the economy had "no momentum of its own," he wrote, "no inner power" to right itself.[19] The entire structure of society needed to be changed. The new conditions demanded a more permanent, structural solution, a fiscal policy of public investment through which the government could create conditions of full employment and constantly moderate the business cycle.[20]

To put this discussion back into the context of architecture, Walter Gropius arrived at Harvard in 1937, just as Hansen, his new colleague and almost exact contemporary, first articulated the mature economy theory. The immigrant architect grew acclimated to his new surroundings in a moment of sustained national emergency that saw the theory bloom into a vogue among progressive economists and cultural critics like Lewis Mumford. Mumford's analysis of the London County Council's County of London Plan of 1943 comes out of the same set of ideas about population on which Hansen based his mature economy theory. Hansen knew Mumford's work and even consulted with him in 1941 for the economist's work at the Federal Reserve.[21] With characteristic overstatement, in 1943 Mumford wrote of "the close of the world frontier."[22] Mumford's colleague, Henry Churchill, an important architect-planner with the Regional Planning Association of America who had worked on the Syracuse Project, based his 1945 book, *The City Is the People*, on the idea, as did Washington, D.C., planner, Louis Justement, in his 1946 book *New Cities for Old*.[23] Churchill's book was republished in 1962, and Justement, who headed the AIA's Committee on Urban Planning from 1946 to 1949 and created a prominent wartime plan for Washington in "19XX," carried these ideas into the postwar period.[24] The "old" cities of Justement's title nodded to the mature economy theory, and his subtitle, *City Building in Terms of Space, Time, and Money,* gave a practical corrective to Giedion's *Space, Time and Architecture* by way of urban reconstruction as a form of fiscal policy.

Keynesians also filled Roosevelt's "brain trust," including Marriner S. Eccles, and headed many of the high-profile initiatives of the New Deal. A few historians, Alan Brinkley foremost among them, have noted the importance of the mature economy.[25] The phenomenon, however, ran much deeper than scholarship acknowledges, spreading through Hansen and his followers into the NRPB and the Federal Reserve. George W. Terborgh, Hansen's primary antagonist, called the theory "an official creed" of the Roosevelt administration and "an unstated assumption of governmental policy and planning: . . . this theory has emerged into the arena of public propaganda and practical politics. It threatens, through its impact on mass opinion and public policy, to influence the history not only of ideas but of social and economic institutions."[26] Terborgh was not far off. As noted in chapter 1, Guy Greer, Hansen's closest ally at the Federal Reserve, marbled *Fortune* magazine with the rhetoric and spread the idea in his many wartime articles and lectures on postwar housing and urban planning. The mature economy theory played a central role in discussions on urban planning, through NRPB staffers assisting planning boards, schools, and government agencies across the nation.

The idea met great resistance, as well, especially in Congress, in business, and among classical economists like Friedrich A. von Hayek and Terborgh, something more fully detailed in chapter 4.[27] Yet the idea survived, fed by genuine fears that the United States would fall into depression again after World War II. In fact, the war seemed to prove the theory: a massive influx of government deficit spending for war production rapidly created full employment, lifting the nation out of the Depression. Keynesians viewed the war itself as a monumental instance of deficit spending, splendid proof of their theories, since the war created such a dramatic recovery from depression. Fears continued into the postwar period. In July 1946, a Gallup poll reported that 60 percent of the people interviewed believed there would be a "serious business depression" within a decade.[28] As late as 1948, economist Leon H. Keyserling, then vice chairman of the President's Council of Economic Advisors, warned of a depression following the postwar economic boom: "Unless substantial changes in popular attitudes and economic practices occur, the new prosperity era will be followed within three to ten years by a depression which might be as much larger than the one commencing in 1929 as the second World War was larger than the first."[29]

On the home front, economists, architects, and planners alike easily extrapolated the mature economy to the whole of society, embodying the fears of cultural senescence in the city, seeing it as "mature," having reached the end of its life cycle, or dying.[30] The rhetoric provided architect-planners with a moral argument for the destruction (understood as surgery) of the city (understood as a dead or diseased body). Long-standing organic and biological metaphors for buildings and cities gained new power. In effect, the mature economy hypothesis translated nineteenth-century biological and organic metaphors into twentieth-century planning ideology, inflecting the language that planners used for decades to "rehabilitate" urban areas.

Sick Cities: Architects and Maturity

Armed with the language of maturity and related body and illness metaphors, architect-planners went to war with cities. Once understood in terms of the mature economy, the sick city became a compelling argument for grand planning proposals, including those of the International Congress of Modern Architects, or CIAM. In *Can Our Cities Survive?* a book commissioned by CIAM, José Luis Sert, more than any other architect-planner of the period, carried the metaphor through his writing in a sustained manner.[31] The Spanish architect, who had arrived in the United States in 1939, pronounced urban planning obsolete. "In its place," he wrote, "must be substituted urban biology, or the study of the life of cities and of the living conditions within them."[32] He represented the city as a living organism, a thing that is born, develops, and eventually dies, a metaphor so ubiquitous at the time that architects and planners treated it like a truism. Taking the reader through the entire life cycle of the city, he linked age and disease directly and, grafting it onto Hansen's mature economy rhetoric, wrote: "[W]hen a certain degree of maturity is reached in the cities of today, they universally exhibit the same alarming symptoms."[33] As with a human being, the body of the city would begin to fail after a certain unspecified number of years. Maturation manifested itself most clearly in slums and blighted areas.

He likened the former to "the first stage of a protracted malady" and believed that the focus on slum dwellings in planning was "the same as devoting one's attention exclusively to maladies which had reached a crisis. . . ."[34] More radical, preventative measures were necessary.

Although published in 1942, *Can Our Cities Survive?* reflects the desperation of the 1930s, the undisciplined mixing of metaphors being a kind of rhetorical flailing, an effort to find the language to argue for a new socioeconomic system to replace the old one, which seemed to be in the throes of a mysterious disintegration.[35] As Susan Sontag asserted in *Illness as Metaphor,* metaphors help people contemplate the mysterious by placing sickness in a temporary realm that makes sense or over which we have control.[36] This Sert did with uncanny skill, calling planning "a kind of mysterious science," countering the mystery of urban illness with another one. Planning's mystery, however, submitted to "science."[37] Sick-city metaphors allowed Sert to play with the mystery, to suggest a scientific diagnosis without supplying one. Through the illness metaphor, Sert made a leap from calling the blighted areas or slums pathogenic, a point he made many times and backed up with medical "evidence," to calling the city itself diseased. A problem *in* the city—that some areas can be unhealthy and are prone to spread diseases such as tuberculosis—is made an endemic part of its nature, of its physiognomy, so to speak. Sert added that the tightly congested parts of the city, which to his mind were also the sick parts, became sick partly because they had destroyed too much of their natural setting. Good urban health was also a function of the amount of "nature." These ideas led to the conclusion that remodeling was impossible. The city had to be totally replanned and replaced: "The only remedy for this condition is the demolition of the infected houses and the reconstruction upon the reclaimed land, of sanitary dwellings surrounded by open areas, so that air and sunshine can penetrate into their rooms without hindrance."[38]

The desire for open areas and sunshine, a reasonable and humane plan for the city, derived from the treatments doctors prescribed for the most mystified disease of the nineteenth century: tuberculosis. Open space and sunshine warded off the spread of urban ills much in the way rural sanitariums and exposure to the sun and air were meant to cure tuberculosis sufferers of their illness. It is clear that this prescription confused the disease with the environment associated with it: the city. We know now that the high-rise in open space does not in and of itself cure the urban ills that "infected" the slums of Sert's day. Space, sunshine, and good design are about as effective at preventing slums, urban anomie, and social dysfunction as sanitariums were at curing tuberculosis. In adapting the human treatment to the body of the city, Sert in effect tried to take the nineteenth-century city (by definition, diseased) out of the city and replace it with new forms inoculated against disease with the injection of doses of nature, space, and rational planning. At the heart of this mysterious science lies the rhetorical alchemy of the mature economy, which allowed one to place new cells into the old city body. Behind Sert's language lay the desire to destroy the city and create an urban tabula rasa, an effort to create the conceptual framework necessary to uproot people and confiscate private property.

As with Gropius and Hansen, his theory of urban pathology was ultimately politi-cal. Disorderly growth itself promoted disease, Sert argued, and was, in fact, part of the disease. The unplanned city, inherently susceptible to illness, referred obliquely to the absence of planning policies under the laissez-faire capitalist system that prevailed until the 1930s and led, in his view, to wild speculation and uncontrolled urban growth. His generation paid the price for the disorder of previous generations. More importantly, he implied that planning acted as a prophylactic against the spread of urban ills and, by impli-cation, against laissez-faire. Moving from tuberculosis to a more insidious disease, he called slums the "*obvious* cancer of city growth" (his emphasis), yet the cure required more than "treating one small section of the urban organism."[39] The old system itself caused disease just as the new system would cure it. Rid the world of the old system (laissez-faire capitalism) and cities would be restored to health by the new system (planning).

Following the American Keynesians, Sert attacked the free enterprise system as a major obstacle standing in the way of planning, in fact, as its antithesis. He wrote: "The first objective will be that of *removing the interference of laissez-faire policies,* which still hold sway everywhere" (his emphasis).[40] In Sert's account, capitalism, like the city it en-gendered, no longer reflected contemporary conditions. When the city was young and vigorous (and people "could not foresee the blind alleys into which, with the coming of depressions or economic crises, it would be led"), it could handle the free enterprise sys-tem.[41] The argument relied on the loose metaphor of maturity to gain a purchase not just on the city but also on the whole of society. According to Sert, the city (and the society that had created it) had aged and could no longer sustain the unplanned speculative growth of capitalism without dying. This demanded a more comprehensive redistribution of urban land, in fact, a complete replacement of the urban body. Sert broached the deli-cate politics of planning in the United States, but this time with more subtlety. He tried to overcome the limitations of eminent domain (and the hostility of capitalists) by pro-posing a joint-stock solution. People who owned land in an area slated for replanning would be given a share in the new neighborhood in return for moving out and allowing the land to be "reassembled."[42] Sert's euphemism and the larger joint-stock idea hardly concealed the fact that privately owned land would be claimed under the auspices of a powerful centralized government bureau, which would also impose a new model of living on the city and its residents. Whether or not people were fairly remunerated, the govern-ment rather than market forces would coordinate a major forced migration and demo-graphic shift. Sert was not alone.

Eliel Saarinen also merged urban destruction with biological metaphors. "No ethi-cal hesitations should exist," wrote Saarinen in *The City: Its Growth, Its Decay, Its Future* (1943), "to question why the present property . . . could not be changed to another . . . or condemned . . . by virtue of advanced civic legislation, and passed to the community af-ter a certain length of time."[43] The work provided the background for J. Davidson Stephen's "organic" plan of Detroit that Greer published in *Fortune* (Plate 4). Saarinen compared the form of the city to the form of the cell, handling the analogy so literally that

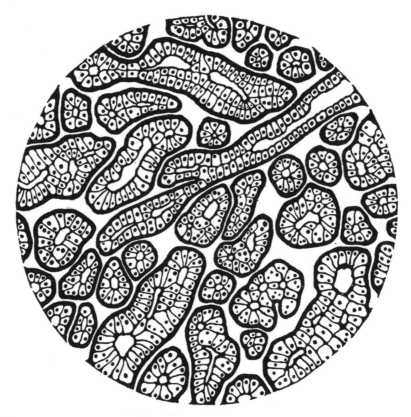

Figure 2.1. Eliel Saarinen, "microscopic 'community planning,'" *The City: Its Growth, Its Decay, Its Future* (1943), 10. Courtesy Robert Saarinen Swanson and Ronald Saarinen Swanson.

it disappeared almost completely as a metaphor. In the captions to the images, "healthy cell tissue" became "microscopic 'community planning'" and "disintegrating cell tissue" became "microscopic 'slum growth'" (Figure 2.1 and Figure 2.2). Saarinen believed that cities were organic, that they obeyed the same principles as living things, and like Sert, he thought of the city in terms of the life cycle, which explains his subtitle. In his estimation, the city had reached senescence and needed to be replaced with what he called "organic decentralization," a term that justified the vogue for decentralization as a biological necessity. Saarinen also despised the city of industrial capitalism, the same unplanned, disordered, and diseased agglomeration that Sert hoped to do away with. This city represented an outmoded system, one that had reached the end of its life cycle. As with Sert's imagined city, the new city would be highly planned, with green swathes to ward off the spread of slum.[44]

Similar arguments found their way into wartime advertising, as well. An advertisement for Revere Copper and Brass gave graphic form to this language (Figure 2.3).[45] The ad featured a project for Lower Harlem, New York, by William Lescaze, with the copy: "Sure Surgery for Sick Slums," echoing what had become a common metaphor of the day. The image plays off of the headline: the dirty children on the balcony, framed by

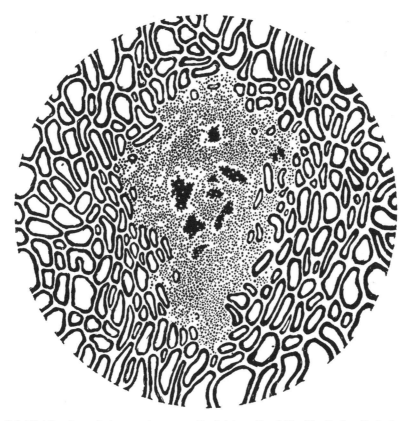

Figure 2.2. Eliel Saarinen, "microscopic community disintegration," *The City: Its Growth, Its Decay, Its Future* (1943), 16. Courtesy Robert Saarinen Swanson and Ronald Saarinen Swanson.

the proscenium arch of their laundry, behold the drama of 194X, the future looming on the clean, white horizon of expectation. Through Lescaze and Revere Copper and Brass, these ideas found a wider and more popular audience in the *Saturday Evening Post,* where the ad ran. Obscure economic theory thus made its way from threatened government agencies to progressive architecture and, finally, to mass circulation magazines.

Mature Pittsburgh

Not surprisingly, the maturity metaphor carried special resonance in the aging industrial cities of the United States. In 1945, Pittsburgh, Pennsylvania, like many cities during World War II, finished a postwar plan sponsored by a nonprofit planning organization called the Allegheny Conference on Community Development (ACCD).[46] In the *Civic Clinic for Better Living,* an oversized pamphlet published to promote the plan, Benjamin Franklin serves as the allegorical figure for Pittsburgh, the core of Allegheny County (Figure 2.4). The aging Franklin receives a "check-up" from a doctor, only to find that while he looks "hale and hearty as ever," middle age has brought on "certain disquieting symptoms" such as "hardening of the arteries" and "low morale" (Figure 2.5).[47] "This

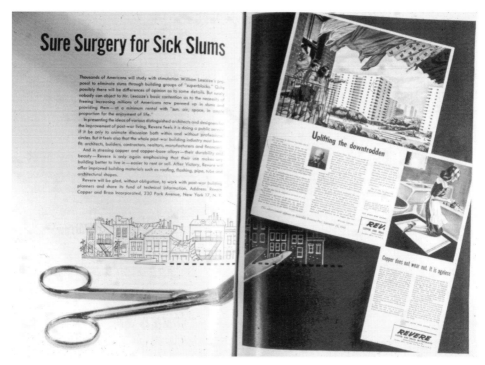

Figure 2.3. William Lescaze, advertisement for Revere Copper and Brass, *Architectural Forum* (October 1944): 46–47.

great industrial entity," the pamphlet claims, "has reached maturity."[48] The pamphlet runs through the various planning solutions that would stave off old age for Allegheny County (and Franklin). The amiable founding father reappears frequently in the narrative as a reminder of the analogy of body to city or to body politic. In the first frame, he paternalistically places his hand on the shoulder of a man who sets down a model factory on a large map of Pittsburgh's industrial infrastructure (Figure 2.6), the moral being that "Diversification of industry is the nourishment needed." Next, an almost "beefcake" Franklin, his chest straining the buttons on his vest, rolls up his sleeves, grabs a hammer, and begins building a house because "*more* homes, *better* homes vitalize the community's life-span" (Figure 2.7).[49] Likewise, a new transportation system "determines the pulse of the region," and clean air and streams are "health and welfare tonics." Franklin, slimmed down and back in his Colonial garb, takes two children on an outing to the park, a picnic basket in each hand (Figure 2.8). "Recreational facilities," we learn, "supply the vitamins for health." Finally, a younger, slimmer, and smiling Franklin, once the patient, becomes the authority. He stands before a town meeting and gives "the PEOPLE" (as in Kahn's diagram) the diagnosis: "community partnership" (Figure 2.9). Through participatory planning, Pittsburgh would reverse its "disquieting symptoms," unclog its arteries, and rejuvenate its aging body—an allegorical treatment of what Gropius and Wagner had called "relieving the sick bodies of our cities from their high blood-pressure and congestion."

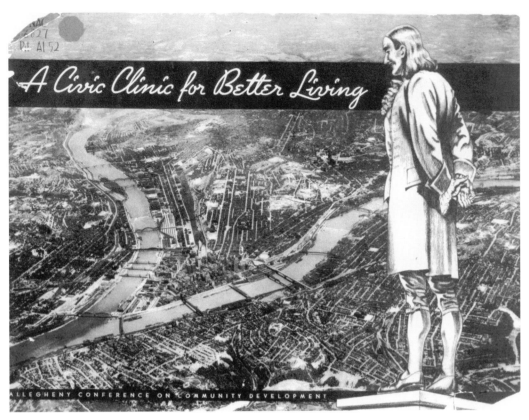

Figure 2.4. Benjamin Franklin as the allegorical figure of Pittsburgh, *A Civic Clinic for Better Living*, Allegheny Conference on Community Development, 1944.

The unusual document is a period piece. The language is dated and forced, the images almost endearing in their naïveté, the sort of cartoons and strategies one still finds in cheaply produced religious brochures passed out in bus stations. The parallel is not gratuitous. The Civic Clinic is a piece of proselytism for planning. Franklin, the ultimate citizen, replaces Christ, the ultimate Christian, and in a "second coming" of sorts leads the people toward a miraculous recovery from old age in 194X, a kind of millenarian resolution. The messy allegory, which variously makes Franklin the figuration for the ailing Pittsburgh and for the body politic, as well as a citizen and a civic leader, creates a vital ambiguity akin to Christ's ambiguity. Flesh and spirit, past and future, city and citizen, all become transmutable, transfigurable. Franklin waves away the intractable urban problems of the Depression in a rebirth through the formation of a new, activist social body, which finds new life by following his model. Pittsburgh is essentially born again. The assonance with Christian allegory, whether intended or an unconscious use of a vernacular narrative, surely made the pamphlet accessible. In other words, the Civic Clinic translated economic and architectural rhetoric to a lay audience in an effort to make planning palatable.

Figure 2.5. Franklin gets a checkup. *A Civic Clinic for Better Living.*

Figure 2.6. Industry as "nourishment." *A Civic Clinic for Better Living.*

Figure 2.7. "*More* homes, *better* homes vitalize the community's life-span." *A Civic Clinic for Better Living.*

When the Civic Clinic claimed that Pittsburgh had reached maturity, it drew directly on the mature economy theory. In fact, as early as 1939, two economics professors at the University of Pittsburgh, Glenn E. McLaughlin and Ralph J. Watkins, had argued that Pittsburgh was a mature city and used a combination of population and industrial studies to question "the ability of an enterprise system to produce a progressive evolution of the economy under conditions of maturity."[50] Following Hansen's basic argument, they wrote: "The Pittsburgh district is a mature industrial area whose growth trends began to taper off almost thirty years ago," an oblique reference to Frederick Jackson Turner's Frontier Thesis. The authors saw the city as an "instructive case study of the problem of industrial growth in a mature economy" and studied the "clinical records of [its] regional economy" in an effort to make more general claims about the state of the U.S. economy.

Figure 2.8. "Recreational facilities supply the vitamins for health." *A Civic Clinic for Better Living.*

While the authors seem to have had no direct connection with the *Civic Clinic for Better Living,* the Allegheny Conference on Community Development turned to these same "clinical records" for its own "clinical analysis," taking on the rhetoric as much as the material, of the economists.[51] McLaughlin and Watkins, moreover, both served the NRPB and consequently would have had close contact with Hansen's ideas.

The would-be citizen-planners of Pittsburgh, and the rest of the nation, would have been prepared for the reception of the Civic Clinic in a number of other ways, from the dissemination of the word *planning,* as discussed in chapter 1, to the American response to economist John Maynard Keynes in the New Deal and on the home front. Pittsburgh in particular endured the stinging critique of Frank Lloyd Wright, who told residents

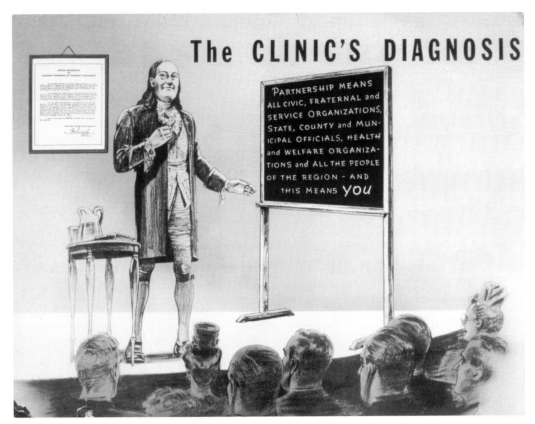

Figure 2.9. Franklin leads the Civic Clinic. *A Civic Clinic for Better Living.*

that the city "is obsolescent and is slowly dying as surely as humanity is growing. In all probability the town will have to be abandoned, eventually to become a rusty ruin and tumble into the river, staining the waters with oxide of iron."[52] Pittsburgh also entertained a plan by Robert Moses in 1939, and the Pittsburgh Regional Planning Association hired one of Moses's planners, William Sellew Chapin, as chief engineer.[53] The Civic Clinic used still more available imagery in the figure of Franklin, a founding father with ties to Pennsylvania history and to Yankee ingenuity, but also to pragmatism and entrepreneurship. As an institution builder, Franklin provided a great model for a fledgling organization composed mostly of businesspeople attempting to convince the rest of Pittsburgh to buy into a comprehensive plan. Franklin gave planning an enduring, ancient American paternity and a sense of revolution, getting to the heart of the paradox of planning in 194X.

Theories of Maturity and the Frontier

Maturity alone provided a compelling way of thinking about historical and urban change, but when grafted onto the myth of the frontier, it gained special poignancy. In forecasting a dramatic end to the Industrial Revolution, Hansen grew his mature economy theory directly out of Frederick Jackson Turner's frontier thesis, an account so foundational to conceptions of American history and reform, and so often repeated, that historian Kerwin Klein has likened it to an origin myth.[54] At the annual meeting of the American Historical Association in 1893, the young Turner read his paper, "The Significance of the Frontier in American History," and explained the development of American culture as a product of the westward expansion of Euro-Americans in the United States. According to Turner's elastic sense of an expanding frontier, where "civilization" repeatedly met "savagery," waves of American settlers improvised new social, political, and economic practices and thereby sloughed off inherited European conventions. This energy, he held, carried back from the West, modifying the more entrenched establishment on the East Coast. To put the thesis simply, the frontier made Europeans into Americans, and the frontier thesis created an intricate and convincing case for the uniqueness of the American experience. As Klein has written, the theory "reshaped historiography" in America, positioning the "European and Euro-American occupation of North America . . . [as] the central topic in United States history. . . . For decades Turnerian history dominated the profession as no other field ever has."[55] By the 1930s, the frontier thesis had become the nearly unquestioned paradigm of historical explanation. The most pressing part of Turner's hypothesis in 1893, however, came when he declared the end of the frontier. The end of free land spelled the end of this improvisation and thus the end of those forces that had shaped American character, culture, and most of all, democracy.

From the vantage point of the 1930s, with economic depression at home and the rise of fascism abroad, Turner's rather pessimistic prediction from 1893 resonated strongly. Other parallels gave his thesis renewed relevance in the 1930s, as well. He delivered his talk in the midst of the depression of 1893, one so deep that it almost did in plans for the World's Fair where he spoke. In turning to the frontier thesis in the 1930s, Americans looked back to the last major depression and to a moment that launched the Progressive era, the Progressive tradition of history, and a narrative about American culture that once again could be useful for the New Deal and for pressing the case for a planned society. With these parallels in mind, Hansen leveraged the frontier hypothesis into an explanation of the Depression and a plan to relieve it. The economist's riff turned the origin myth of the frontier into a cautionary tale (not unlike Turner's): after decades of boom and bust in the nineteenth century, in which the availability of free land and cheap resources had sopped up the excess labor force and capital, America had reached a plateau. With the frontier closed and the development of the interior virtually finished, the Depression corrected for the extravagance of laissez-faire capitalism, especially the overspeculation of the 1920s.

Hansen's economics were part of a broader return to the frontier in the 1930s. Richard Slotkin has written of the revival of the Hollywood Western in 1939 as a renewed engagement with the idea of the frontier at precisely that moment when the United States had to negotiate its role in the new war in Europe. The frontier, as a myth about expansion, boundaries, borders, or more generally about national identity understood in terms of territory, provided a fertile trope for filmmakers to editorialize on the politics of the day.[56]

The frontier, as an inherently American experience, provided a conceptual border between Old World Europe and native traditions. As Slotkin argues, repetition over time conventionalized the frontier myth, creating a "deeply encoded and resonant set of symbols, 'icons,' 'keywords,' or historical clichés. In this form, myth becomes a basic constituent of linguistic meaning and of the processes of both personal and social remembering."[57]

In architecture, the frontier provided a ready myth for embodying the mature economy, inverting it into the urban frontier. For instance, linking mature economy rhetoric to the planning ethos of the home front, *Architectural Forum* publisher Howard Myers wrote (using language suspiciously close to Hansen's): "With population stabilized, with few new frontiers to open and with millions of decrepit structures," Americans had reached maturity "as a people."[58] Turner's own ambiguous use of the word *frontier* set the stage for this sort of slippage between the economy and national identity. The historian manipulated the idea of the frontier to encompass "place, process, population, and period, . . . holding in combination a mixture of warring elements: migration and colonization, town building and warfare, competitive individualism and cooperative community."[59] In these incarnations, it served as an ideal metaphor for depression and war. Like Myers, economists like Glenn E. McLaughlin and Ralph J. Watkins framed maturity in cultural terms, as well, seeing it as part of "the rhythmic surges of the human spirit."[60] In short, the mature economy implicated a mature society. The rhetoric suggested a nation tapped of its energy and power. Or, as Howard Myers put it, a middle-aged or senescent body "beyond the point where homeopathic remedies can cure the ill[ness]."[61] Myers condensed all the clichés out of which a popular mythology of the Depression might be constructed and used them to advocate a radical shift toward planning. First, in his mythic narrative, the Depression grew naturally out of the end of the frontier. Second, he represented maturity as an affliction, something that would continue to get worse without radical, invasive treatment. Third, this sickness, embodied in the Depression, was a cultural predicament, not merely an economic state, and therefore entailed a much deeper response than simple cosmetic changes could effect. Americans could no longer expect the "automatism" of the "natural" business cycle, previously kept resilient and virile by the bounty of the frontier, to right itself. These three forms of maturity—the frontier, sickness, and cultural renewal through radical change—were part of the conceptual framework of the home front.

New Frontiers, Native Frontiers

While Myers was American, Gropius, Sert, Saarinen, and even Lescaze were all foreign-born architects writing in a moment of intensified xenophobia in wartime America. As propagandists for planning with clear roots in European modernism, they had to contend not just with what Greer had called a "truculent Congress" bent on curbing planning on grounds that it was "un-American," but also with American architects and planners with strong nativist tendencies intent on finding an *American* form of planning. And yet battle lines were rarely drawn clearly. Ralph Walker, for example, a passionate advocate of postwar

CORBUSIER——Find the citizen. A hive of the irresponsible. Shelved community ready to swarm to the
charms of a Hitler. "Stupendous Megalomania"

Figure 2.10. Ralph Walker, commentary on Le Corbusier's Plan d'Algiers. From "Planning for Peace," *New Pencil Points* (June 1942): 41. Reprinted with permission of Penton Media.

planning during the war, excoriated European modernist solutions. In an article in which he supported a commonsense version of the Hansen-Greer Plan, he used unrelated images to lambast Le Corbusier's Plan d'Algiers: "Find the citizen. A hive of the irresponsible. Shelved community ready to swarm to the charms of a Hitler. 'Stupendous Megalomania'" (Figure 2.10).[62] And above an unlabeled Alvar Aalto plan he added: "Disintegration of community form. Might be a mobile by Calder. Cubist relations rather than life" (Figure 2.11).[63] Walker buried his ideology in these slurs. Americans were to think collectively, his article suggested, but not to live that way, in "a hive of the irresponsible," where they might submit to the rhapsodies of mass rallies.

The home front turned to the frontier as a persuasive keyword that helped "Americanize" planning by couching it as a modern, urban descendent of manifest destiny, the next stage in the development of "American Civilization."[64] Linking planning to the frontier connoted expansion, progress, freedom, and rugged individualism, all of which posed important counterpoints to the Depression and to the totalitarian associations of fascist or communist planning. Frontier rhetoric also fed American desires to frame their experience as exceptional, rooted in the character of the land itself and therefore inevitable.

Already in the 1930s, the frontier had become a ubiquitous reference for New Dealers searching for familiar terms to express the complex socioeconomic shifts of the period. The Depression inflected the idea of the frontier with new meaning, and New Dealers conscripted Turner's thesis to narrate the collapse of industrial capitalism and to navigate a way out of it. By the beginning of World War II, the frontier had been linked closely with the fate of cities, as in Hansen's adaptation of Keynesian thought. The urban

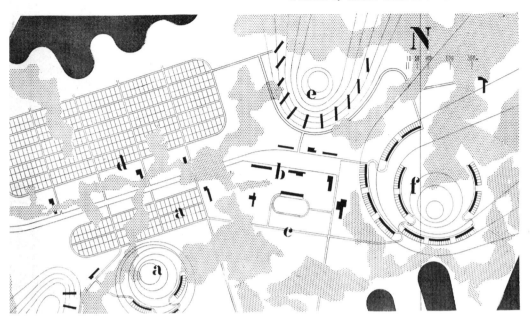

AALTO—Disintegration of community form. Might be a mobile by Calder. Cubist relations rather than life

Figure 2.11. Ralph Walker, commentary on plan by Alvar Aalto. From "Planning for Peace," *New Pencil Points* (June 1942): 42. Reprinted with permission of Penton Media.

spaces freed of Gropius's "endangered production" would open up new frontiers, an idea that continues today in terms like "urban homesteader" and "urban pioneer," commonly used for someone who begins the process of gentrification by moving into a so-called blighted neighborhood.[65] Applying the frontier to purportedly unproductive, disused, and by association "uncivilized" urban land transformed areas considered devoid of value and strapped with an intractable population into an untapped resource, free for the claiming. Drawing out the parallel, the strategy clears the slum rhetorically before razing it physically, undermining the value of its population as preparation for its displacement, a process akin to the displacement of Native Americans from the actual frontier. The use of the frontier creates a very particular tabula rasa, one rife with the associations of the American West as a crucible of American culture, individualism, and economic vigor. The frontier, detached from its historical context in the West, becomes an invisible force, not unlike the invisible hand of laissez-faire, but brought to bear on collective, planned action. The eddying waves of energy that Turner saw flowing back from the frontier and creating a dialectic of cultural formation with the eastern establishment in the nineteenth century, rolled beyond the regional or sectarian boundaries of east and west that began to dissolve with the end of the frontier, and issued into and out of the urban frontier.

The language conveyed nativist ideas that were bound to age metaphors. At the core of Turner's thesis lay a claim about American exceptionalism. As "settlers" shook off conventions inherited from Europe, an intrinsically American civilization took shape implicitly in terms of a conceptual framework of age, as the New World abandoned Old World ways. In his book *New Frontiers* (1934), Henry A. Wallace, then Roosevelt's secretary of agriculture who would go on to be vice president (1941–1945), began with a classic age metaphor: "The United States is like a boy eighteen years old, possessed of excellent health and strong body, but so unsettled in his mind and feelings that he doesn't know what to do next."[66] This optimistic precursor to the more dour mature economy theory soon broke down: "The tragic joke on the United States is that we went to bed as a pioneer debtor nation in 1914 and woke up after a nightmare of world madness as a presumably mature creditor nation in 1920."[67] Mixing maturity and body metaphors in anticipation of Hansen, Gropius, Saarinen, and the ACCD in Pittsburgh, he framed the Depression in terms of generational tension:

> The people of my generation, those born from 1880 to 1895 [the same generation as Gropius, Hansen, Giedion, Lescaze, Myers, and Robert Moses], can see and feel the inevitable pressure. We want to see the new world safely born, but we do not want the old world destroyed. The new world must be born from the body of the old world; for if the old is destroyed prematurely the new will also die and chaos will ensue.[68]

Wallace sketched out an early sounding of the mature economy theory and called for a new frontier as the resolution, a frontier that "cannot be found on the maps. . . . Some people call it a state of mind."[69] Comparing the old and new frontiers, Wallace wrote:

> The keynote of the new frontier is cooperation just as that of the old frontier was individualistic competition. The mechanism of progress of the new frontier is social invention, whereas that of the old frontier was mechanical invention and the competitive seizure of opportunities for wealth. Power and wealth were worshipped in the old days. Beauty and justice and joy of spirit must be worshipped in the new.[70]

Wallace, a farmer turned politician, then spatialized the new frontier in terms of "thousands of self-subsistence homestead communities properly related to decentralized industry," out of which would develop the "New World."[71] This Jeffersonian vision—soon to tour America in the form of Frank Lloyd Wright's Broadacre City, which he unveiled the same year—was then taking shape, according to Wallace, in the Resettlement Administration homesteads on which Louis Kahn and others were then working.[72] Even the name of the bureau suggests a link with the frontier. The earliest programs of the New Deal thus manifested the frontier thesis and mature economy in terms of urban theory and planning practice.

Contemporary historians noted the connection between the mature economy and the frontier, as well. In his 1934 essay, "Frederick Jackson Turner and the New Deal," Curtis Nettels wrote: "[E]verywhere one sees evidence of the influence of the frontier interpretation in current discussion of the new order."[73] Roosevelt, according to Nettels, "realized that the economic policies suitable for an expanding nation are not wholly suitable for maturity" and cited examples among many leading scholars, such as historian Henry Steele Commager and economist Rexford Tugwell, a member of Roosevelt's brain trust who ran the Resettlement Administration and later the Tennessee Valley Authority.[74] In fact, Benjamin Stolberg of the *Nation* wrote of the National Resources Board: "[It is] a true social revolution in the simple sense that it expresses the most significant thing in our national life—the realization that the social frontier is also over."[75] New Dealers saw in the frontier more than a metaphor for the uncharted future; they connected the economic turmoil of the 1930s directly with the closing of the frontier.

As early as 1936, Hansen himself linked the Great Depression to the frontier in his review of Keynes's *General Theory*.[76] He would go on to put the frontier to use causally, metaphorically, and historically. This meant emending Turner's theory that the frontier had closed around 1890. "With respect to the frontier," he wrote,

> the economic development of the last frontier had scarcely started in 1890. It is true that the political historians have used 1890 as the date for the closing of the frontier, and this is correct in the sense that free homesteads after that date were no longer available, but the *economic* development of the last frontier had a full generation to go after 1890. The land had to be broken, buildings had to be erected, railroads built, warehouses, commercial establishments and houses constructed. The frontier in terms of frontier *development* lasted until World War I. It is wholly incorrect to say that the economic frontier ended in 1890.[77]

A classic Keynesian and New Deal formulation, it explained the Depression as a lag between the end of the "land grab" and the slowing of intensive development of that land. The lag theory allowed economists to represent the Depression as a natural phenomenon, the maturation of the economy's life cycle, rather than an abrupt and irregular break in capitalist expansion—a subtle and useful distinction from the Marxist account of the end of capitalism. Simultaneously, the frontier could be used as a historical construct, assimilating Keynesian measures to American traditions. As late as 1945, Hansen likened his plan for full employment to the homestead movement and the Homestead Act of 1840, as Wallace had done a decade before: "Just as the right to free land was the watchword of economic opportunity a hundred years ago, so the right to useful, remunerative, and regular employment is the symbol of economic opportunity today."[78] The parallel fabricated a pedigree for full employment, giving fiscal policy the air of a "natural right" and rooting it in a historical and mythic American experience and in the land. Hansen used the frontier to make New Deal ideas that critics branded as socialist—social, economic, and national planning—into American ideas, as self-evident and inalienable as the other rights accorded the natural community of men by the Enlightenment.[79] By this way of thinking, laissez-faire capitalism had disregarded these rights, an acceptable state of affairs so long as the free land and resources of the frontier existed as counterweights to the imbalances of the system.

Hansen came by these rhetorical strategies and ideological connections at the University of Wisconsin, where he studied with Richard T. Ely, who, among many distinctions, briefly taught the young Frederick Jackson Turner there in the 1890s. An economist like Hansen, Ely created the Wisconsin School of Progressive Reform, an interdisciplinary department of social science before the word interdisciplinary existed. The department linked history, economics, and sociology, a fertile cross-pollination for Turner and later for Hansen. Turner caught the beginnings of Ely's synthesis, bringing insights from social science into history, and Hansen went through the same system, graduating when it was well established in 1918, an auspicious year for the young economist, whose first professional work dealt with reconversion after World War I. Hansen followed Ely's example in other ways, as well. In the teens, Ely turned his attention to urban conditions, writing popular tracts on the city and land use, later founding the Urban Land Institute (1936), a nonprofit group that gave impetus to the field of land-use planning to which Hansen owed a great deal of his thought.[80] Turner and Hansen thus shared both an alma mater and a mentor. Hansen's colorful rhetoric married Turner's language to the ideas and language of Keynes, producing one of the most fertile hybrids of American economic history. In the late 1930s and especially during the war, Hansen applied it to urban rehabilitation.

Planning as Frontier

Considering Hansen's ties with Gropius, Hudnut, and other architects, as well as Greer's wide lecturing and publishing campaign, it is not surprising that the frontier metaphor filtered into architectural and planning circles during the Depression and war and continued long after World War II in discussions of cities. A number of wartime pamphlets published by Revere Copper and Brass replaced the lost frontier with the house, a proxy for the romanticism of pioneering and settlement. Published to accompany the firm's wartime advertising as a form of corporate responsibility, each one featured anticipatory designs and ideas for the postwar world. As an answer to the problem of a mature economy (and society), several of these pamphlets proposed a metaphorical frontier beyond the closed western frontier and let that powerful idea do its work reinvigorating American culture and thought as earlier frontiers had presumably done. Paul Nelson's pamphlet of 1942 spelled out some of these themes.[81] Nelson looked back to the 1930s for answers to problems particular to the postwar house. He rehashed visions of prefabrication and the development of a Fordist architecture, but in the context of the apocalypse of war. Prefabrication itself linked up directly with the first possible response to a mature economy, the creation of a new industry to supplant flagging industries. In this case, prefabricated houses, rolled out on assembly lines and delivered to the site, were modeled on the industry it was meant to replace: the automobile. Nelson recycled his "La Maison Suspendue" (or the Suspended House), developed in France between 1936 and 1938 (Figure 2.12).[82] Nelson wrapped the house in a permanent steel cage formed of an exoskeleton on which he hung the internal structure. From the cage, which, in theory, made the house unusually adjustable, he suspended mass-produced rooms connected by a system of interconnected ramps. When the rooms went out of style, the owners could alter, move around, or discard them.[83] The arrangement followed a familiar fantasy of total flexibility and mobility: "A truck could back up to your house and a complete sleeping

Figure 2.12. Paul Nelson, Suspended House, 1936–38. Acrylic, metal, paint, stone, textile, wood, 14 x 26½ x 28½ inches (35.6 x 92.7 x 72.4 cm). Gift of the Advisory Committee (MC 14), Museum of Modern Art, New York. Digital image copyright Museum of Modern Art; licensed by SCALA/ Art Resource, New York.

room, bathing room, cooking room or eating room, for example, could be unloaded and set in place."[84] When one moved, the cage was still saleable, and "the old rooms could be shipped to your new house . . . sold on the 'used room' market, or they could be traded in for the newer, better models which had since been placed in production."[85]

Nelson's experience with the European avant-garde in the 1930s, including Fernand Léger, Joan Miró, and Le Corbusier, clearly influenced his work, but his rhetoric remained attached to a uniquely American experience. "The exterior shell of the house," he wrote, "should be a frontier between the individual and the surrounding community."[86] He posed his Suspended House as a complex metaphor, playing on the tension between public and private, inside and outside, *suspending* the idea of the house between old and new, the individual and the community. Through the frontier metaphor (and the house as its primary example), Nelson attempted to work out these unresolved dualisms. He linked the geographical frontier to the temporal and cultural frontier of 194X implicit in the Revere Copper and Brass series. Applying the idea of the frontier directly to the modern home, Nelson imagined the skin of the house as a symbolic frontier, mitigating the harsh encounter with modernity, with the new. He even suggested that the exterior would admit any choice of styles from Cape Cod to Georgian, in this case as much a matter of consumer preference as the need to soften the harshness of prefabrication. In so doing, Nelson went further, redefining modernity itself as frontier and positioning the house on the tenuous line between frontier and settled territory, future and past, or collective experience and individual identity. In Nelson's hands, the modernist homestead combined the promise of modern architecture with a quasi-historical idea of the unlimited frontier, transposed to the individual home.

The creative ferment of the frontier myth could also be found in the interior arrangement of rooms. The unit rooms segregated the "specialized functions" from the rest of the house. Nelson drew a clear spatial distinction between necessities such as eating, sleeping, and bathing, on the one hand, and leisure on the other hand, leaving a "free area remaining which is not the product of the machine. This can be furnished and decorated, used and enjoyed, with absolute freedom from all restrictions imposed by the specialized functions, which are at present carried out throughout our homes."[87] He used the machine to create a space that was free of mechanization, allowing people to move and behave outside of its regimentation: "The machine has now become the liberator," he wrote, echoing Lewis Mumford.[88] It "frees the individual and enables him to shape his surroundings according to his needs and desires. In this way it accentuates the individual and opens before all of us wholly new opportunities for self-enrichment in our homes."[89] But the machine was more than a liberator. According to the pamphlet, a new civilization would grow in those free spaces, in this interior frontier. It was not in the new forms, per se, that a new spirit would evolve, but in the spaces between the built forms. Here lay the new frontier, at least for Nelson, in the flexibility his house gave people to plan and shape their personal environments, just as the western frontier in Turner's theory had produced American civilization.[90] Nelson interiorized what had been an idea or ideology and whipped this highly individualistic, if not antisocial, spin on the frontier into a utopian ideal.

Another Revere Copper and Brass advertisement by housing expert Carl Boester presented a similar isolated modernist homestead. The illustration provocatively depicted the breadwinning husband stepping out of his private personal aircraft to greet his expectant family at their prefabricated house, situated in the middle of a verdant, rural landscape (Figure 2.13).[91] Boester coupled two of the industries on which some industrialists pinned their hopes of reversing the Depression: the prefabricated house and the personal flying machine. Although the illustration depicts a nuclear family in its modern homestead, the domestic idyll of the illustration had little to do with Boester's agenda. "The experts," he wrote, echoing the reports of the NRPB, "say we must have extensive development of our cities, complete rehabilitation on a square-mile basis, not a building-to-building remodeling."[92] His solution moved beyond the realities of urban blight and slum clearance to the modern homesteads of Frank Lloyd Wright or Henry Wallace, but constructed in a manner that would stimulate the sort of high consumption the emerging economy demanded.[93] Following the model of the automobile industry as Nelson had done, Boester wrote: "[W]e must accelerate obsolescence. If housing is to take first place in our national income, as economists believe, then we must have constant obsolescence and ever-new production in housing."[94] The ad's headline reinforced the message, claiming that his design was "helping to open new frontiers." Essentially, with the frontier exhausted, business would have to simulate the mechanism of its productivity in the form of obsolescence. Cities had to adjust to changing economic doctrine and realities. A mobile population, set in motion by the Depression and by the war, was not merely modern but an economic necessity.

Figure 2.13. Carl Boester, advertisement for Revere Copper and Brass, *Architectural Forum* (February 1943): 12–13.

Boester considered the house that lasted longer than its mortgage a liability. Longevity in a house was wasteful, stalling production by inhibiting consumption.[95] He envisioned houses built to last three to five years, equivalent to the life span of a car, and with this he boldly pronounced the automobile age finished. As the illustration suggests, commuters would fly to work. In fact, in Boester's view, technological liberation allowed the family to be completely self-sufficient, altogether free of the city and its problems:

> We don't need the road, because the "Cloudcar" will move through the air and then onto the paved highway of the individual area, eliminating the private road to our door. Sewers—an unscientific and unsanitary method of waste disposal, besides requiring costly quantities of water for operation, when water can better serve irrigation purposes—can be eliminated by a simple process of waste incineration. Water—with the amount we need greatly reduced by the solution of the waste disposal problem—can be rain or well water. . . . Some of it will be condensed right out of the air.[96]

Solar energy, radio phones, and education by television would all reinforce the independence (and isolation) of the postwar family, the modern homesteaders. Boester used fashionable economic theory and the resonance of the frontier to address the urban conditions of his day, seeing in a self-sufficient, decentralized housing scheme a neat—perhaps much too neat—solution to urban problems. Both Nelson's and Boester's ads, and many others of the war years, updated the homestead movement, inventing a personal frontier in which new lives would be cut not out of the wilderness of nature but out of the personal unknown of the future, out of 194X. The rhetoric of the frontier animated the otherwise cold or "foreign" idea of the prefabricated house and its equally cold or obscure economic underpinnings. The transformation generally promised in the ads and by the frontier, a millenarian change after the war, fit well with the larger social projects of modern architecture and planning.

Planning with You: Architectural Forum's Urban Frontier

In 1943, under the guidance of Howard Myers, *Architectural Forum* (which ran the Revere Copper and Brass ads) started "Planning with You," a new section, and published a pamphlet by the same name aimed at teaching the public about planning. The pamphlet, a primer in the mold of the NRPB's *Action for Cities,* didactically instructed people about why planning was a necessary and patriotic duty of every citizen on the home front.[97] An advertisement for the pamphlet informed the readership that "The New Frontier Is Right Where You Live."[98] In a society wary that its material and cultural energies had matured, the promise of a new frontier, especially in an unexpected domain, made for a good promotional strategy. The *Forum* passed off planning as a new frontier, a new democratic social structure that would transform American cities and towns. In case the frontier reference were not enough, the *Forum* compared its efforts to Thomas Paine's *Common Sense* (Figure 2.14).[99] Paine's pamphlet fomented the revolution, leading to the establishment of the first democracy; *Planning with You,* the ad would have us believe, fomented the new

In which we invite you to join us
in the useful art of PAMPHLETEERING

". . . . the pungent pen of the pamphleteer played its part in rousing the spirit of the nation

Washington's day was Tom Paine's day, but Tom Paine's way was the pamphlet. Again and again, when things looked their darkest, Paine's militant pamphlets appeared to turn a faltering, famished Revolutionary army from despair to determined attack and final victory.

Today, the pamphleteer is with us again. In England pamphlets on a dozen subjects claim the avid attention of millions. Wendell Willkie's "One World," almost too ambitious in form and price to be so classified, is nevertheless one of the truly great and successful pamphlets of any time.

Undeterred by this impressive tradition, the Editors of THE ARCHITECTURAL FORUM have set down certain convictions on city and town planning in a modest sixteen-page pamphlet. "Planning With You," addressed to the whole public, is not designed to make its readers expert in this technical field. Rather, it introduces the U. S. citizen to planning, it advocates that planning-on-paper must be done now.

Rebuilding every U. S. city and town is an issue of great dimension —just such an issue as would have claimed the attention of the pamphleteers of the past. It is *the* challenge to postwar America. It stands or falls, as all great issues do, on public opinion.

But this pamphlet cannot influence widespread public opinion unless copies by the thousands reach people by the thousands—your friends and neighbors, your fellow townsmen. "Planning With You" in quantities is available to individuals and organizations at five cents a copy. Checks should accompany orders. If you believe that planning now is imperatively necessary, you can take no better first step than to place a few or many copies of "Planning With You" before people without whose support there will be neither great plans nor great enterprises to follow.   —THE EDITORS

Figure 2.14. Promotion for *Planning with You* comparing *Planning with You* to Tom Paine's *Common Sense, Architectural Forum* (September 1943): 64.

revolution in planning, the next stage of democracy. The pamphlet attacked the slum as "the breeding place of crime, disease and death: . . . Blight is malignant and unless stopped moves on to make slums of once good neighborhoods."[100] These were the terms that Hansen, Gropius, Sert, and others used in their wartime writing on cities: growth, decay, death, and replacement through planning.[101] The *Forum* used the pamphlet and related articles to further Luce's interest in planning, drawing attention to the *Forum*'s and *Fortune*'s Syracuse Project and other important ventures in planning, but now in terms of the frontier.[102]

More than anything, *Planning with You* staged a publicity campaign for planning. Even before disseminating the pamphlet, the *Forum* ran its "New Frontier" broadside as full-page advertisements in the *New York Times, Washington Post,* and *Cincinnati Enquirer* to coincide with architecture and planning conferences in these cities (Figure 2.15).[103] The advertisement distilled the pamphlet down to its essence, arguing for planning as an essential part of postwar business and as a democratic process that demanded the full participation of American society. "Planners are not crackpots," it claimed: "These technicians are not screwballs or dwellers in ivory towers," rebuffing the stereotype of Robert Moses's "long-haired planners" label. "They are hard-working, trained, skillful people." Not only architects and planners planned. "They are Engineers. And they are Builders, Real Estate Men and Bankers. A few of them are Government officials," it added tactfully, "but most of them are private 'professionals,' expert in giving your community what it needs."[104] The pamphlet itself sketched out a short history of the American town, glossing over its descent into blight, and then rallied the public to get involved with planning. The tone reveals the level of distrust they anticipated the public would have. "Planners, like doctors, like to use big words, but they both get results. And since you are the patient in both cases, you might as well be a smart one and learn how to help the planners."[105] This was tantamount to Franklin's check-up, turning the citizen into the patient as a means of creating participation.

The *Forum* promoted *Planning with You* almost as fiercely as it promoted planning. In spite of a small budget at the Time Advertising Department, which allowed only a limited distribution and publicity, publisher Howard Myers aimed to send copies of the much cheaper advertisement to local businesses in all cities with fifty thousand people or more, asking them to sell the campaign. He distributed copies of the pamphlet to all the attendees at the AIA and American Institute of Planners conferences in 1943. He also mailed out six thousand copies of the pamphlet and appealed to Time for more funds in order to send one to all thirty-five thousand subscribers.[106] Within a month, the *Forum* ran ads praising its own program by reproducing the dozens of checks written by architects, planners, organizations, and businesses, essentially underwriting the cost of distributing the free pamphlet (Figure 2.16).[107] The savvy Myers condensed some of the comments, publishing them in the *Forum* and distributing them around Time, Inc., in order to garner support for his program.[108] The commentary shows an extraordinary response, especially considering it was just an advertisement. Business leaders applauded the effort, including executives at Johns-Manville Corporation, Westinghouse Electric, Revere Copper and Brass, and the Ruberoid Company. Real estate corporations, nonprofits,

THE NEW FRONTIER
IS RIGHT WHERE YOU LIVE

one of several full page newspaper advertisments published in support of postwar planning and rebuilding

When people talk about rebuilding America they do not mean some other town.

They mean your town, whether you live in Manhattan or Manitowoc.

Nor do they mean some other "third" of the nation than the third you happen to be in. Rebuilding America means rebuilding it for three-thirds of the nation—for each town and for everyone in it.

The important thing about postwar planning is not the jargon the planners talk but what the planners do. Without your help there is precious little they can do but talk.

Planning, like Democracy, needs more than the experts

There are two kinds of postwar planning. One kind could only result if the citizenry shrugs its shoulders and leaves the job to the experts. Not many people, certainly not the planners, want that. The other kind of planning will result if an informed group of active citizens in every community arouses public opinion and guides the planners in gradually making over each community into a better place for your wife, your children, your neighbors and you.

Planners are not crackpots

These technicians are not screwballs or dwellers in ivory towers. They are hard-working, trained, skillful people. They are Planners. They are Architects. They are Engineers. And they are Builders, Real Estate Men and Bankers. A few of them are Government officials, but most of them are private "professionals," expert in giving your community what it needs.

Maybe your town does not need changing—maybe?

Maybe your town has no traffic problem?

Maybe it has no slums and no blighted areas soon to become slums?

Maybe most of the houses are not over 50 years old?

Maybe there are enough safe places for your children to play in? And enough modern schools for them?

Maybe your hospitals are model 20th Century medical plants?

Maybe there is a fine municipal swimming pool for all the kids?

Maybe your water supply and sewage system are up to date?

Maybe these questions are not for you? Maybe you live in the town nobody knows?

Slow planning is better than fast planning

It takes time to replan even a small town.

First you have to assemble all the facts about the kind of town it is. Next the town has to decide what kind of place it wants to be in the future. Then you have to figure out the steps to get there. And only after that can you even begin to plan on paper.

If the war lasts two more years, your planners would have to hurry to have any decent plans ready. And if the war ends sooner, you are likely to be behind the job, even if you start tomorrow.

Replanning and rebuilding your town is a good business proposition

A badly planned town—and almost every town was built before autos and planes were thought of—if allowed to shift for itself will not be able to compete with progressive postwar communities.

Trade will fall off. Sooner or later, people will move to more attractive places. And as your town goes downhill, the cost of community services will go up and taxes will follow, without any compensating features. In other words, you pay no more to rebuild your town than if you do nothing. Of course, planning and rebuilding cost money. But you get something that the town next door cannot take away from you, something your neighbor next door deserves to share with you.

The essentials of a planning program are simple

Planners, like doctors, like to use big words, but they both get results. And since you are the patient in both cases, you might as well be a smart one and learn how to help the planners. To help many people make replanning of the U. S., and your particular piece of it, a truly democratic and successful enterprise, the Editors of THE ARCHITECTURAL FORUM are preparing an inexpensive 12-page booklet. This booklet "Planning With You," is almost a primer, but not quite. It counts on your civic spirit and sees you as a responsible adult anxious to play an active part in postwar planning. The booklet is free. Send for it. Read it. It is the first step you personally can take in doing something for the future of your town now.

WHY THE ARCHITECTURAL FORUM is steamed up about replanning and rebuilding your town

This is no philanthropy. This magazine has perfectly sound and selfish reasons for printing this message. For 612 consecutive months THE ARCHITECTURAL FORUM has been talking to its regular audience which now numbers more than 33,000, among them most of the professionals who will lead the way in replanning and rebuilding America. They need a voice to reach the people who will decide how much and what kind of rebuilding should be done. This message is their voice. No one will lose by heeding it.

THE ARCHITECTURAL FORUM is published by TIME INC.
19 WEST 44TH STREET, POSTAL DISTRICT No. 18, NEW YORK

Figure 2.15. Advertisement for *Planning with You, Architectural Forum* 79 (August 1943): 81.

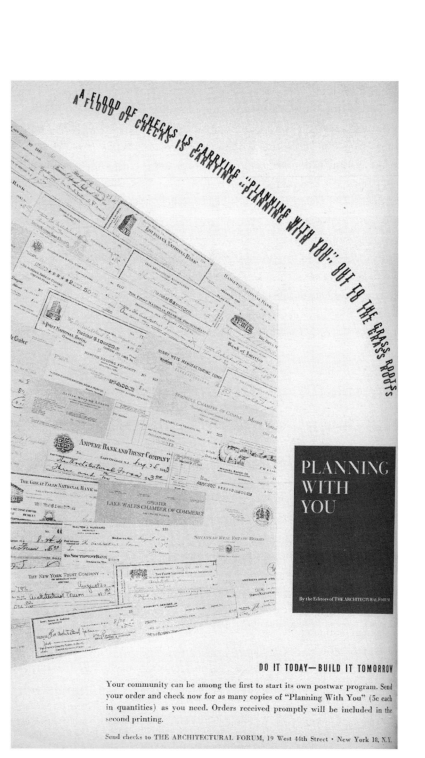

Figure 2.16. Flood of checks, advertisement for *Planning with You, Architectural Forum* 78 (June 1943): 157.

planning organizations, and leaders of government agencies, including Alvin Hansen and Charles W. Eliot of the NRPB, also supported the *Forum*'s campaign.[109] People ordered "Planning with You" by the thousands—the *Forum* quickly ran out of copies and money for reprints.[110] Wallace Richards, the executive secretary of the Pittsburgh Regional Planning Association, ordered one hundred copies, one for "each member of the Allegheny County Conference on Postwar Planning."[111] This was the same organization that would later publish the *Civic Clinic*, suggesting the possibility that the *Forum*'s pamphlet served as a model. By May 1944, over one hundred fifty thousand copies had been distributed.[112]

Architects and planners registered their approval, as well, requesting copies for local distribution and rightly seeing *Planning with You* as an important bridge to the public. Hugh Ferriss posted the ad at the Architectural League of New York, and Robert D. Kohn, a former president of the AIA and an important member of the Regional Planning Association of America, called it "horse sense" planning and hoped it would start a nationwide movement that would "make our people realize that local, regional and national Planning alone can provide the setting for economic welfare."[113] The responses display the broad support for a planning society (as opposed to a planned society): "In many people's minds, [planners] have been thought to be something akin to the parlor pinks of a decade ago who were composed mostly of long-haired men and short-haired women. Planning is perfectly respectable and I believe we must bring the public to believe that the planning of cities and of housing is no different from the planning which industry must do every time it decides to change the model of a car."[114] The author steered planning away from bohemian or socialist stereotypes and instead conflated local citizen efforts at postwar planning with the completely accepted industrial planning of Ford, the sort of planning that both drove capitalism and was winning the war.

Planning with You also offered a step-by-step program for running a local planning campaign, which it clearly drew from the NRPB's *Action for Cities*, simplifying the terms and emphasizing elements of publicity. The *Forum* encouraged readers to apply its lessons in "grass roots" planning efforts in their hometowns, much in the manner of the "Civic Clinic."[115] Publicity played a major role. The first step was to sell the town on the program by publishing a notice, provided by the *Forum*, in the local newspapers and distributing the pamphlet in the community. The magazine went so far as to outline the cost of the promotion, by chance citing the cost in Pittsburgh at $7,500. This step would be followed up with talks on radio stations, feature stories in the newspapers, and exhibitions of models and plans.[116] *Planning with You* thus brought together frontier rhetoric, planning, and the tactics of consumer culture.

Conclusions

The mature economy recast planning as American in a moment of ideological suspicion and rupture. Hansen's poetic economics helped architects and planners mix earlier organic metaphors with the "harder" rhetoric of social science, which they then applied to the modern city. The mixing of organic and scientific metaphors shows a transitional moment between the organic thinking of the nineteenth century and the social science–based planning of the postwar period and contributes to our understanding of how architects turned to social science as a form of authority. The co-option of economic theory reveals the subtlety of disciplinary influence, which, in the case of architecture and planning, reached beyond the rigors of methodology to the magic of rhetoric. Sert, Saarinen, Gropius, Churchill, and others all used economic rhetoric without being economists, applying the latest controversial economic ideas to a much more physical or material understanding of the built environment. The consequences for this deserve further examination. The way the two fields intersected with one another ends up being an important study in how systems of authority are constructed within architecture.

Modernist architecture, born both of an economy of means and of aesthetic economy, found inspiration in hard economics. The connection stems in part from the predictive function of economics. Since the 1880s, Dodge Reports had been tracking the building industry and helping to rationalize the flow of materials, manufacturing, advertising, and design. These reports in effect charted the business cycle as reflected in building; the same cycles prompted Alvin Hansen to propose the mature economy theory, linking the fate of the economy with full employment in cities. City planning became the centerpiece of a centrally planned workforce and economy, and this demanded a clean slate on which to start. Darwinian laissez-faire economics, "red in tooth and claw," would have been just as apt a metaphorical partner for progressive architects seeking a "natural economy" for urban renewal. But they associated the purported automatism of market forces with the unplanned chaos and dysfunction of nineteenth-century cities. The encounter between the two economic systems, interpreted through the myth of the frontier, shaped up as a conflict between "Old World ways" and "the American way," as in the Herman Nelson Corporation ad of 1944 (Figure 2.17).[117] The advertisement compares the hubbub and haggling of a European market, with its chaos of unfixed prices and disorganized produce, with the rationalized and hyperorganized abundance of the American supermarket. The Old World way—that of a mature society—suggested evolution (and cities) at a bottleneck, lacking standards and stuck in outmoded forms and practices. The New World way—thoroughly planned—suggested a kind of progress based on predictability, honesty, and, of course, planned capitalism. Here were two visions not just of the economy but also of the city. The mature economy theory rooted this progress in "nature" by co-opting the natural metaphors of laissez-faire for planning via the frontier thesis. On one level, this was purely rhetorical: mature cities needed rejuvenation. On a deeper level, the rhetoric came laden with historical implications drawn loosely from both Darwin and Marx. The crisis of industrial capitalism, as witnessed in the Depression, led "naturally" to a new stage of development in the evolutionary sense of that word: social crisis, as cataclysm in nature, produced new social forms, a synthesis of laissez-faire and the totalized planning of, say, the Soviet Union. Democratic planning thus carried with it the sense of a third way, an inevitable resolution of forces. Self-consciousness, instead of posing a dilemma of human intervention with natural processes, became part of the evolution. Building on the esprit de corps of war, the newly mobilized citizenry (acting through Stonorov and

Figure 2.17. Old World way, New World way, advertisement for Herman Nelson Corporation, *Architectural Forum* 81 (July 1944): 52–53.

Kahn's chart, *Action with Cities*, the *Civic Clinic*, or *Planning with You*) would shape the next stage of participatory democracy, creating a planned society from the grass roots. This sort of thinking meshed well with both the sense of social responsibility of the Modern Movement and its idealistic vision of social transformation through reshaping the built environment.

The economic rhetoric of the late 1930s and the war years, as interpreted by architects and planners, played an important role in translating the desperation of the Depression into the urban renewal of the postwar period. The most conspicuous case is the famed Pruitt-Igoe public housing project in St. Louis.[118] *Architectural Forum* first covered the project in 1951 with the headline "Slum Surgery in St. Louis," an overt use of the sick-city metaphor in a scheme that came close to the square-mile planning sponsored by the NRPB and Hansen (Figure 2.18).[119] Ironically, when Pruitt-Igoe failed twenty years later and met the fate of implosion, writers again turned to the same rhetoric to explain the problem. By that time, the mature economy had returned from exile. As Theodore Rosenof has shown, twenty years after the postwar economic boom discredited the mature economy theory and secular stagnation, they reemerged as explanatory models for the economic turmoil of the 1970s, and they have continued to play an important role.[120] The mature economy continues to furnish a language of pathology to discuss urban problems, as well. For instance, *The Mature Metropolis* came out of a 1977 conference

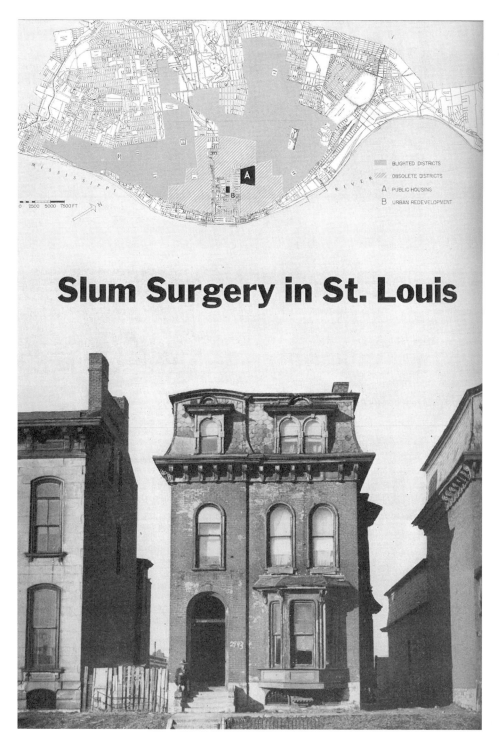

Figure 2.18. "Slum Surgery in St. Louis," *Architectural Forum* 94 (April 1951): 128.

of the Institute for Urban and Regional Studies in St. Louis, Missouri, and another report from 1980 on "rustbelt" cities in the Midwest was called *New Direction for the Mature Metropolis.* The latter emerged from two conferences in Ohio, one devoted to "Managing Mature Cities."[121] The language again spread into the public sector, used in congressional discussions of urban problems.[122] The theory is more than the defeatist philosophy of laggard moments. It grants economic authority to grand liberal visions, especially large public projects that require deficit spending, as do many urban planning projects. The mature economy theory failed to direct postwar planning policy not because it failed to stimulate public officials or the imagination of the public at large—the Civic Clinic provides an important counterexample—but because the building boom prevented the depression on which so much of secular stagnation theory depended. Cities and the built environment were transformed after the war, but as much by private enterprise as by public programs of urban rehabilitation along the lines recommended by the NRPB. Industry created near full employment without the need for dramatic fiscal policy, which rendered urban rehabilitation as a public spur to full employment irrelevant. Laissez-faire capitalism, checked and sometimes aided by planning agencies much more limited in scope than Hansen had hoped, performed its own surgery on postwar cities.

3 Advertising Nothing, Anticipating Nowhere
Architects and Consumer Culture

194X might be seen as a temporal frontier in which the rhetoric of maturity narrated a tale of destruction and the possibility of a new world after the war. While the metaphor of maturity prepared a postwar tabula rasa, advertisements in the building industry filled it in. Architects, who had been shunned by the armed forces in military building and planning operations, found themselves in league with one of the major forces behind home front morale and postwar anticipation: magazine advertising. The alliance boosted architecture's prospects in small but significant ways. It created commissions for paper architecture in high-profile magazines and the trade press, and more importantly, it gave a particularly generous airing to progressive architecture, which leaped from its narrow base in mostly elite cultural circles to a much wider public. The pages of magazines became theaters in which citizen-consumers watched the drama of war unfold explicitly in terms of goods and imagined the world of 194X in terms of architecture.[1] Here readers gained a preview of "the postwar," represented as the tangible aggregation of appliances, steel, glass, plastic, lighting, and copper flashing that combined to make the houses, neighborhoods, and sparkling new cities promised after the war. Articles on the war nestled up to pieces on the postwar home. Interspersed throughout, readers found vivid advertisements that completed the calculus between the war effort and postwar consumption, the temporal gap between them bridged by savings bonds and planning, and the conceptual gap between them narrowed by slogans like 194X or "better living."[2] Admen recruited architects to serve as actors in this drama and posed them as experts and prognosticators on housing, civic and commercial buildings, neighborhood and urban planning. Together admen and architects invented the world of 194X, stoking the anticipation of life after the war.

The complex, intertwining interests of publicity, propaganda, and public service inspired the new campaigns. Desperate for publicity while their products were off the market, corporations in the building industry turned to advertising.[3] The ads were also an economic boon for architects who were hit hard by wartime restrictions. They provide a window into the work of a number of architects at pivotal moments in their careers. Taken as a whole, considered as a body of work by a profession working under extraordinary conditions, they become the forgotten oeuvre of the war years. In addition to being a neglected corpus of architectural designs and ideas, the ads are among the most compelling forms of cultural anticipation in the period, supplying a vision of the future that appeared in both the architectural and mainstream press. The campaigns came in different forms. The emerging genre of architectural advertising rapidly found a conventional form, with a portrait of the architect, a testimonial, an anticipatory design, and a show of support for the war. United States Gypsum, a manufacturer of gypsum-based building materials, pioneered these sorts of ads in early 1941.[4] The company commissioned architects to create paper architecture for its ads, an innovation appropriate for those months when the United States backed into the war. Revere Copper and Brass tightened U.S. Gypsum's multiple-page ads into a more legible format, which Barrett Roofing, Pittsburgh Plate Glass, General Electric, and other companies adopted. Soon such ads filled magazines with the work of Stonorov and Kahn; William Lescaze; George Fred Keck; William Wurster; Harwell Hamilton Harris; Eero Saarinen; Walter Gropius; Skidmore, Owings and Merrill; and other leading progressive architects.

Other companies, especially Bohn Aluminum and Stran-Steel, offered more generalized visions of postwar architecture, using a single visual aesthetic created by an ad agency artist to describe the future and often resorting to visual cliché rather than using the original ideas of a specific architect (see Plate 12 and Figure 3.39). These clichéd—perhaps even willfully clichéd—visions of modern architecture presented an accessible image of modernity to a public unschooled in the brief history of the Modern Movement but familiar with world's fairs and wartime buildings like the Quonset hut. The architectural advertisements reveal a deep cultural engagement with contemporary architecture, both as architecture and as a figure for the future. One of the foundational beliefs of the Modern Movement—a kind of material determinism that architecture could be a form of social reform—became an important advertising strategy and consequently enjoyed widespread publicity.

Architects and Advertising

The search for the tools of persuasion to sell planning to the public came as American architects confronted long-standing professional discomfort with advertising and public relations. In fact, depression and war precipitated the fall of a professional interdiction against advertising in architecture. While this is a complicated story, and one larger than can be told here, suffice it to say that during the war architects made their peace with Madison Avenue. This was not always the case. For much of the twentieth century, architects faced censure from their professional bodies if they advertised their services. While architects frequently worked around this prohibition, nonetheless it reflected the widely held view that the very definition of professionalism depended on rising above the "low" world of commerce, despite the fact that architects themselves could not practice effectively without intimate knowledge of and deep immersion in that world. As Mary N. Woods has shown, "[C]apitalism . . . was the milieu of American architectural practice" in the nineteenth century.[5] As professions emerged in the nineteenth century, they grounded their codes of conduct in an aversion to internal competition. Professionalism thus came to contradict competition, yet this was the central mechanism of capitalism, along with one of its key corollaries, consumer seduction. In the nineteenth century, the American Institute of Architects (AIA) had already erected safeguards against competition between individual architects for commissions, much in the spirit of the old gentleman-architect tradition, which precluded architects from accepting money for their work. Such safeguards, in addition to recalling the genteel origins of architecture, distanced the professional world from the commercial sphere. Reputation, as opposed to Barnumesque self-promotion, acted as the invisible hand directing architectural practice.

Architects, however, were swimming against the current. Already in the late nineteenth century, the increasingly national scope of the American economy placed architects in the midst of an ever more intricate and expanding complex of anonymous business relationships. The conditions of Depression and World War II complicated this state of affairs, drawing architects closer to consumer culture. The meager prospects of wartime employment forced architects to confront the realities of self-promotion, from which they had been shielded by their high-minded ideals of professional practice. In January 1941 *Pencil Points* started a regular section called "Public Relations," choosing D. Knickerbacker Boyd, the head of the AIA's Committee on Public Information after World War I, to write it.[6] Boyd weighed in monthly on how architects could improve their standing and educate the public about their skills. The magazine also ran advertisements in *Advertising Age,* one of the key organs of the advertising industry, in order to publicize the role of architects in defense building. At about the same time, *Architectural Record* began a comparable section called "Architecture Meets Advertising," with architect Ronald Allwork as section editor. Of greater consequence, the AIA began to open up to the possibilities of public relations and to relax its rules against the involvement of architects in advertisements.

As many of the advertisements already discussed in this book demonstrate, during the war, architects for the first time worked with advertising agencies in a sustained manner, weaving their ideas for postwar architecture into wartime advertising campaigns that propagandized the war and prepared the public for postwar consumption and, in particular, for the building boom. Architects remained several steps away from using advertising directly for self-promotion, but professional resistance to advertising weakened, and architects found themselves moving in new circles, their photographs and designs circulated in new contexts. Here lay a largely untapped domain for architecture. A younger generation of architects, who came of age in the 1930s and grew up within a mature consumer culture, met less ethical hesitation as they threw themselves into the emerging matrix of architecture and advertising. Even months before the war, ads like those by Revere Copper and Brass would have violated the AIA's policy.[7] The war would change that.

Advertising and World War II

Architects wrestled with advertising in the much-altered context of the home front. It is well known that when America went to war, Madison Avenue followed.[8] In fact, advertising emerged from the Depression as wounded as architecture, and its wartime prospects looked equally bleak. As the United States edged its way into war, Roosevelt, advised by a brain trust deeply antagonistic to the advertising industry, considered banning ads completely. For New Dealers who already disdained advertisements as an unnecessary cost in production, such promotion seemed particularly indulgent in wartime. The idea got as far as proposed legislation to curb all advertising for the duration, which would have decimated an industry still reeling from the effects of the Depression.[9] But in late 1941, the Roosevelt administration unexpectedly reversed course to embrace advertising as a way of avoiding some of the propaganda debacles of World War I. Roosevelt's support came only after animosity between admen and New Deal officials threatened to become a national issue.[10] Admen and advertisers met in November of that year in Hot Springs, Arkansas, to determine what tack to take during the war and, in particular, how to handle government restrictions. Manufacturers, who were then giving up their peacetime production for emergency war production, worried about staying in the public eye. The proposed change also threatened advertising agencies with extinction. Just as architects prophesied the end of their profession, so did admen doubt whether there was a place for them under the conditions of depression, war, or in a postwar world given over to large-scale public works. Addressing the Hot Springs conference, New Dealer Leon Henderson, newly appointed administrator of the Emergency Price Control Board and an avowed enemy of the advertising industry, put their immediate fears to rest, assuring the admen that the Roosevelt administration would back advertising during the war.[11] Soon after, Roosevelt himself came out publicly for reconciliation between the government and advertising.[12]

During the remainder of 1942, the administration concretized its support into law. Lawmakers battled over the extent to which manufacturers could invest war profits into advertising, a key issue given that many corporations were then devoting their entire plant to war-related production. A rule of thumb developed that allowed a generous and unspecified percentage of profits taken from war contracts to be put back into advertising, overturning earlier restrictions and using such vague language that corporations had carte blanche and a clear conscience to advertise as they pleased. One writer commented that the Roosevelt administration maintained "what has been characterized by executives as a 'beneficently indefinite' rule against allowing excessive advertising expenses as tax deductions."[13] By September 1942, legislation allowing "ordinary and necessary" advertising was "so generously construed . . . that virtually any kind—and often any amount—of advertising was permitted" by military contractors.[14] Moreover, any advertising that promoted the war bonds campaign was tax deductible, a great boon for corporations that needed to offset war profits. They could now do so under the guise of patriotism. In fact, the Department of Commerce encouraged widespread tax-free advertising.[15] Money now flowed into the advertising sector, and new ad campaigns filled magazines.

Advertisers seized the opportunity. A War Advertising Council formed, which organized the vast number of new ad campaigns, made space available in magazines for government messages, and spearheaded the war bond campaign.[16] As Frank W. Fox has written, "[W]hen advertising did go off to war, it went more resolutely, more evangelically, than all of the entertainment media combined, and it wound up taking its morale-building responsibilities much more seriously."[17] The War Advertising Council became a key player in American war propaganda. Over the next three years, it contributed the equivalent of over one billion dollars in space and time to propagandize the war.[18] The mobilization of the advertising industry played an important part in the war, but it also revived the industry itself, boosting long-declining profits, and more importantly, cleaning up advertising's reputation while it simultaneously restored the reputation of corporate America. The War Advertising Council performed an unusual public service to the nation, demonstrating a sense of social responsibility not normally associated with advertising. Public service and institutional advertising exploded, providing the context for the building industry to commission architects to envision the world after the war.

United States Gypsum

The United States Gypsum Company created the prototype for these architectural advertisements in a campaign that built on the tight connections between advertising, architecture, and the architectural press. At the very moment that embattled architects observed the narrowing of professional opportunities as the United States prepared for defense in 1941, U.S. Gypsum hired New York architect Richard Boring Snow to create designs for defense housing. His designs appeared in *Architectural Forum* in March 1941 in one of the first wartime advertising campaigns to use architectural designs that had little to do with the product itself (Figure 3.1).[19] The previous month, a round of letters in the *Forum* angrily took the federal bureaucracy to task for doling out defense housing contracts to its own office of procurement, shutting architects out of the process at the very moment that war production had jump-started the economy. The U.S. Gypsum ad quietly editorialized on behalf of the architectural profession by publicizing ideas for defense housing designed by an established architect.

U.S. Gypsum ads by Cameron Clark, Gardner Dailey, Edward Durrell Stone, George Fred Keck, Eero Saarinen, and others followed in 1941 and 1942. The advertisements played on the ambiguity between advertising and articles in the press. The company's multiple-page ads paraded as news, even emulating the graphic layout and informational bias of an article, thus confusing the boundary between editorial content and advertising

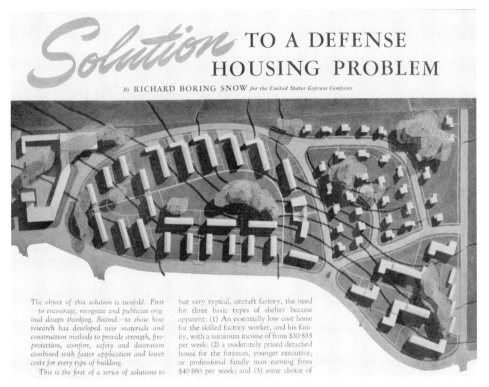

The object of this solution is twofold. First —to encourage, recognize and publicize original design thinking. Second—to show how research has developed new materials and construction methods to provide strength, fire-protection, comfort, safety and decoration combined with faster application and lower costs for every type of building.

This is the first of a series of solutions to

but very typical, aircraft factory, the need for three basic types of shelter became apparent: (1) An essentially low cost home for the skilled factory worker, and his family, with a minimum income of from $30-$35 per week; (2) a moderately priced detached house for the foreman, younger executive, or professional family man earning from $40-$60 per week; and (3) some choice of

Figure 3.1. Richard Boring Snow, advertisement for the U.S. Gypsum Company, *Architectural Forum* 74 (March 1941): 37–40.

content.[20] U.S. Gypsum packed each ad with explanations of the product and specification data in addition to a range of more fanciful illustrations of the possible uses of the product in wartime or postwar projects.

In August 1941, U.S. Gypsum quickly moved from housing, which promised a direct use of its products, to an almost unfathomably large urban project, which held little hope for direct marketing of its products. The company's fourth ad featured Edward Durrell Stone's plans for Sixth Avenue in New York City (Figure 3.2).[21] Since 1878, an elevated train had run up the middle of Sixth Avenue, but in 1939, after almost thirty years of debating its fate, the city dismantled the tracks, leaving the scarred and dilapidated street free for new development. What to do with Sixth Avenue became an important local issue, debated "in the executive offices of the larger stores, in the shifting knots of men around the bulletins of employment offices . . . over bolts of cloth, over shocks of cut flowers . . . in the hodge-podge of second-floor flats, in hardware stores, jewelry shops, printing plants and the dark caverns of warehouses."[22] The issues transcended New York parochialism, becoming a national issue because it offered a model for planning in a dense urban fabric. Like the more recent multiple rounds of design and planning for the World Trade Center site, the plan for Sixth Avenue went through many iterations on paper, including at least two exhibitions, which played out over a period of several years between 1939 and the end of the war. Critics saw it as *the* greatest urban planning opportunity to emerge in many

STUDY FOR AN AVENUE OF THE AMERICAS

by EDWARD D. STONE FOR THE UNITED STATES GYPSUM COMPANY

Pan-American Solidarity is in the news, both politically and commercially. What would be a more practical expression of the entire idea than a central market place for the Americas?

To the vision of a prominent New Yorker we owe gratitude for this study. As President of the Sixth Avenue Association, Colonel V. Clement Jenkins fought an 18-year battle to remove the elevated structure from New York's Sixth Avenue. In 1939 his hope became a reality—the elevated came down!

But Colonel Jenkins' fight had just begun. The removal of one eyesore, created another.

The outmoded buildings of the seventies which lined both sides of the Avenue were revealed in all their ugly unfitness for life today. But Colonel Jenkins visions an avenue of buildings to constitute the commercial capital of the Western Hemisphere. Ambitious? Yes, but both desirable and feasible.

The United States Gypsum Company takes pleasure in presenting Mr. Stone's capable treatment of this stupendous vision as the fourth in its series of solutions to architectural problems. As always, your comments on the design or structural considerations are solicited.

The United States Gypsum Company

Edward D. Stone (at left) studied architecture at Harvard and Massachusetts Institute of Technology and has won, among other honors: the Rotch Traveling Scholarship in architecture; the Architectural League medal for domestic architecture; and the grand prize in House and Garden's competition for 1939. Associated in the design of the Museum of Modern Art in New York and the Foods Building at the recent New York World's Fair, he was archi-tect for Collier's Home of Ideas and one of the Life homes in 1940. His work includes many homes in New England, Long Island, the Carolinas and Florida. Colonel V. Clement Jenkins (at right) is president of New York's Sixth Avenue Association. For 20 years he has been one of the Association's most active members. Colonel Jenkins' keen interest in city planning has been a major factor in past Sixth Avenue progress.

ADVERTISEMENT

Figure 3.2. Edward D. Stone, advertisement for U.S. Gypsum Company, *Architectural Forum* 75 (August 1941): 35.

generations. Lewis Mumford vividly described the corridor as "two solid miles of avenue suddenly relieved from the noise and dinginess of an ancient Elevated structure; two miles of sordid shops, mean apartments, vacated shooting galleries, decrepit loft buildings; a mass of rusting iron cornices, cracking plaster, bedaubed woodwork, much of it without adequate fire protection, all of it waiting to be carted to the dump."[23] Mumford bemoaned the first exhibition, held in December 1940, seeing mainly "muddling and remodeling" as the chief "inspiration" of the architects involved. "This is not a case for piecemeal plans," he wrote, urging the city to "understand the possibilities of the avenue as whole."[24]

By 1941, a comprehensive plan emerged. In June, the Sixth Avenue Association appointed Edward Durrell Stone to create a design for the street (Figure 3.3). Stone had been catapulted to architectural celebrity by the success of his Museum of Modern Art, which had opened in 1939. The architect turned the project into an assignment for his studio class at New York University, which created the exhibition.[25] U.S. Gypsum supplied materials for the exhibition and, two months later, used the work in its ad campaign.[26] The Sixth Avenue Association pitched the idea for an "Avenue of the Americas," transforming the twenty-seven midtown blocks between Thirtieth and Fifty-Seventh Streets into a tree-lined boulevard to "house the Manhattan interests of all the Latin-American republics."[27] Yet the idea went far beyond a monumental gesture to international trade in the Western hemisphere: the new avenue would form a cultural spine for Manhattan, with new centers for music and the arts, a fashion district, buildings for recreation and health, a new hotel and convention center, a railroad terminal, and a host of restaurants, shopping areas, office space, and parking garages, all linked together aesthetically and functionally (Figure 3.4). Stone laid out the modern corridor as "the commercial capital of the Western Hemisphere."[28] Between Fifty-Seventh Street and Fifty-First Street at Rockefeller Center, a new cultural center would be built, including a concert hall, a music museum, a gallery, and a health museum and center. Between Rockefeller Center and Times Square, Stone envisioned a "Plaza of the Americas," with buildings representing "the twenty-one American Democracies," each with its own exhibition spaces, consular services, travel bureaus, and offices to conduct international trade (Figure 3.5). From Times Square to Thirty-Second Street, a new merchandising district with shops, style centers, and a new garment district would take shape. No street in the world looked as completely modern as Stone's vision, which he hired Hugh Ferriss to render, a mark of the seriousness with which he took the project.[29]

Here was a modernist prodigy, the architect of the Museum of Modern Art, working with a manufacturing company with little or no vested interest in urban reconstruction, publishing the most comprehensive report of the architectural scheme. The unusual alliance between Stone and U.S. Gypsum made a topical story, one that used news and corporate social responsibility as a form of publicity. The unusual four-page ad assumed the format of an article and included technical information on U.S. Gypsum products and text explaining the idea. It responded directly to issues then emerging in the architectural press. In the same issue in which the ad ran, the *Forum* initiated "Building's Post-War Pattern," a harbinger of the obsession with postwar planning that would dominate the home front.[30] U.S. Gypsum may have planned Stone's "Study for an Avenue of the Americas" to dovetail with the new section, a practice that the *Forum* encouraged throughout the 1930s and 1940s as a way of bundling its editorial content with its advertising into a coherent package.

AN AVENUE OF THE AMERICAS

In this study involving the redesign of some 20 city blocks, we have attempted to provide a framework sufficiently flexible to serve as a pattern on which future studies for the completion of the entire task can be made.

In our conception of the problem, which offers a unique opportunity, both to the property holder and the public, we have tried to secure a practical, economical and feasible solution.

In the beginning we could have advocated the dedication to the city of every other block for park purposes, but feasibility demanded that we consider the large property values and enormous investment in existing structures. Rather than a continuous planting area or series of parks disposed at intervals along the street, we

have retained the sidewalk trees now proposed and suggest, in the interest of variety, that each block or series of blocks contribute their court or open area for both the utility and esthetic effect of light, air and greenery more frequently and effectively disposed.

The familiar conglomeration of one-story tax payers and 30-story skyscrapers should be prevented if Sixth Avenue is to become a true street of the future—an "Avenue of the Americas." Our plan restricts building heights to six stories on the face of the Avenue with the privilege of building higher after suitable setbacks at this level. Constructing these six-story structures would create an immediate improvement—the higher setback portion of the design would follow as the needs for space required.

The necessary movement of trucks and cars is facilitated by providing ample garage space at regular intervals along the Avenue, with entrances sufficiently removed from the traffic artery to avoid congestion and stalling. All deliveries to the buildings would be made through these garages, reducing traffic and parking on the Avenue and facilitating quick delivery for both tenants and their suppliers.

FLEXIBLE DESIGN

Unity in exterior design is achieved by expressing the usually concealed column and beam construction of New York's commercial buildings in the facades; creating an impression of large scale design with full flexibility in fenestration, but without the small scale effect of large walls, perforated with thousands of double-hung windows. The interior design will, of course, be flexible in order that it may be readily adapted to the widely varying demands of occupants.

Page 2 (Continued on Page 3)

The Elevated goes down—and a new era begins for New York's Sixth Avenue —an era that holds great promise.

Removal of the 6th Avenue "L", for years a landmark, enables the citizens to see the street for the first time.

ADVERTISEMENT

At 34th Street progress has already modernized the street. But see the next picture.

Obsolete buildings house a miscellany of business. To bring order out of this chaos is the problem.

Figure 3.3. Edward D. Stone, Avenue of the Americas, advertisement for U.S. Gypsum Company, *Architectural Forum* 75 (August 1941): 36.

Where the *Forum* started out tentatively, calling on the architectural profession to absorb the idea of postwar planning as its contribution to the war effort, Stone boldly envisioned a form of urban reconstruction of near Haussmannesque proportions.[31] The anti-Victorian copy stated: "The outmoded buildings of the seventies which lined both sides of the Avenue were revealed in all their ugly unfitness for life today."[32] After years

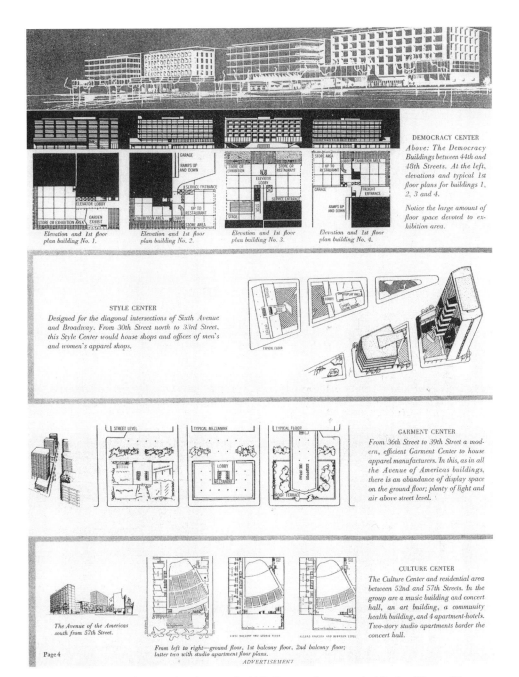

DEMOCRACY CENTER

Above: The Democracy Buildings between 44th and 48th Streets. At the left, elevations and typical 1st floor plans for buildings 1, 2, 3 and 4.

Notice the large amount of floor space devoted to exhibition area.

Elevation and 1st floor plan building No. 1.

Elevation and 1st floor plan building No. 2.

Elevation and 1st floor plan building No. 3.

Elevation and 1st floor plan building No. 4.

STYLE CENTER

Designed for the diagonal intersections of Sixth Avenue and Broadway. From 30th Street north to 33rd Street, this Style Center would house shops and offices of men's and women's apparel shops.

GARMENT CENTER

From 36th Street to 39th Street a modern, efficient Garment Center to house apparel manufacturers. In this, as in all the Avenue of Americas buildings, there is an abundance of display space on the ground floor; plenty of light and air above street level.

CULTURE CENTER

The Culture Center and residential area between 52nd and 57th Streets. In the group are a music building and concert hall, an art building, a community health building, and 4 apartment-hotels. Two-story studio apartments border the concert hall.

The Avenue of the Americas south from 57th Street.

From left to right—ground floor, 1st balcony floor, 2nd balcony floor; latter two with studio apartment floor plans.

Page 4

Figure 3.4. Edward D. Stone, advertisement for U.S. Gypsum Company, *Architectural Forum* 75 (August 1941): 38.

Figure 3.5. Edward D. Stone, Plaza of the Americas, advertisement for U.S. Gypsum Company, *Architectural Forum* 75 (August 1941): 37.

of fighting over the fate of Sixth Avenue, an actual tabula rasa seemed possible, and given the context of America's entry into the war, Stone's particular response to it is of special interest. In August 1941, the United States still clung tenuously to its neutral status. Stone's Sixth Avenue project sketched out a symbolic narrative of the place New York would play in a world with an isolationist America steering the Western Hemisphere peaceably through the war and positioning itself as the center of the free world (and free enterprise) in the postwar era. As European cultural institutions were being destroyed, Stone planned a whole cultural district in America's first city. As the fragile balance of power drew all of Europe into World War II, Stone imagined a street that would show off the international solidarity of the Americas. These ideas came to the public, or at least to readers of the *Forum,* through an advertisement.

While none of the other U.S. Gypsum ads matched the scale of Stone's project for Sixth Avenue, the rest used a similar approach, melding progressive architecture, news, and public relations with a sense of anticipation. Eero Saarinen's project of March 1942 for a "Demountable Space," a kind of instant community center, responded to issues of community in temporary, demountable war workers' housing (Figure 3.6).[33] The young architect moved beyond the teachings of the elder Saarinen, elaborating instead the wartime vogue for demountable construction and R. Buckminster Fuller's ideas for mast houses, which had appeared most recently in the previous month in one of the first ads in the Revere Copper and Brass series. Like Fuller's houses, the demountable social center employed a central column, acting both as chimney and erection crane, to hold up a system of suspended construction like a mast (Figures 3.7 and 3.8). Standardized and prefabricated floor, wall, and roof panels provided seemingly endless flexibility, including the rearrangement of interior spaces as new needs arose. The social center could hold recreational facilities, conference rooms, exhibition spaces, nursery and health care services, and a library.

But Saarinen's real concerns were social. Even before the debacles of some ill-conceived defense "communities," which led to the well-documented race riots in Detroit and to the social problems in many housing projects reported by Agnes Meyer, the deluge of workers living around defense plants stressed cities to the point of chaos.[34] The Detroit-based Saarinen had one of the most miserable examples nearby in Willow Run, Michigan, where as early as February 1942, impromptu "shack towns" and "trailer camps" housed some 250,000 new workers who descended on a housing market already filled to 99 percent of its capacity *before* the start of the war economy.[35] The month before Saarinen published his project, Detroit erupted into race riots that made national news.[36] A two-hundred-unit defense housing project called the Sojourner Truth Settlement, built by the United States Housing Authority and set aside for "Negro tenants," became a battlefield as over twelve hundred white people armed with knives, clubs, rifles, and shotguns blocked the new tenants from moving in. After authorities estimated that it would require three thousand policemen to protect the tenants while they moved in, Detroit's mayor called off the move.

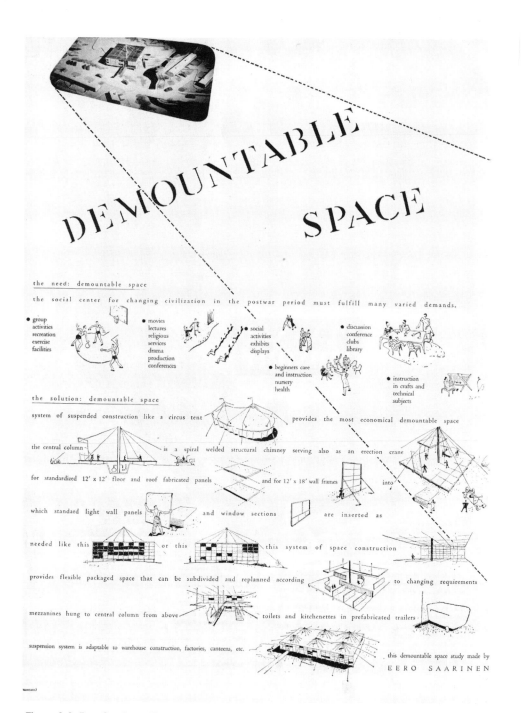

Figure 3.6. Eero Saarinen, "Demountable Space," advertisement for U.S. Gypsum Company, *Architectural Forum* 76 (March 1942): 50.

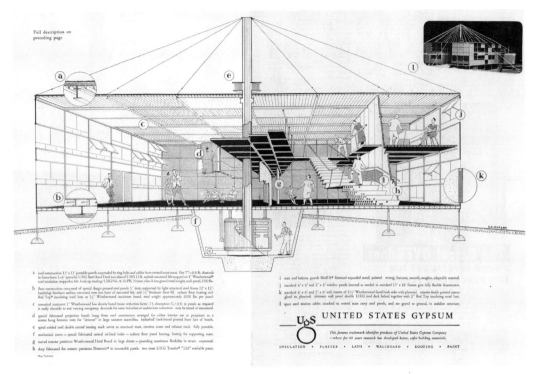

Figure 3.7. Eero Saarinen, section of "Demountable Space," advertisement for U.S. Gypsum Company, *Architectural Forum* 76 (March 1942): 51.

Such problems turned people's attention from the question of quick housing to the more nettlesome issue of how to shape these nearly spontaneous and intentionally impermanent developments into coherent communities. The postwar world, Saarinen proposed, might be just as migratory and demand the same flexibility. His demountable "social center for changing civilization in the postwar period" promised to address the social instability that first arose as a result of the displacement of the Depression, with Hoovervilles and other inadequate forms of housing, and later with the dislocation caused by the war.[37] Populations shifted too rapidly for conventional architectural solutions. Under the conditions of war, it was easy to heroicize a transient lifestyle, to see it as a new stage of modernity, and to equate it loosely with freedom. The social center, it followed, needed to cater to an extremely mobile culture, one whose needs were constantly changing. Flexibility, understood in terms of prefabrication, interchangeable parts, an open plan, and the ability to expand and contract the building's square footage and to alter functions as needed, responded to a population at loose ends, but it also reflected another set of concerns. The unknown quantity of 194X often led architects to plan buildings that were physically adaptable. With the coming of war, a great sense of impermanence had descended on American culture. Saarinen conceded to the unknown, incorporating it into architecture.[38] Only the most flexible of designs would work in the new civilization. This rhetoric of flexibility also fended off one of the standard attacks on planning: the equation of planning with totalitarianism.

Figure 3.8. Eero Saarinen, model of "Demountable Space," advertisement for U.S. Gypsum Company, *Architectural Forum* 76 (March 1942): 52–53.

Saarinen drew attention to his project as a demountable *space*—not architecture—as the radical solution to the problem of planning for the unknown. The section (see Figure 3.7), drawn by fellow Cranbrook architect Ralph Rapson, showcases this flexibility, with "curved interlocked partitions" (g), a pivoted basketball hoop (d), and a hanging booth that could project films inside or outside the building (d). Rapson peopled the space with intergenerational groups at play and at rest and with people watching within the same subdivided space. With a host of cheap, prefabricated, interchangeable materials serving as their kit of parts, Saarinen traded in the crafting of the wall—arguably the nineteenth century's primary site of architectural manipulation—for the sculpting of the space. Materials and methods, as much as ideologies, determined the shift.[39] Space also distinguished Saarinen's use of the mast from Fuller's, whose mast houses and grain bin houses focused on prefabrication, mobility, and maximizing resources. Grain bins, after all, are made for grain, not people, and while they were demountable, they were not particularly flexible. Fuller's Dymaxion ideas were quite opposite in spirit from Saarinen's demountable space. With Fuller, people were meant to concede to the ingenious architectural solution. New civilizations would arise out of new forms, not the reverse.

Other U.S. Gypsum ads married new research in the social sciences to house design (George Fred Keck), proposed the supermarket as a social and commercial nucleus for suburban development (Gardner A. Dailey), and explored ideas for wartime communities and postwar schools, which also became the focus of community development. Together they set the tone for the culture of architecture during the war and stimulated a new crop of ads that presented topical, progressive ideas grounded in present conditions but oriented toward the future. In addition to their anticipatory designs, most of them ended with extensive technical data and specifications, the sort that architects routinely tore out of magazines and filed for future use. In other words, U.S. Gypsum reinvented the trade catalog, slipped it into the magazine in the guise of news, and played it off of the buildup to war.

The persistent interest in moving beyond buildings to community development and large-scale planning issues also became an important theme in ads, as other companies realized how potent the appeal to a vision of postwar cities could be. These efforts to explore (and exploit) the world of 194X fall ambiguously between corporate propaganda and a genuine interest in corporate social responsibility. Not only were the two seemingly disparate strands bound together by home front patriotism, but also they encountered an architectural profession uncannily crossed up by the same forces: public relations and social responsibility. The absorption or co-option of modern architecture by corporate America was not born of some postwar loss of faith in the mission of modern architecture, a "selling out" of ideals to big business. It was born of deep instabilities in big business, advertising, and architecture, and the shared necessity to reshape public opinion—and to do so posthaste in anticipation of the building boom.

Revere Copper and Brass

Following U.S. Gypsum's lead, Revere Copper and Brass began its own "Revere's Part in Better Living Series" in late 1941. The manufacturer of copper building materials, which ran the ads for over three years, commissioned prominent progressive architects and established the form of the architectural testimonial, pairing designs and text with a photograph of the "celebrity" architect. Each of the ads promoted a pamphlet in which the architect expanded on his ideas in terms that the lay public could understand but without sacrificing their value as professional information. Revere's campaign took a significant step beyond U.S. Gypsum's. In addition to running ads in *Architectural Forum* and *Pencil Points*, the company ran them in *Time* and *Saturday Evening Post*, the top national weekly magazine in terms of advertising revenue.[40] These two popular magazines were also the most read magazines by architects and planners, according to a 1943 survey by Time, Inc.[41] So popular was the series that the *New York Times* covered the pamphlets as news several times.[42] The exposure contributed to the popularity of the series. Architects collected the pamphlets and in some cases aggressively initiated contact with the company in order to take part in the series, although typically the advertising firm, St. Georges and Keyes, approached architects directly.[43] Revere turned to many of the architects championed by the *Forum*, especially those whose work appeared in the 194X issues—although in some cases Revere used them first.

Ads and pamphlets like these provided an unexpected forum for the dissemination of architectural and planning ideas. Some of the most exciting material in the architectural press could be found in ads for U.S. Gypsum, Revere, and other companies. Advanced architectural ideas spread well beyond architectural circles; their distribution far

FOR THE REALTOR

FOR THE BUILDER

FOR THE ARCHITECT

FOR THE MANUFACTURER

FOR THE FINANCIER

IMMEDIATE ACTION...

When guns cease firing, and the production lines for munitions can at last come to a halt, there will come a time of re-orientation when America prepares to build once more the things her people want.

As an example of the way every factor in the building industry can find immediate action, Revere presents the Teague house which is designed for mass production with existing tools and equipment.

Revere believes publication of such projects can help prepare a mass market for prompt acceptance of the new contributions of the architect, the builder, the dealer, the realtor, the manufacturer, the financier.

In presenting these various concepts by leading architects and designers, Revere Copper and Brass Incorporated seeks only to stimulate public interest in better housing, confident in the knowledge that the greater use of copper and brass makes any house better to live in, better to own, better to rent or sell. The Revere Technical Advisors are always ready to help with your problems.

Figure 3.9. Walter Dorwin Teague, advertisement for Revere Copper and Brass, *Architectural Forum* (January 1942): 58.

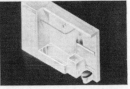

Figure 3.10. Walter Dorwin Teague, advertisement for Revere Copper and Brass, *Architectural Forum* (January 1942): 59.

outstripped that of the architectural press. And the arrangement was lucrative for architects, saving them from the dim prospects of war. Oscar Stonorov and Louis Kahn received five thousand dollars for *You and Your Neighborhood: A Primer of Neighborhood Planning,* the largest of the Revere pamphlets.[44] Five thousand dollars was a princely sum in 1944 considering that a typical house in the Revere series cost less than that. The median income for an architect of Kahn's age in 1950, when such statistics were first systematically surveyed, was just under ten thousand dollars. This number would naturally have been lower during the war, when commissions had sagged and before postwar inflation set in.[45] Revere, moreover, could write off the cost of the pamphlets as a tax break. The results of the campaign must have exceeded the company's expectations. By July 1944, over two hundred thousand people had requested one or more of the pamphlets, a fact proudly displayed in Revere's advertising throughout the campaign.[46]

Revere's campaign also differed from U.S. Gypsum's in other ways. It made no effort to obscure its commercial status. Revere's two-page ads were ventures in propaganda, implicitly knitting the company's role in the war effort to anticipations of a better world after the war. The ads subordinated the text to the drama of the images and key headlines, persuading through direct appeal. In spite of running shorter ads than U.S. Gypsum, Revere produced a more ambitious campaign, enticing some of the most important modernists of the day to contribute to the series, including William Wurster, Louis Kahn, Harwell Hamilton Harris, William Lescaze, Antonin Raymond, and George Fred Keck. Visionaries and industrial designers like Buckminster Fuller, Norman Bel Geddes, and Walter Dorwin Teague joined modernists of every stripe, from California regionalists to the more radical Paul Nelson, recently back from working with Le Corbusier in France. But the company took pains to represent the building industry fairly, including the ideas of Fritz Burns, a successful builder and head of the National Association of Home Builders, and Carl Boester, a young, unknown housing expert with the Purdue Research Center.

For the first nine months, Revere's ads concentrated on postwar housing, especially on low-cost prefabricated housing solutions, an issue then dominating the architectural press (Figure 3.9).[47] Industrial designers Walter Dorwin Teague, Norman Bel Geddes, and Buckminster Fuller, and architects George Fred Keck, Paul Nelson, and A. Lawrence Kocher offered competing visions of mass-produced houses that could be delivered to the site by a truck and assembled in hours with unskilled labor. Many of these were gadgets-cum-houses that applied the lessons of the automobile industry to the house. For Walter Dorwin Teague's house, the advertising firm represented prefabrication and mass production through the unsettling image of a woman holding the same roofless model of his design, leaving ambiguous whether it is the house or the expanding woman who is promised to the architect, builder, realtor, manufacturer, and financier. On the second page of the ad, Teague joins the woman and together they offer the "house of tomorrow" (Figure 3.10).

By 1941, the mass-produced, Fordist house reflected depression-era thinking, not the world of 194X, which moved beyond the individual house to larger concepts of

Figure 3.11. Walter B. Sanders, advertisement for Revere Copper and Brass, *Architectural Forum* (April 1942): 51.

planning. The one exception among the early Revere ads was Walter B. Sanders's project for an apartment block, which began with the premise of a permanent shell that could be filled as needed by occupants with expansible, flexible apartment units (Figure 3.11).[48] Residents would be able to buy and sell rooms on the used apartment market as their families expanded or contracted. The idea attempted to solve some of the issues that concerned the younger Saarinen. In the pamphlet, Sanders drew parallels between architectural flexibility and freedom, linking it with an appeal to American individualism, the great impediment to prefabrication and much mass housing (Figure 3.12).[49] But even this vision for 194X had its genesis in Le Corbusier's much earlier idea of the Maison Dom-ino of 1914, in which the young Swiss architect responded to the destruction and housing shortage of World War I in France with an open vessel of concrete that inhabitants could fill in as needed (Figure 3.13). Sanders married the Dom-ino to Le Corbusier's later ideas for housing blocks, although it was certainly new to *Saturday Evening Post* readers and predated Le Corbusier's Unité d'Habitation in Marseilles.

While these projects deserve attention in their own right, in late 1942, the Revere ads shifted their focus to larger issues of community and urban planning. Houses would continue to be of interest in the campaign, but plans for community centers, urban reconstruction, and planning came to the fore. Lawrence B. Perkins's ad of October 1942 for a community center marked the first decisive shift in attitude (Figure 3.14).[50] It also

Figure 3.12. Walter Sanders, from *Apartment Homes for Tomorrow's Better Living* (New York: Revere Copper and Brass, 1942).

corresponded with a sharp about-face in the advertising world, which "suffered through the dark spring of 1942, bottomed out in June and then unexpectedly embarked upon a growth phase which would last throughout the war."[51] Many of the new campaigns that romanticized planning started late in 1942 or early in 1943, when the War Advertising Council infused the advertising world with energy. Emotional rather than economic indicators sparked the change in the industry, something the new campaigns reflected.

The illustration in the Perkins ad shows a well-dressed couple overlooking a new town, with teardrop cars; boxy, white houses with flat roofs; and a new community center. The copy reads: "After total war can come total living."[52] The image prompts a narrative that begins in 194X, after "the violent impact on . . . intellectual and national life" of total war had changed "the pattern of our existence."[53] A man, presumably back from war, claims his wife and finds a town in which to settle. The bluff from which they survey the town, a park, or open space beyond their community operates temporally as a stand-in for the war. It separates the couple, or really the reader, from the future and helps flesh out the clichéd story: he went to war a boy and came back a man; she waited for him dutifully to return and gets her reward, a new home. A national narrative about community runs parallel to the personal one. "Total living," a play on "better living" and total war, sounds a false note half a century after its use, but in the context of war, the usage must have been

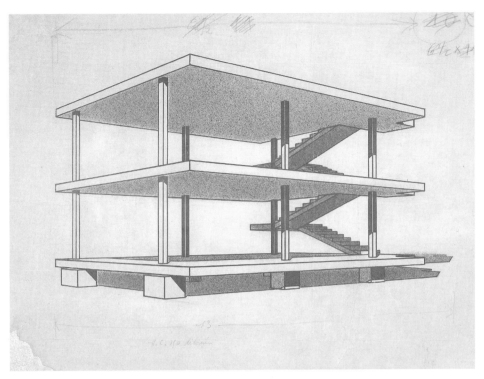

Figure 3.13. Le Corbusier, Maison Dom-ino, 1914. Plan FLC 19209. Copyright 2008 Artists Rights Society (ARS), New York / ADAGP, Paris / FLC.

more apt, if not disarming. Total war necessitated both a physical and spiritual mobilization. It galvanized people on the home front, joining them in a common cause. Even if ads and the media concocted the idea of home front harmony, war harnessed the energies and focused the attention of the nation, ripening the potential for myths about American consensus. This drove the interest in larger planning issues over the individual house in advertising appeals. Total living suggested a nation applying the same mobilizations and commitments of war to postwar living, lending symbolic power to reconversion. The potent fantasy directed people on the home front to convert the deprivations and obligations of war into a seductive vision of postwar life. By creating an image for the rewards of sacrifice, total living translated collective duty into personal, material terms and then reflected it back onto a vision of collective life.[54]

Perkins's community center became the focus of total living. "What a single family cannot possibly afford," the ad exhorted, "a group of families can easily possess."[55] The war itself gave Americans a model for collectivity: "By working together to win the war, groups of us are learning to be teammates and friends."[56] The community center itself would be the agent of total living. Perkins wrote: "[L]eaders in every field of endeavor have already sensed this swing in values; their signposts and 'blueprints' are legion."[57] He offered his design as a "realistic bridge over the abyss which lies between nebulous faith and actual fulfillment."[58] "'Total living' is more than a fine phrase," he continued:

"After total war...total living"

You could read, relax, hold First Aid and other courses, in this comfortable meeting room.

You and your neighbors could produce plays and concerts in this little theatre of your own.

You could have a hobby shop with work benches, power tools, potter's wheels and looms.

A neighborhood fun center for children in the daytime—a gymnasium for grownups at night.

Floor plan of the complete community building, showing how the rooms would be arranged, with the swimming pool outdoors.

"What a single family cannot possibly afford, a group of families can easily possess. After the war we will make the discovery of what this can mean for happy living. Neighbors can have a swimming pool, a gymnasium, a little theatre, a hobby shop with power tools, in a community building within walking distance of tomorrow's home.

"By working together to win the war, groups of us are learning to be teammates and friends. By acting together afterwards, we can create a new community spirit through which we can secure buildings to house the recreations and hobbies we have in common, to make them more satisfying and more fun.

"In such a building, rust-proof metals and new plastics will make possible the admission of daylight wherever wanted, while beams of artificial light and heat may be focussed where they're needed—not scattered wastefully in the hope of reaching the right spot by accident. Already I am helping to plan several such neighborhood centers, and I know how well we are mastering new techniques and economics that can bring this kind of total living to communities everywhere."

LAWRENCE B. PERKINS
Perkins, Wheeler and Will, Architects
Chicago, Illinois

Almost daily, out of the tremendous effort we are making to win this war, come new reasons why our sacrifices are worth while. New inventions, new ideas that can be used for peace as well as war, new production techniques and materials—all of these can bring us new homes and better living in days to come.

In this rebirth of living, copper will play an even more important part than it does today. Not only will it protect tomorrow's homes and buildings against weather and termites, insure rust-free water, help reduce heating costs, but it will also help to make possible the new comforts and conveniences which American inventive genius is already planning for us all.

Today the copper industry is working all-out for Uncle Sam. There is no copper available for any purpose except winning the war. But in Revere's laboratories, research is steadily pressing forward in preparation for the better homes and better living that victory can bring.

Naturally, in this limited space, Mr. Perkins could only begin to tell you about his conception of a community home. So Revere has prepared an illustrated booklet giving more information. This, and former booklets describing the low-cost homes conceived by other leading architects, will gladly be sent to you free. Write us.

★   ★   ★

REVERE
COPPER AND BRASS INCORPORATED
Executive Offices: 230 Park Avenue, New York

Figure 3.14. Lawrence B. Perkins, advertisement for Revere Copper and Brass, *Architectural Forum* (October 1942).

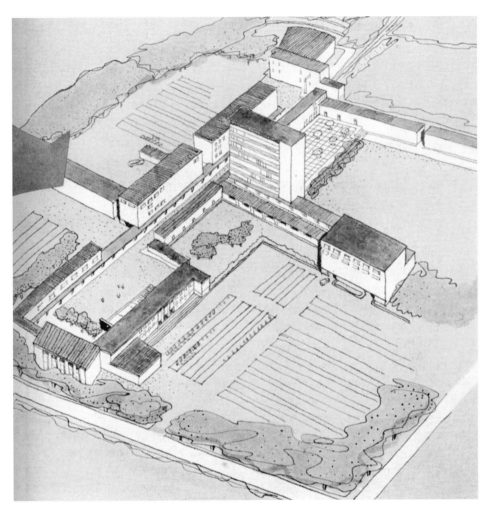

Figure 3.15. George Nelson, view of hypothetical town, from *Your Children Could Romp Here While You Shop* (New York: Revere Copper and Brass, 1943).

"It is a stupendous concept of groups, neighborhoods, communities and an entire nation more closely knit than ever before."[59] Home would still be the "hub" of society, but in the future, all activities would radiate around the "Community Center," a site for interaction and a symbolic site for the formation of democratic values.[60]

Other architects in Revere's series offered alternative visions of how to use architecture to seed community. In March 1943, *Architectural Forum* editor George Nelson redesigned a "Main Street" for a city of 50,000 as a model for similar cities (Figure 3.15). As managing editor of *Architectural Forum*, his Revere pamphlet may have served as a prototype for the *Forum*'s pamphlet *Planning with You*, which debuted that May at the annual convention of the AIA.[61] "Competition for attention," he wrote in his Revere pamphlet, "has turned Main Street into the ugliest thoroughfare in the world, with garish fronts next to over-age derelicts, with signs of all sizes and shapes creating a picture more discordant than the most raucous and cheap of amusement parks"[62] (Figure 3.16).

Yesterday . . . a show place

Today . . . a "white elephant"

Tomorrow . . . a rooming house

Figure 3.16. George Nelson, the decline of Main Street, *Your Children Could Romp Here While You Shop.*

Figure 3.17. George Nelson, promenade, *Your Children Could Romp Here While You Shop.*

Nelson blamed Main Street's problem on its piecemeal development. It was unplanned, which made it particularly susceptible to urban decay. He proposed to replan Main Street dramatically, girding it against the threat of cars and development. He first turned congested blocks in the heart of the city into green promenades for shopping (Figure 3.17). Nelson placed important civic buildings as pendants at both ends of the commercial artery, diverting traffic into a miniature urban beltway, and pedestrianized the shopping district in the city.[63] Main street had become a shopping center, anticipating the influx of malls into downtowns in the postwar period under the influence of Ketchum, Gina, and Sharp, Victor Gruen, and others (Figure 3.18).[64] A small greenbelt surrounded the commercial center, an added touch appropriated from the work of the Regional Planning Association of America, forming a buffer between the shoppers and the streets.

Nelson had grand plans for Main Street. The new shopping center would also be a municipally controlled civic center, with arcades, cafés, plantings, fountains, a playground for children, a theater, and other civic buildings, a harbinger of the pedestrianization of urban streets after the war. The old Municipal Plaza, once crossed by trolley tracks and wires, would become a quiet square with a new Town Hall fronted by a large pool and fountain. Behind the fountain, Nelson placed a "massive monument, a sheer wall of smooth dark granite." Carved into the surface, he envisioned a plan of the business district, "a very reasonable thing to do, for the pride of the citizens in their achievement is very real and completely justified"[65] (Figure 3.19). Literally a monument to planning, it turned the commercial overhaul of Main Street into a communal planning project.

Figure 3.18. George Nelson, pedestrian shopping zone, *Your Children Could Romp Here While You Shop.*

The young architect-editor's idea garnered wide attention during the war. For instance, Joseph Hudnut used Nelson's Revere material in an article in the *Magazine of Art* predicting the nature of postwar architecture.[66] Echoing not just Nelson, but Perkins, the Harvard dean believed it unlikely that the United States would "return after the war to that form of individualism which characterized the era of expansion and exploitation."[67] The new society would temper and control the individualism of prewar America, and future architecture would derive from the architect's ability to translate these new impulses into form. That Hudnut illustrated his point with Nelson's pamphlet for Revere Copper and Brass from the previous month demonstrates how the ads prefigured, or at very least disseminated, important architectural ideas. Nelson's plan to turn Main Street into promenades and grassy pedestrian areas, anchored with commercial and cultural institutions, went beyond the proposals made by Eero Saarinen and Perkins on community centers. Nelson believed that any city could be transformed by turning aging strips

Figure 3.19. George Nelson, memorial, *Your Children Could Romp Here While You Shop.*

of commercial urban land into nuclei for the different areas of the city, a form of neighborhood planning with commerce at its core. Thus the city might be decompressed and reorganized into a series of small, interconnected towns, much like the London County Council's County of London Plan of 1943. With Nelson's pamphlet, Revere moved from the narrow interests of community planning to the larger realm of urban and regional planning.

Robert Alexander, a young architect who had made his name working with Richard Neutra on Baldwin Hills Village in Los Angeles, advanced the idea still further, proposing an idea for the planting of towns (Figure 3.20).[68] The architect had worked out his plan independently of his commission from the copper company, and after consulting with Lawrence B. Perkins, pursued the opportunity with dogged persistence, sending an unsolicited manuscript for the pamphlet to the advertising company and following up on his unanswered submission.[69] His initiative paid off. The pamphlet assumed the form of a mock letter from a soldier to one of his platoon mates as they were settling in to their postwar lives. His town, Oakpark, evoked Wright and suburban Chicago (even though he changed the original site from Santa Barbara), and, following Perkins's pamphlet, he added a community center. Alexander stocked Oakpark with a prefabricated house, much like those in the earlier pamphlets, and loaded it with gadgetry in order to smooth the unexpected move from California to Illinois. "We practically live outdoors," he stated.

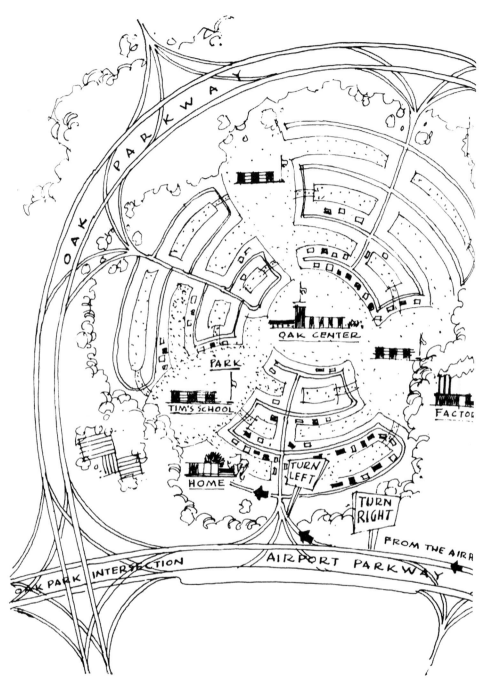

Figure 3.20. Robert Alexander, Oakpark, *Preview of a New Way of Life* (New York: Revere Copper and Brass, 1943).

"In fact we hardly realize that there is a roof on this house. The other night the electric-eye failed to close the copper louver at dawn and I had to get up to close them by hand. Of course we don't care what the weather is outside, since we make our own weather in the house to suit us."[70] Whether disingenuous or not, the faith put into new technology was common in the period. In this case, the architect attached it to a larger set of concerns.

In placing this postwar house in the planned community of Oakpark, Alexander provided a context for the earlier ads of Bel Geddes, Teague, Fuller, Paul Nelson, and others. The self-sufficient town had its own active political setup and a cooperative farm, reiterating the theme of collectivity. A park greened the center of town, Oak Center, which he cut off from traffic, like Nelson's Main Street, and stocked with the schools and shopping. A greenbelt surrounding the town inhibited dangerous growth, a similar use of nature against the spread of urban illness deployed by Saarinen, Sert, Nelson, and others. Instead of creeping suburbs, little Oak Centers would establish themselves in networks across the landscape, "each one to be a self-contained living and working part of the entire body of the city," a rather conspicuous nod to Wright's Broadacre City and to neighborhood unit planning.[71] But unlike Broadacre, or Radburn and the Greenbelt towns of the 1930s, Oakpark intervened in the center of a populous city. Beneath the placid surface of Oakpark lay a mountain of legislation on eminent domain, contentious ideas about the displacement of people, and a nihilistic view of the architecture of the past. The town simultaneously cleared the unwanted urban blight, provided a model for future growth, and retarded overspeculation.

Alexander connected his plan with broader national planning projects, explicitly linking them up with a version of American democracy. With a thinly veiled reference to the great New Deal planning project of the Tennessee Valley Authority, he wrote: "[D]on't fail to look at the Central Valley River Development; you will pass right over it. They have had a pretty free hand in developing something new and better there, without all the difficulties we have had in planning Oakpark in the very center of the city."[72] Alexander tried to imagine how planning and democracy might work together, settling on a form of spontaneous activism:

> While you and I were on the fighting front, my dad and a few of his friends had enough foresight to see that victory would be empty if we failed to do some tall thinking and planning for the peace. They formed a Citizens Planning Council and studied the many proposals which were then being written for post-war development.[73]

But the architect's democratic spirit and patriotism came out in a repetition of Perkins's earlier use of the phrase "total living." He concluded: "The only answer to total war is total planning for peace." Here was Kahn's chart on comprehensive planning—in fact the entire culture of planning—condensed into a single slogan.[74] Alexander also articulated what Nelson only hinted at: planning was the means of beating American cities back. Their approaches reveal a kind of antiurbanism, one aimed at the existing city, presenting its destruction as a patriotic ideal, part of American democracy. Ideas like this must have contributed subtly to suburbanization and the rejection of the city in the United States after the war.

Students of city planning will also notice the resemblance of his concentric design to Ebenezer Howard's diagrams of the Garden City or to the plan of Democracity at the 1939 New York World's Fair. Where the eye sees a fixed diagram, however, the mind should perceive a critique of the grid. In progressive circles in the 1930s, the rigidly right-angled city, "obligatory," according to Le Corbusier, because of its rationality, had acquired a stigma. It was an expedient of capitalism for the creation of profit. And those who attempted to throw curves around it were no longer romantics nostalgic for the medievalizing effects of Camillo Sitte but rather were progressive architects of a new stripe. Robert Alexander could allow elliptical excursions in Oakpark and escape the fate of being labeled a rearguard romantic—his citizens, after all, were moderns: they owned personal airplanes and demountable houses that they could take with them on vacation. But Alexander embraced a kind of formal fallacy: eradicate capitalism's urban form—the grid—and the system would dissolve into oblivion. A rounded form would thwart capitalism's logic of intensive land use. Cul-de-sacs and green spaces face down the capitalist bully on the new village green. In place of an urban form driven by laissez-faire's invisible hand, Alexander approached urban form as a physical determinist. The hand of the architect, guided by social ideals, would arrange a town in such a way as to encourage desirable social forms. Schools, hospitals, houses, places of work, all would find their sanctum, protected from ulterior motives (like profit). Perhaps this is why we frequently find images in this period of hands presenting new buildings to the world—a modernist donor's portrait that creates an allegorical representation for public money (see Figure 3.11).[75] Instead of embodying the invisible hand of the market, given the views of the architects, these hands glorified, and even deified, public spending.

Total planning could take many forms. Returning to William Lescaze's Revere advertisement that played into mature economy rhetoric ("Sure Surgery for Sick Cities"), we find the predictable use of the tall building in open space as a remedy for prevailing urban problems in Harlem (see Figure 2.3). The ad came from an actual project for the rehabilitation of Lower Harlem, an area bounded by Morningside Park and Fifth Avenue, and Central Park and 126th Street, about eighty blocks in America's largest city. Lescaze had already published the plan in one of the *Forum*'s 194X issues.[76] After completely razing the existing city, Lescaze proposed a massive modernist project, the "superbuilding unit" in the "superblock," ostensibly meant to free up the space below (Figure 3.21).[77] To his credit, Lescaze did not send hundreds of families into his housing project to fend for themselves entirely. He optimistically believed that the community center he placed at its heart would be "the life center of the project" (Figure 3.22).[78] The illustration shows the community center to be a variation on what the architect had called a "citizen's country club" in an earlier Revere pamphlet, a crucial element of many housing projects in the period.[79] Although the "slab-block" had plenty of precedent in the 1930s—Lescaze himself had helped design the Williamsburg Houses in Brooklyn, New York—his megablocks were prophetic. Scores of postwar housing projects look and act like them.[80]

Figure 3.21. William Lescaze, "Superblock," *Uplifting the Downtrodden* (New York: Revere Copper and Brass, 1944).

The commercial venue intrigued Lescaze, who had also done wartime ads for Monsanto, Pittsburgh Plate Glass, Kawneer Window Company, Halsey-Taylor, and, before the war, an Alexander Smith and Sons carpet ad. As a prominent exponent of public relations for architects, he may have seen the ads as serious studies. A major part of the project involved encouraging private enterprise to take the initiative.[81] The city would entice private funding by leasing the land at a low cost, skipping over the need for vast public financing and control, and establishing instead a public–private, for-profit venture meant to rid the city of slum. The idea represented a compromise for Lescaze, who had called for a National Department of Planning and a Cabinet Post in Town and Country Planning.[82]

The ad firm St. Georges and Keyes dramatized Lescaze's plan with a narrative of transformation (see Figure 2.3). In addition to reflecting the mature economy theory, as chapter 2 explored, the image engaged in contemporary conventions in advertising. "Uplifting the downtrodden" works with the theatrical device of the "curtain" of dirty laundry to represent the temporal gap between war and 194X. It signals the transformation from the tawdry, prewar tenements to the pristine whiteness of Lescaze's postwar superblocks, the objects of the children's attention and desire. Similar narratives of uplift suffused advertising in the 1930s.[83] The Lescaze ad grafted it onto another prominent technique that advertising historian Roland Marchand called the "ensemble movement":

> The notion of "uplift" infused the entire ensemble movement. The argument that ensemble merchandising, carried to its logical conclusion, required a new, and harmonious image, and the presentation of oneself as an esthetic masterpiece, had their sources in elite sensibilities. They connoted the bringing of order out of chaos, the molding of an image of "fittingness" and harmony—traditional concerns of social elites. . . . Creative advertising men and women, as representatives of a cultural elite, had hoped to impose their esthetic vision on the rising consumer masses.[84]

Figure 3.22. William Lescaze, community center in Lower Harlem Heights, *A Citizens Country Club or Leisure Center* (New York: Revere Copper and Brass, 1943).

Revere's ad echoed the ideology of the ensemble movement, pairing the tattered rags of the poor family—an airing of dirty laundry on the balcony of their slum apartment— with the clean, modern, white building, stocked presumably with washing machines. Chaos and tatters turns to order and an urban ensemble; the dysfunction of the tenement becomes the mechanical efficiency of the machine for living in. Whatever rhetoric Lescaze brought to his project, St. Georges and Keyes dressed up his building in the visual raiment of the ensemble movement. The public, tutored by reading magazines to recognize this sort of allegory, could now insert modernist architecture into their narratives of uplift.

Allegories born of consumer culture thus met Le Corbusier's ideas on the common ground of anticipation. American architects, however, had gone a long way toward modifying his vision. Stonorov and Kahn's two Revere pamphlets bring out some of the complexity of city planning during World War II, especially in the context of advertising. Both were done in a larger and more elaborate format than the typical Revere pamphlets. *Why City Planning Is Your Responsibility* (1943) elaborated on Nelson's pamphlet, calling for a sensitive, selective form of neighborhood planning.[85] Because cities were not uniformly blighted, some sections deserved to be saved from the postwar bulldozer and conserved. The architects offered a strategy to make safer neighborhoods with improved housing stock, accessible shopping, and adequate recreational facilities. Like Robert Alexander, the architects chose the core of the city, in this case several blocks in Philadelphia, as their model.

Figure 3.23. Stonorov and Kahn, advertisement for Revere Copper and Brass, *Saturday Evening Post* (July 3, 1943): 57.

The image in the ad gives a privileged view of a smartly dressed woman who stands on the balcony of a modern high-rise aiming a model airplane at a group of kids playing at the community center below (Figure 3.23). From their pristine balcony, in contrast to the soiled balcony in the Lescaze ad, the adults can easily monitor what goes on at the community center, which includes recreational facilities, a children's clinic, and a pool. As with Nelson's Main Street, the streets have given way to grass and pedestrian paths. In the background, typical nineteenth-century Philadelphia rowhouses show that the graphic artist worked from a real site or photograph or perhaps a composite aided by Kahn's intimate knowledge of the city.[86] But high-rises like this and open spaces were oddities in the dense plan of Philadelphia neighborhoods. The anomaly reveals the architects' plan. Taking a strikingly sensitive position compared to Lescaze, Stonorov and Kahn retained the functional parts of the city and cleared out slums that could not be salvaged. In their place sprout green spaces, community facilities, and tall buildings to concentrate the population, thereby relieving the pressure put on the street by unbroken regiments of rowhouses. The architects favored thinning out the dense urban core of the city, a plan for true physical decentralization rather than desertion and destruction, the method most often employed de facto after the war.[87] They suggested that certain streets be turned over to the school system and converted into parks and kindergartens, a discrete form of pedestrianization.

The Housing Authority would destroy substandard housing, remodel all reparable housing, and build a new public housing project. Small shopping centers, an idea perhaps derived from Nelson, were to replace the chaotic array of corner grocers. The city would extend a ninety-nine year lease on reclaimed "street-land" to private enterprise to construct the shopping area. Stonorov and Kahn injected a dose of reality into the otherwise fantastic images and plans that filled most advertisements: "Remember," they wrote, "that the millennium of a mechanized miracle world is not just around the corner. It will take a lot of work and many years to bring it about."[88]

Revere distributed 110,000 copies of the pamphlet within a month, over five times the number of architects in the country, with distribution continuing for years.[89] This sort of popularity deserves an explanation. Neither architect had achieved fame enough to warrant the swell of public interest. Both struggled during the war. The pamphlet's success hinged on its practical advice about how to conduct local planning efforts. But behind the scenes, a publicity campaign took shape. Alexander Crosby, the executive director of the National Public Housing Conference and a friend of the architects, championed the pamphlet, requesting thousands of copies for the three hundred directors of local housing authorities, the twenty-five thousand parent–teacher associations, and for libraries, women's organizations, and other civic groups.[90]

Crosby could be devastating in his letters to local planners. Chiding Edmund Bacon, then managing director of the Philadelphia Housing Authority, he wrote:

> You have impressed me as a man of vision and action, with a stance that enables you to look outward even to the fringes of the rabble in the slums. And now, sir, you tell me that you have ordered a mere 25 copies of the Revere pamphlet by Messrs. Stonorov and Kahn, a quantity that would barely suffice as one week's reading matter for a brace of lavatories.

He then embarrassed him with the fact that the Chicago Housing Authority had ordered twenty-five hundred copies, "and that's no typographical error," he wrote; "Newark ordered 250, and so it has gone with Tacoma, Tampa, Detroit, Buffalo, Knoxville, New Haven, any number of other cities. A pamphlet full of Philadelphia pictures, written by two of her most distinguished sons! I ask, sir, what the hell?"[91] Crosby worked closely with Revere's advertising firm, St. Georges and Keyes, in order to demonstrate the value of the pamphlet and consequently its promotional value. He wrote to everyone to whom he had sent copies of the pamphlet, urging them to request more and presumptuously providing a model letter that praised the work of Revere and the ad firm.[92] Stonorov and Kahn also strenuously pushed their pamphlet, carefully tracking where it was sent and sharing letters praising their work with St. Georges and Keyes and Revere Copper and Brass. They thus created a covert promotional campaign within Revere's own promotion. The strategy paid off handsomely. Within a couple of months, they were working on a second Revere pamphlet, *You and Your Neighborhood* (1944), which emerged directly out of the success of the first pamphlet as well as Crosby's publicity campaign.[93]

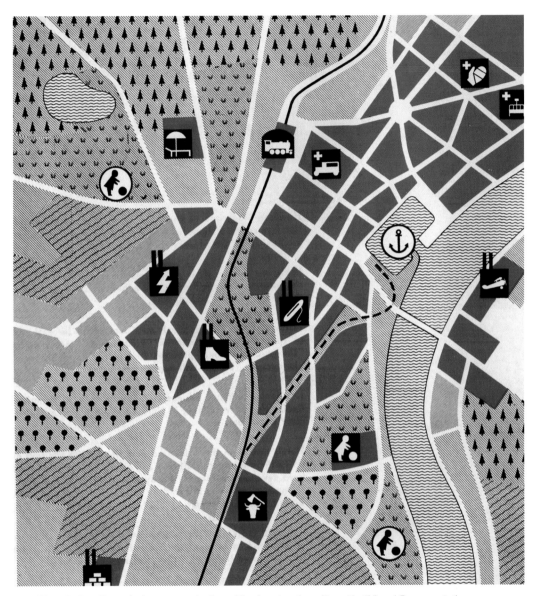

Plate 1. Otto Neurath, isotype method used in planning, from Neurath, "Visual Representation of Architectural Problems," *Architectural Record* 8 (July 1937): 56. Reprinted with permission of the Otto and Marie Neurath Isotype Collection, Department of Typography and Graphic Communication, University of Reading.

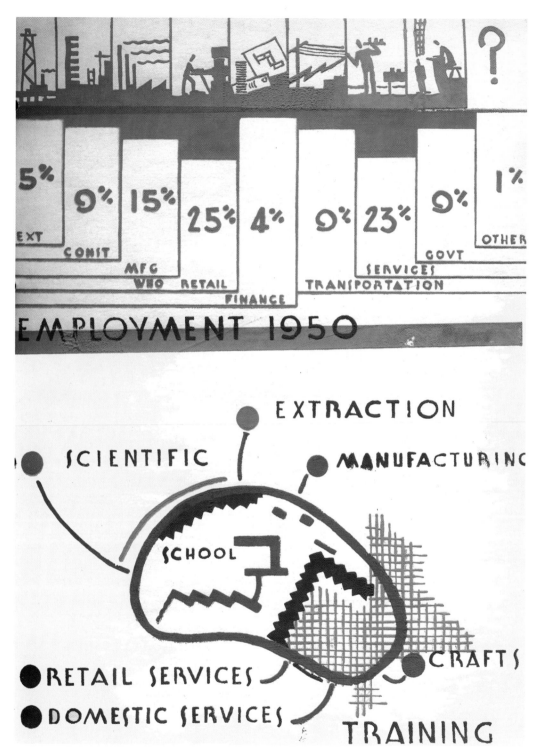

Plate 2. A. C. Walker and R. S. Colley, *Sketch Plan for the Development of Metropolitan Corpus Christi* (Corpus Christi: Clyde Rainey Printing Co., 1943).

Plate 3. Cover of *Pencil Points*, March 1945. Reprinted by permission of Penton Media.

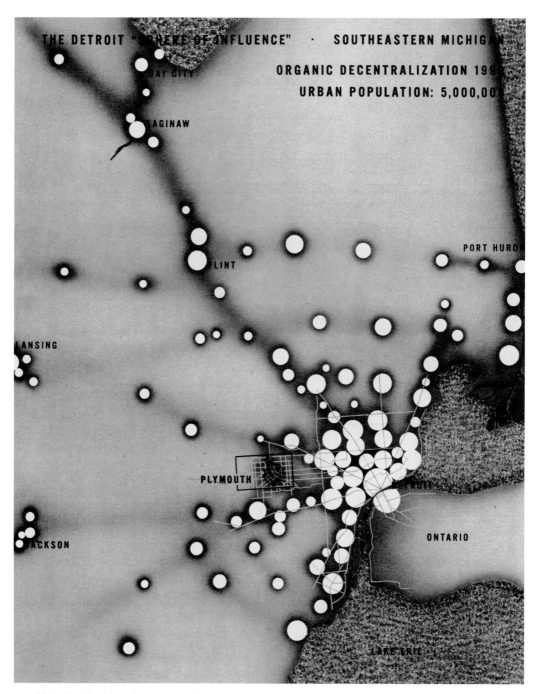

Plate 4. J. Davidson Stephen, plan for postwar Detroit, from *Fortune* 29 (January 1944): 122. Courtesy of the J. Davidson Stephen papers, 1942–45, Archives of American Art, Smithsonian Institution.

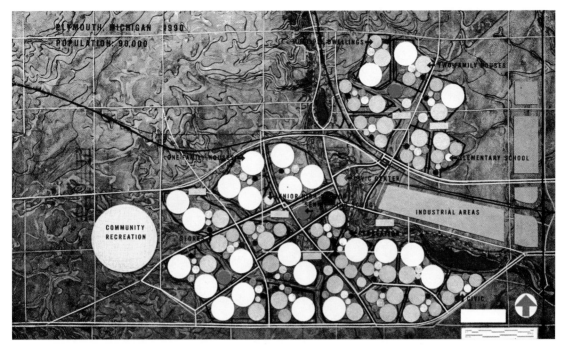

Plate 5. J. Davidson Stephen, plan for postwar Plymouth, Michigan, from *Fortune* 29 (January 1944): 123. Courtesy of the J. Davidson Stephen papers, 1942–45, Archives of American Art, Smithsonian Institution.

ONE DOLLAR A COPY JANUARY 1944 TEN DOLLARS A YEAR

CITY PLANNING

Plate 6. Peter Vardo, "City Planning," cover of *Fortune* 29 (January 1944).

Plate 7. London County Council, plan of London, 1943. J. H. Forshaw and Patrick Abercrombie, *County of London Plan* (London: Macmillan and Co., 1943).

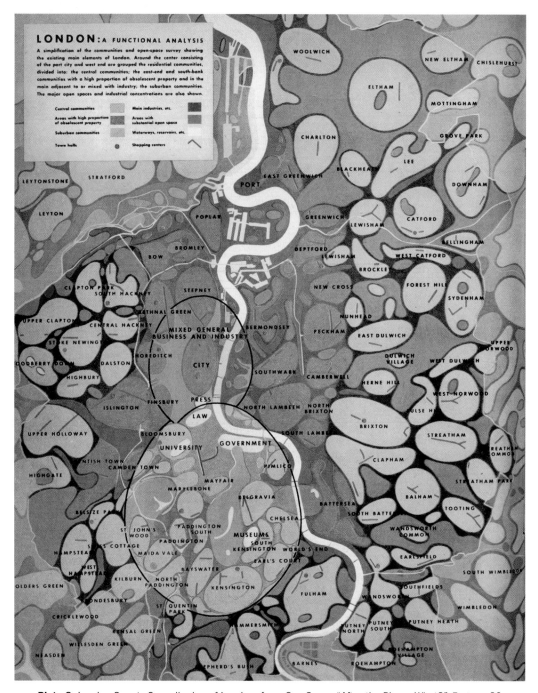

Plate 8. London County Council, plan of London, from Guy Greer, "After the Plans, What?" *Fortune* 30 (July 1944).

Plate 9. Pieter Breughel, *Battle between Carnival and Lent,* 1559. Kunsthistorisches Museum, Vienna. Reprinted with permission of Kunsthistorisches Museum, Vienna.

Plate 10. Advertisement for General Electric, *Architectural Forum* (December 1944): 66–67.

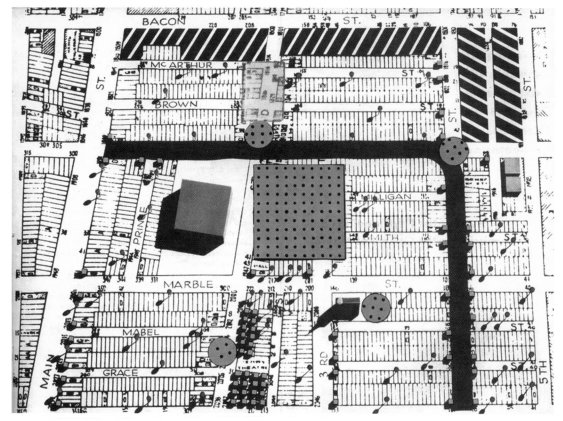

Plate 11. Stonorov and Kahn, plot map planning, *You and Your Neighborhood* (New York: Revere Copper and Brass, 1944).

COMING LAWNMOWERS

Power lawn-mowers of tomorrow will combine real beauty with utility. Lawn-mowers are only one of the products that will be made more attractive and more readily useable, through the use of light alloys in substitution for much heavier metals. Aluminum and magnesium alloys combine lightness with great strength and will supply the answer to many problems in design. Consider Bohn as the source to which you can come for advice and assistance in helping plan your new products to meet post-war requirements.

BOHN ALUMINUM AND BRASS COPORATION
GENERAL OFFICES—LAFAYETTE BUILDING • DETROIT 26, MICHIGAN
Designers and Fabricators
ALUMINUM • MAGNESIUM • BRASS • AIRCRAFT-TYPE BEARINGS

Plate 12. Lawnmower of the future, advertisement for Bohn Aluminum and Brass, *Fortune* (May 1945): 173.

Plate 13. Cover of *Pencil Points* 25 (August 1944). Reprinted with permission of Penton Media.

Figure 3.24. Stonorov and Kahn, the simple tools of planning, *You and Your Neighborhood* (New York: Revere Copper and Brass, 1944).

The pamphlet gave the citizen-planner step-by-step instructions about how to create a grassroots neighborhood planning council, including how to work with local government, set up a storefront office, and begin planning. Stonorov and Kahn presented "simple tools" that one could find around the house (Figure 3.24), and how to use them on a site map, including a schematic graphic language for planning (see Plate 11). Their diagrams instructed the would-be citizen-planner how to compose the planning council and how to think about the relationship of neighborhood to community. Aware of the possibility that city planning might seem esoteric or intimidating, the architects familiarized the concept of city planning by comparing city to house. They likened the bedroom to the "quiet areas of the city," the study to the "cultural areas," the living room to the "get together areas," and the hallways to the "corridors of the city" (Figure 3.25). The pamphlet ends with a plea to include city planning in primary education, placing it between civics and art. "There is no better way," they wrote, "to acquaint [students] with the economic problems of their city and to make them aware of their future responsibility as citizens."[94] Classes like this would create a generation of planners, institutionalizing planning within the education system when the profession was just beginning to establish itself within the universities.

Both pamphlets strike the genuine tone of a grassroots agitation, but Stonorov could also be cynical about the whole affair. In a letter to Edward Carter, then librarian of the Royal Institute of British Architects, he sent copies of the first pamphlet and added:

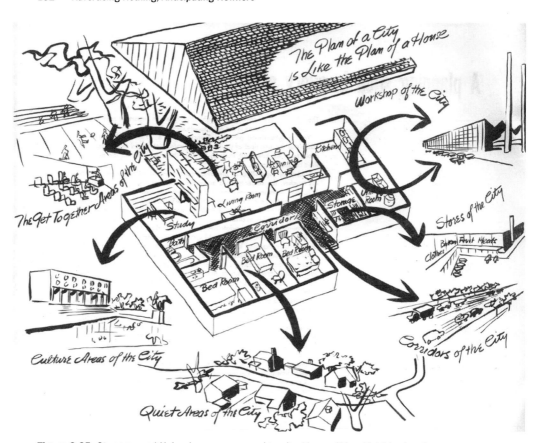

Figure 3.25. Stonorov and Kahn, house compared to city, *You and Your Neighborhood.*

"We are writing a primer on planning for the same people [Revere Copper and Brass] which probably is an indication that the American industrialists are replacing the intellectual liberal in whatever his role is as a defender of the intangible that never materializes."[95] Nonetheless, they carried out the second pamphlet with even more promotional relish, sending it to schools, women's organizations, universities, realtors, home builders and the Home Builders Association, chambers of commerce, the American Federation of Labor, and the Museum of Modern Art. Even the Girl Scouts received copies.[96] From the beginning, Stonorov and Kahn imagined a media blitz to go along with *You and Your Neighborhood,* including feature stories in *Time* magazine and the *Ladies' Home Journal* that would represent city planning as "home-making for the community"; radio broadcasting with Catherine Bauer and others; a newsreel that showed how neighborhood planning was a "natural step toward 'retooling for peace'"; reprinting the primer in the large-format *Life* magazine; an editorial in the *New York Times;* and luncheon meetings with editors, local chambers of commerce, the AIA, the Producers Council, and citizen planning and housing groups. The architects would take to the road, giving speeches from New Orleans to San Francisco.[97] Not surprisingly, the pamphlet equaled the success of *Why City Planning Is Your Responsibility.*

Figure 3.26. Stonorov and Kahn, bulldozer fists replacing neighborhoods, advertisement for Revere Copper and Brass, *Architectural Forum* 81 (November 1944): 45.

Its influence, however, seems to be at odds with the illustration in the advertisement that promoted it (Figure 3.26).[98] The artist subverted the architects' message. The left leaf of the advertisement reads "Neighborhoods are living things," reflecting the biological metaphors rampant in architectural writing at the time. In the right leaf, a hand perversely scoops up a neighborhood of rowhouses, viciously crumpling it up in its bulldozer-like fist, while another delicately replaces it with a prefabricated, orderly, white neighborhood, complete with a communal garden plot and a Quonset hut community center or school.[99] Planning, personified as an omnipotent and fearless destroyer, ambidextrously demolishes and replaces whole blocks of the city. Slum clearance took on a violence quite opposite to their warning that planning would not bring about an instant millennium.

The Stonorov and Kahn ad operated effectively with little text, providing visual arguments when textual description might have been less accessible. Where narrative and statistical accounts of the slum and of urban blight could be numbing and inaccessible, the images made it palpable, and replaced slum instantly, even magically, with a clean, organized, and less dense urban fabric. They also created representational strategies for eminent domain and slum clearance that condensed the laborious and politically delicate textual description and argument of organizations like the National Resources Planning Board (NRPB). Yet the text accompanying the Stonorov and Kahn ad headed, "Let YOURS be these helping hands," complicates this reading. The phrase lionizes the emergence of the citizen-architects, the local activists who gathered to form a planning council and usurped control of their local built environment. They had become the visible hand of planning (Figure 3.27).[100]

Roofs, Windows, Lights

The advertising campaigns that followed Revere's format flooded the architectural press and certain trade and popular magazines in 1943 and 1944. Companies conscripted many of the same architects to represent their products within the context of planning for the postwar building boom. The modernist interest in the rooftop as a "fifth façade" that could be better utilized for recreation and other activities provided the format for the Barrett Roofing Company, not surprisingly, a manufacturer of asphaltic roofing materials.[101] The company borrowed *Architectural Forum*'s slogan, 194X, and its managing editor, George Nelson, for its first ad, a "Department Store in 194X" (Figure 3.28).[102] The ad ran in *Pencil Points,* but also, conspicuously, in the *Forum*'s "New Buildings for 194X" issue, suggesting Nelson's role in stimulating the series. Nelson drew a rooftop café and housing department with model homes for sale, translating Le Corbusier's rooftop culture into American terms. Nelson's rooftop also might be seen as a transposition of the Town of Tomorrow from the 1939 New York World's Fair, where visitors could "window-shop" for houses, onto a Corbusian rooftop. The New York–based Nelson would have known the Fair well. In one sense, the idea undermines the social urgency of postwar housing, placing the single-family house in a site of leisure and consumption. How, for instance, would the NRPB and the more radical comprehensive planning schemes intersect with this rooftop? All of these ads, however, participated in a mode of forecasting that intersected with the larger culture of planning. Whether roof, window, light, kitchen, or refrigerator, the anticipatory designs directed the home front's attention to planning the future.

Month by month, Barrett Roofing ads imagined a different building type by leading modernist architects, following the spirit of *Architectural Forum*'s "New Buildings for 194X" issue.[103] The ads imagined a new civilization budding on the rooftops of America, from a factory by Richard Bennett and an airport by Caleb Hornbostel to a "multiple dwelling" by Harwell Hamilton Harris and a hospital by Hugh Stubbins Jr., compiling piecemeal what the *Forum* had done in its "New Buildings for 194X" issue.

One Barrett Roofing ad by Charles Platt for "Public Housing in 194X" used the tall building in open space (Figure 3.29).[104] The text provided an economically ambiguous argument for the project, one that could use either classical economics or Keynesian theory as justification while fitting into modernist ideals. Platt called for buildings that would not outlast their mortgage so that land use remained flexible, creating, in effect, an ever-renewable tabula rasa. Classical economists would have supported the free rein the impermanent building gave to the purported automatism of market forces, and Keynesians would have applauded the emphasis of consumption over production as the driving force

Figure 3.27. Stonorov and Kahn, Neighborhood Planning Council, advertisement for Revere Copper and Brass, *Architectural Forum* 81 (November 1944).

in the most intractable of industries—the building industry. We are now, of course, far from Le Corbusier's justification for the tall building in open space: the concentration of population, the clarification of urban disorder, the freeing up of open space, and the establishment of social and economic hierarchies, although all of these remained important factors in urban design.

Also for Barrett Roofing, Oscar Stonorov and Louis I. Kahn imagined a "Business 'Neighborhood' in 194X," which combined the vogue for neighborhood planning with a plan for pedestrianization (Figure 3.30).[105] Although the details of the plan are murky

DEPARTMENT
STORE
IN 194X

Aᴺ outdoor selling department that is *actually* out of doors ... prefabricated houses for sale on the roof of a department store . . . This is just one example of the many functional possibilities of roofs in the post-war building era ahead. Designed by architect George Nelson of New York City, this project opens new horizons in department store roof design. Space is provided for assembled prefabricated houses, arrangements of outdoor game equipment, garden furniture and pools, where they may be exhibited in their proper surroundings. Featured also are an attractive soda fountain and

restaurant with tables indoors and out. The roof is appropriately finished to protect the waterproofing membrane and utilize important roof areas which are generally neglected.

*   *   *

This is the first of a series of architectural designs providing greater utilization of roof areas, a development forecast by the Barrett Roofs which support roof-top gardens in Rockefeller Center, New York, and elsewhere.

In post-war buildings, traditional limitations of design will be put to test, and many new practices and techniques will unquestionably be developed. Just as Barrett Specification Roofs proved their adaptability to new architectural forms in the decades since 1854, so too will these famous coal-tar pitch and felt roofs continue to provide the maximum in dependable, long-lasting waterproofing and weather-proofing protection for the buildings of tomorrow.

THE BARRETT DIVISION
ALLIED CHEMICAL & DYE CORPORATION

40 Rector Street, New York

2800 So. Sacramento Ave.   Birmingham
Chicago, Illinois   Alabama

*Trade-mark Reg. U. S. Pat. Off.

Figure 3.28. George Nelson, advertisement for Barrett Roofing, *Architectural Forum* 78 (May 1943): 53.

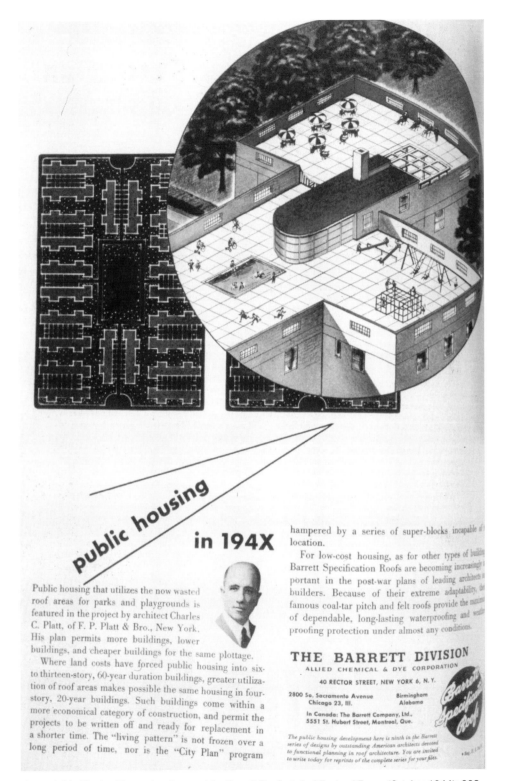

Figure 3.29. Charles Platt, advertisement for Barrett Roofing, *Architectural Forum* (October 1944): 228.

business

"neighborhood"

in

194X

How the roof space of a group of office buildings might be put to functionally cooperative use is suggested in this sketch of a business "neighborhood" in 194X, which has been planned by Oscar Stonorov and Louis I. Kahn, prominent Philadelphia architects.

Limited roof areas of the individual office buildings are planned so that their uses are complementary to each other. On the tallest structure is placed a sub-post office with facilities to land fast mail helicopter planes. Another roof accommodates a garden restaurant, and a third features midday recreational facilities for the neighborhood...

Thus, variety of ground use finds its corollary in intelligent utilization of roof area, which if served by special express elevators, would establish new commercial values for the roofs of office buildings.

* * *

This project extends the pattern of roof functionalism as it has already been developed at New York's famed Rockefeller Center, where Barrett Roofs serve a variety of purposes—from observation decks to rooftop gardens. Here as elsewhere, Barrett Roofs have demonstrated their complete adaptability to new building techniques. These coal-tar pitch and felt roofs offer the maximum in dependable, long-lasting protection. Standard since 1854 for flat roof construction, they are destined to play an even greater part in post-war building.

THE BARRETT DIVISION
ALLIED CHEMICAL & DYE CORPORATION
40 Rector Street, New York 6, N.Y.

2800 So. Sacramento Ave.   Birmingham
Chicago 23, Ill.   Alabama
In Canada: The Barrett Company, Ltd.
5551 St. Hubert Street, Montreal, Que.

*Reg. U. S. Pat. Off.

This business center development is the twelfth in a series of designs by leading American architects devoted to functional planning in roof architecture. You are invited to write for reprints of the complete series for your files.

Lou. K. '45

Figure 3.30. Stonorov and Kahn, advertisement for Barrett Roofing, *Architectural Forum* (June 1945): 179.

and an analysis of a fragment like this has obvious limitations, the image already shows in embryo some of the architectural ideas that would make the mature Kahn famous. The tallest building is essentially a space frame capped by a massive heliport for the post office that seems to act as a roof for an outdoor space, not unlike the one made popular by Edward Durrell Stone at the top of the Museum of Modern Art. But Kahn left the buildings schematic. His real fascination here was urbanism, the experience of the city as lived from above. The layered horizontal surfaces become the primary tissue connecting the architectural solos together, a vast and motley supraterrestrial urban strata given over to people, cafés, recreation facilities, small parks, and monumental sculpture. The idea recalls Le Corbusier's idea in *The City of To-Morrow and Its Planning* for terraced buildings that created a visual and functional gradient leading up to his impossibly tall skyscrapers.

Kahn, however, was more concerned with creating a complex space than a rational order of the whole. The main axis asserts a strong identity. Its paving distinguishes it from other surfaces, a manipulation of materials that Kahn would apply to differentiate spaces and uses in his postwar buildings, most eloquently at his buildings at Yale University. The monumental metal sculpture also defines the axis, providing a gesture (and no more) toward shelter. The architect adapted the piece from his essay on monumentality that appeared in *The New Architecture and City Planning* of 1943. Answering Sigfried Giedion's call for monumentality, Kahn offered a vision of public space free of classicizing elements and overt symbolism but deeply imbued with powerful forms and a sense of place (Figure 3.31). In the Barrett Roofing ad, he used similar tactics. The giant sculpture frames space. It leaps out from the building on the right to shelter a long platform of cafés and restaurants, and then tiptoes one shorter step to frame the promenade. The three curled toes of the monument suggest the idea and syncopation of an arcade, further defining the axis and, through the longer limbs, stitch it to the secondary spaces that spill off of it. The scheme brilliantly reworks the rational, beaux-arts organization of spaces that Kahn knew well from his training at the University of Pennsylvania under Paul Philippe Cret. The tension between the axis and the radically asymmetrical dispensation of spaces, both horizontally and vertically, shows Kahn reinventing the old method in a modernist vein but not without carefully maintaining its genius for clarity and order and without forfeiting the attention to scale (especially human changes in scale) that lay at the heart of Giedion's search for monumentality.

Here monumentality is not just about objects in space but also about the capacity for space to frame human gesture, especially the collective gesture of the crowd in public space. Where Ralph Walker bemoaned Le Corbusier's Plan Algier as a potential haven for fascism, and Giedion counseled architects to find appropriate symbols for the age, in part to counter the power of fascist architecture over the crowd, Kahn sketched out the alternative in spatial terms.[106] While we cannot be sure that the architect titled the ad, the idea of a business neighborhood drives this point home. Business, not the state, would create the free spaces of democracy, and it would do so in the familiar and domestic terms of the *neighborhood.* The ad thus brought together several loaded ideas and

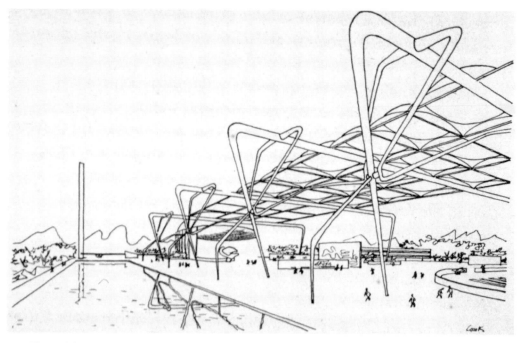

Figure 3.31. Louis I. Kahn, design for monumental sculpture, from Paul Zucker, ed., *New Architecture and City Planning* (1944). Reprinted with permission of the Louis I. Kahn Collection, University of Pennsylvania, and the Pennsylvania Historical and Museum Commission.

keywords of the moment, resolving them in a modernist urban plan whose spatial complexity looks forward to Kahn's mature work. In June 1945, with the Axis on the verge of defeat and the beginnings of reconversion, the dreamy visions and radical rhetoric of 1942 to 1944 gave way to the much more conventional-sounding business neighborhood.

Much like the Barrett Roofing ads, Pittsburgh Plate Glass Company's campaign, "There Is a New Trend in Store Design," assembled architects such as Pietro Belluschi; Walter Gropius; Skidmore, Owings and Merrill; Saarinen and Swanson; and Gruen and Krummeck to envision postwar store design. The company poached several U.S. Gypsum and Revere architects, including Gardner Dailey, who also did a market for the glass company, and Lawrence Perkins, Stonorov and Kahn, and William Lescaze. The designs deserve attention in their own right, but as a group they suggest a revision of Main Street or downtown, a thoroughgoing replacement of the old fabric with contemporary architecture. This holds true in spite of the misleading idea that these were mere storefronts, cosmetic alterations of Main Street's face and a rethinking of display within. Indeed, they were storefronts, but when *Pencil Points* published a collection of the designs in 1944, the magazine understood the series in terms of the overall rehabilitation of downtown— not unlike the *Forum*'s "New Buildings for 194X" issue (Figure 3.32).[107] The bird's-eye view reveals a covered "shopping district," before the idea of the mall had made significant inroads into American culture.[108] Woven into the highway system, connected to a civic center with a reflecting pool and public buildings, topped with parking and a heliport,

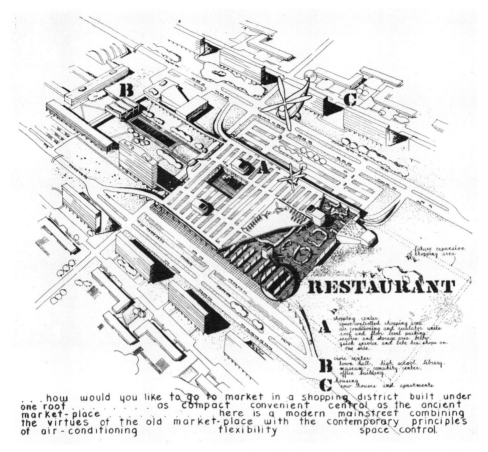

Figure 3.32. Plan of business neighborhood, from "Store Designers Don't Suffer from Traditional Fixations—Thank God," *Pencil Points* 25 (August 1944): 42. Reprinted with permission of Penton Media.

and surrounded by Corbusian high-rises in open space, the "modern mainstreet" was as "central as the ancient market-place," but "contemporary principles of air conditioning, flexibility, and space control" improved it.[109] In other words, the new trend in store design looked beyond hermetic design problems to the nature of cities in 194X, examining consumption and the spaces of consumption as an urban design problem.

The individual ads demonstrate a strong commitment to contemporary design, including, naturally, the wonder of plate glass. William Lescaze's use of plate glass in his design for a florist shop, for instance, at first appears extravagant, a superfluous use of an expensive material (Figure 3.33).[110] But by lifting a rectangular box of glass and tilting it at a forty-five-degree angle above the sidewalk, Lescaze created a three-dimensional experience of window-shopping, an appropriate gesture for a florist or plant shop. At the same time, he provided a modicum of shelter without resorting to the usual overhang. The design was republished in color in the *Pencil Points* issue on the Pittsburgh Plate Glass series (Figure 3.34).[111]

Figure 3.33. William Lescaze, florist shop, advertisement for Pittsburgh Plate Glass Company, *Pencil Points* (April 1944): 31. Reprinted with permission of Penton Media.

Figure 3.34. William Lescaze, florist shop, *Pencil Points* 25 (August 1944): 50. Reprinted with permission of Penton Media.

When *Pencil Points* made the Pittsburgh Plate Glass ads the focus of an entire issue, it did so with high seriousness. The magazine treated the work as a formidable exploration of postwar design. It placed a movie theater by William Lescaze and a haberdashery by Gruen and Krummeck on the cover (see Plate 13).[112] Not only had advertising become news—the Lescaze design had run first as an ad—but also the attention indicated that the medium was not, in fact, the message. Modern architecture and advertising had reached a point of symbiosis. The cover also reappeared in the magazine's publicity, making the store designs part of *Pencil Points'* attempt to reinvent itself as the "magazine of progressive architecture" (Figure 3.35).[113] Architecture in ads had become the symbol of progressive architecture. The slogan, placed under the subscription chart in the ad, would become the magazine's name after the war.

General Electric ran its anticipatory advertising campaign from April 1944 until December 1945, including designs by Nathaniel A. Owings of Skidmore, Owings and Merrill; Lawrence Perkins; Wurdeman and Becket; and Ketchum, Gina, and Sharp, one of the leading commercial architecture firms.[114] Following the Revere series, it combined an original design, a photograph of the architect, a textual explanation of his work, and upon request, a more extensive pamphlet. The content of the ads hewed much more closely to the product than did U.S. Gypsum's, Revere's, or even Pittsburgh Plate Glass's ads, providing narrow studies of how to modernize or improve a variety of interior spaces

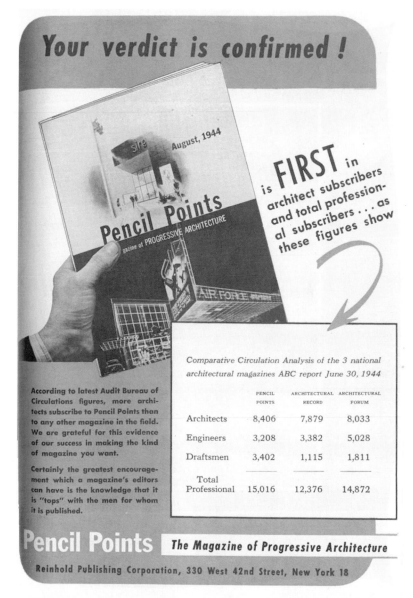

Figure 3.35. Publicity for *Pencil Points* using the Pittsburgh Plate Glass designs, *Pencil Points* 25 (November 1944): 109. Reprinted with permission of Penton Media.

with lighting. A number of modernist ideals found full expression in these studies, flexibility foremost among them. For instance, Lawrence Perkins, who had written about planning for "total living" in a Revere ad, pitched a plan for "flexible classrooms" through the use of light (Figure 3.36).[115] The young Chicago architect had enjoyed modest fame in the early 1940s for his design with the Saarinens for the Crow Island School in Winnetka, Illinois, and he had designed a school in the *Forum*'s 194X issue.[116] From this work, he

Figure 3.36. Lawrence Perkins, advertisement for General Electric, *Progressive Architecture* 26 (October 1945): 24. Reprinted with permission of Penton Media.

learned how rigid classroom design impeded pedagogical innovation. In the future, he explained in his General Electric ad, classes would vary widely in their arrangement, moving beyond the conventional system of rows. The new classroom, arranged "in a semi-circle or a forum, *to fit the student* . . . can increase the interaction of student minds and personalities."[117] Since the classroom was ever changing, lighting had to remain flexible to allow for any kind of seating. His "louvered ceiling-of-light," which used General Electric Slimline fluorescent lamps, purported to provide this flexibility with prefabricated units.

The frequent repetition of flexibility in General Electric ads, and in the appeals of other companies during the war, makes the word sound like a slogan invented by admen. But the idea already had an important pedigree in the Modern Movement. One of the central modernist beliefs, flexibility gave meaning to the open plan and modularity, and it justified the breakdown of the box. It presents both negative and positive faces. The very idea of flexible space implies a previous state of inflexibility; the call for flexibility, therefore, contained a rejection of the fixed or rooted, of impermeable and unmovable walls, of heavy, permanent arrangements of furniture, of the essential nature of rooms with particular uses. Living room, dining room, den, even bedroom, became categories of intransigent thought that had to be broken down in order to excavate to the bottom, to pose the fundamental question about how to arrange space for the quickly changing habits of modern life. So it was for all kinds of rooms. Modern architects frequently lamented the fact that architecture had failed to keep pace with social change. Permanence threatened architecture with irrelevance. Flexibility was a one-word manifesto, revealing the inadequacy of the architecture of the past and replacing it with a nimble, malleable, responsive architecture. "Architecture or Revolution," Le Corbusier posed dramatically at the end of *Towards a New Architecture*.[118] Flexibility called forth the same choice, but in a more moderate tone that translated remarkably well to consumer culture.[119]

While on the surface, General Electric's campaign did little to advance the culture of planning, per se, it adopted ideas like flexibility, naturalizing or assimilating some of the language of the Modern Movement to consumer culture and to the lay public. The pamphlets were sales tools, the sort of materials an architect, builder, or salesperson could show off for a client planning a postwar building. We tend to forget just how ill equipped American buildings remained in the mid-1940s, after more than a decade of depression and war. The great program for electrification of the home in the 1930s had only partially achieved its goal.[120] American homes and many institutions remained in dire need of modernization, which is one reason why many of the Pittsburgh Plate Glass and General Electric ads focused on programs of modernization rather than on ambitious building projects. We also tend to forget how foreign both the aesthetic and the terms of modern architecture could be to Americans, even in the 1940s. Ads like these introduced them gently, Americanized them by inserting them into a familiar context and playing them off of the war effort. Every General Electric ad urged readers to buy war

bonds. The simple statement allowed the company to write off the cost of the advertisement, but it also implicitly linked the war bonds with modern design, making modernization the payoff for the sacrifices of war.

Stran-Steel and Bohn Aluminum

In addition to the campaigns that commissioned architects to envision the world after the
war, several companies offered more generic visions of postwar architecture. Stran-Steel,
the manufacturer of the Quonset hut, created ads that gave people a chance to imagine
themselves in a postwar city made over with the company's products. The ads used a
"split-screen" technique in order to create a "before-and-after" effect (Figure 3.37).[121]
Before the war, a wasteland of junked cars and detritus polluted the landscape. After the
war, with an infusion of Stran-Steel products, a shining white new community supplanted
it. Flat roofs, a rectilinear street pattern, clean plantings, and a sanitized whiteness mark
the postwar as modern. Under the two images, a single, terse word underscored the
transformation: "Rehabilitation," a common term for urban planning from an era when
slum clearance drove the agenda. The term suggests a form of therapy for the "mature"
city, but other images in the series make clear that rehabilitation, like Robert Alexander's
"total planning," was double-speak for destruction. In another Stran-Steel ad, for example, a dark, chaotic slum with smokestacks poking between decrepit houses forms such
a jumble that the street disappears (Figure 3.38).[122] On the postwar side, a community
of orderly, white buildings takes its place. Instead of rehabilitation, this time "Decentralization" explained the change. Many planners considered decentralization an inevitable
and salutary process linked to modern technology, like the car, and one that planning had
to encourage and orchestrate. The idea drove the London County Council's County of
London Plan of 1943, attracted such forceful champions as Lewis Mumford, and was implicit in many of the urban schemes found in advertising. In the ad, the chaos of the slum
gives way to the segregation of residential and industrial areas and the separation of the
automobile and pedestrian routes, a form of urban differentiation or zoning supported
almost universally in this period.

Decentralization, in abandoning areas of urban concentration without specific
plans for the vacated parts of the city, also implied neglect or a form of destruction. At the
risk of overinterpreting what Stran-Steel simply offered as an innocent vision of a miraculous postwar transformation, the ads evince a fear of the people who lived in American
slums. As race riots roiled the home front, the downtrodden slum of the 1930s, which
had been a matter of pathos in New Deal photography and literature, had become a place
of social unrest, violence, and fear, experienced explicitly in terms of race. In a third
Stran-Steel ad, a kind of reactionary pendant to Saarinen's U.S. Gypsum ad, a photograph of an urban slum gives way to an illustration of a clean, white decentralized Quonset
hut community (Figure 3.39).[123] The copy, "Responsibility for Democracy," twins democracy with the destruction of the slum, replacing neutral words associated with urban

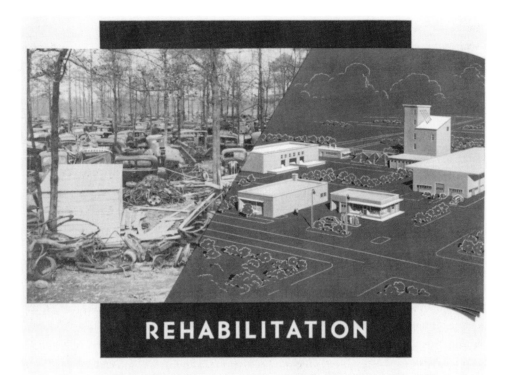

REHABILITATION

The recovery of waste land by creating attractive, livable communities will undoubtedly become an important phase of postwar construction. Such rehabilitation will require ingenuity in planning, progressive design, and high efficiency in building methods and materials.

Stran-Steel light-gauge steel framing systems meet ideally these varied requirements. Strip steel provides a versatile medium for the expression of practical-yet-unorthodox design, and offers such important advantages as great strength, light weight, durability, and economies of time, labor, and materials.

Through current wartime assignments involving the design and fabrication of strip steel, the Stran-Steel engineering staff is acquiring specialized experience which will serve architects and builders well on their postwar projects.

Manufacturer of the U. S. Navy's
Famous **Quonset Hut**

STRAN-STEEL

DIVISION OF GREAT LAKES STEEL CORPORATION, 1130 PENOBSCOT BUILDING, DETROIT 26, MICH.

UNIT OF NATIONAL STEEL CORPORATION

Figure 3.37. Rehabilitation, advertisement for Stran-Steel, *Architectural Forum* (April 1944): 160.

DECENTRALIZATION

Prominent among forward-looking plans for the post-war era is the decentralization of manufacturing areas. Residences and industrial plants will be segregated, with resulting efficiency in manufacturing and pleasanter living conditions for working people.

Stran-Steel framing systems adapt themselves especially well to the construction of residential and industrial buildings. A durable, economical building material, strip steel by Stran-Steel affords exceptional flexibility in design and construction, and permits speedy erection.

The wide experience gained by Stran-Steel engineers in applications of this versatile material on wartime assignments is at the service of architects and contractors for post-war planning.

Manufacturer of the U. S.
Navy's Famous Quonset Hut

STRAN STEEL

DIVISION OF GREAT LAKES STEEL CORPORATION
1130 PENOBSCOT BUILDING, DETROIT 26, MICHIGAN

UNIT OF NATIONAL STEEL CORPORATION

Figure 3.38. Decentralization, advertisement for Stran-Steel, *Architectural Forum* (March 1944): 47.

RESPONSIBILITY FOR DEMOCRACY

What means will be taken to accomplish slum clearance in the post-war world have not yet been determined. Yet accomplished it must be, for on a decent standard of living depends much that is vital to the future of democracy.

Versatile and efficient, Stran-Steel framing systems provide the building industry with an effective medium of construction for all types of housing developments. They speed erection, safeguard the building investment, and lend themselves to the application of modern methods and materials. Stran-Steel's engineering experience, greatly increased by large-scale wartime assignments, will be at the service of architects and contractors.

Manufacturer of the U. S. Navy's Famous **Quonset Hut**

STRAN STEEL

DIVISION OF GREAT LAKES STEEL CORPORATION
1130 PENOBSCOT BUILDING, DETROIT 26, MICHIGAN

UNIT OF NATIONAL STEEL CORPORATION

Figure 3.39. "Responsibility for Democracy," advertisement for Stran-Steel, *Pencil Points* (February 1944): 25.

planning, rehabilitation, and decentralization with the political word *democracy*. Unlike Stonorov and Kahn's appeal for a democratic base for planning, the Stran-Steel ad switched the terms, suggesting that slum clearance would engender democracy. The ads came out of a larger corporate effort that bolsters this reading. During the war, the Detroit-based steel company hired Smith, Hinchman, and Grylls to design a satellite city near Detroit, a project that Stran-Steel pitched as a form of corporate social responsibility in an area stressed by the influx of wartime labor and inadequate housing.[124] Here was a Detroit-based company building a decentralized community outside of a city that was roiled with race riots caused initially by housing shortages. The ads cannot be separated from this political context.

By contrast, Bohn Aluminum avoided social commentary in favor of a kind of "vintage futurism," where streamlined cars, trains, and planes indulged in a safe and, by 1944, outdated science fiction fantasy of the postwar period. The campaign began much in the mode of Revere's campaign, with a design for a car by industrial designer George Walker and a pitch for war bonds. Walker continued to design many of the "Products of Tomorrow" that appeared in Bohn Aluminum ads, although his photograph disappeared from the ads and other unnamed artists contributed to the series, which included an array of planes, buses, refrigerators, helicopters, airports, factories, megastructures, and a lawn mower sitting in a front yard of a modern house like a monumental piece of sculpture (see Plate 12).[125] In its own way, this, too, was a pitch for decentralization through suburbanization. The isolated house on its expansive lawn provides the counterpoint to the stock images of skyscraper cities popularized by Hugh Ferriss and others in the 1930s. These ads ran widely, appearing in *Newsweek, Time, Fortune, Nation's Business,* and *Architectural Forum,* easily outstripping all the other campaigns in terms of circulation. The popular subject matter and aesthetic suited the wide circulation. Little about the ads challenged the public's understanding of architecture or planning, in part because they have too much of the feel of a cartoon to be either menacing or compelling.

The architectural ad campaigns did something for progressive architecture and planning that no collection of articles, exhibitions, and lectures—or, for that matter, actual buildings—could have done. It placed these two still-unresolved cultural phenomena in a common cultural context. The ads worked modernist and in some cases radical designs into a visual and rhetorical environment that belonged to consumer culture. It is not so much that these two worlds were antithetical or distant—they were not. But they had never fraternized so effectively, having never shared such a poignant mission as the war and postwar reconstruction. Architecture, especially modernist architecture, had never been put to such instrumental use by advertising in the United States, nor had it ever been so thoroughly manipulated, tortured into cartoons, fitted into fables, and woven into every shopworn technique of "ballyhoo." The point is worth pausing on. The devices of advertising so carefully explored by Roland Marchand in *Advertising the American Dream* were part of the common literacy of magazine readers. In an age before television, readers came to ads with the ability to take in all the visual clichés and rhetorical tricks of the trade—the use of social tableaux about uplift, parables of the democracy of goods and of civilization redeemed through technology, and tropes about the push-button future.[126] Architecture and cities had always played a role in these techniques, but the wartime campaigns put architecture, and particularly the most contemporary architecture and planning, on the front lines of persuasion. The alliance quite literally transformed architecture, although the consequences of the transformation are harder to pin down.

On the most general level, the anticipatory ad campaigns used architecture as a figure for the future, and they did so in a way that draws attention to the medium itself. By their very nature, these anticipatory designs were a form of paper architecture. Some ads featured the raw renderings and plans of the architects, but the majority of illustrations were filtered through the eye and hand of the ad firm's art director or artist, who routinely used an aesthetic somewhere between a *Saturday Evening Post* cover and a cartoon. This seemingly innocuous fact had important consequences. Cartoons and comic strips were one of the most potent and overused techniques in advertising. Wartime studies had shown the superior "attention value" of comics in advertisements.[127] And while some admen saw them as debasing to the profession, others found in them an appropriate, seductive, and malleable medium, one drawn from mass culture and trained back on the masses. As Roland Marchand has written,

> Enthusiasts for the comic section as an advertising medium quickly discovered that in the comic-strip format, the best techniques learned from other sources could be combined. From the movies came the ideas of continuity of action, quick-cutting from scene to scene, and focusing attention through the occasional close-up. From the confession magazines came the power of personal testimony and the intimate drama. From the tabloids came an emphasis on brevity and pictorial imagery. And from radio came the persuasiveness of a conversational style and the seductiveness of eavesdropping.[128]

While these illustrations differ from comic strips in important ways, they often employed a similar manner of illustration: schematic, fragmentary, and focused on frames that suggest rich narratives and the passage of time. Cartoons were also just as easily combined with other visual modes and narrative devices. Bohn Aluminum resorted to a purely cartoon architecture, the kind of images that readers would have seen in *Popular Science* and science fiction magazines. Stran-Steel ingeniously combined photography and more convincing illustrations of architecture, imitating architectural rendering. The Revere Copper and Brass ads made full use of the more realistic mode of cover art to insert architecture into complex narratives, allegories, and dramas. While not comic strips or cartoons in any literal sense, Revere's ads extracted elements of what by the late 1930s had become an accepted strategy in advertising. The ways in which the artists who worked up the ads for St. Georges and Keyes transformed the architects' ideas reveal the mechanics of the tactic. Lescaze's Revere ad, an allegory for the transformation of Lower Harlem, is a prime example (see Figure 2.3). Revere's cartoon aesthetic avoided dialogue bubbles or a sequential narrative, and it only fictionalized part of the allegory. Each ad inserted some architectural or visual element into a single frame, and each month a new frame would inch the story forward. The infusion of architecture, rather than threatening to dispel the suspension of disbelief, reinforced it with a dose of realism—the reality that would supplant the home front fantasy. The expert architect and his photograph further anchored the anticipatory design in reality. At very least, the ads brought progressive architecture and planning into the realm of magazine illustration, inserting it seamlessly into that aesthetic and the ads that ran in popular magazines. Contemporary architecture's new neighbors—cover girls, Norman Rockwell's folksy pacans to the American family, and the products tantalizing home front consumers—welcomed the European guest to the American family.

The importance of the context of consumer culture deserves more attention as one of the defining elements in the acceptance or mainstreaming of modern architecture in the United States. This is because the ads involved architects with advertising much more intensively than it might at first appear. The process encouraged architects to reframe the nature of their work in terms of consumer culture, which, in turn, invited a backlash. One critique disparaged ads like these as "leg art," while Timken, a manufacturer of heating equipment, proudly defended the practice (Figure 3.40).[129] Such criticism hardly tempered the enthusiasm of the architects, who saw one another's designs and read about their colleagues' ideas in the context of advertisements and promotional materials. More importantly, they worked closely with advertising companies, transforming their work into advertisements.[130] The whole process opened up a window into a world that was, until World War II, mostly closed to architects. Some of the biggest names in the field appeared in ads, their photographs and testimonials granting authority to the marriage of architecture and advertising. All of this occurred in the context of a field desperate to improve its public exposure. The old fear that self-promotion degraded professional standards melted away before the promise of a postwar building boom in which architects would transform the world in the image of the ads.

Conclusions

The culture of planning emerged simultaneously with this growing relationship between architecture and advertising and public relations. After World War II, architecture culture would be indivisible from consumer culture. Many of the architects who had developed an ardent faith in the American interpretation of Keynesian theory as the necessary and inevitable solution to urban problems also produced advertisements for companies committed to resuscitating laissez-faire capitalism and to rebuilding postwar cities through market forces. What seems now like an obvious contradiction, or even a "selling out" of modernist ideals to corporate patronage, carried no such stigma during the war. Although the appropriation of modernist architecture by corporations after the war has often been seen as a pivotal shift in the Modern Movement, in fact, as the corruption of its social responsibility, during the war the alliance meant just the opposite.[131] The relationship between architecture and American corporations that played out in the ads promised something akin to the Werkbund's original belief in reforming society by improving

LEG ART?

Forum:

We quote from page 4 of your August issue:

"Enlightened advertisers like Revere, Celotex, Monsanto Plastics, and U. S. Gypsum have produced designs of practical value. They have done a magnificent job. Beyond this small progressive elite, other advertisers, who unexpectedly rallied around modern design, have largely failed to grasp the

Timken postwar house

implications of planning. To them, by and large, modern design has merely been a fashionable substitute for leg art."

Move over, *Police Gazette*. You have a new bed partner.

R. M. MARBERRY
Advertising Manager
Timken Silent Automatic Division
Detroit, Mich.

Figure 3.40. Modern design as "leg art," Letter to the Editor about a Timken ad, *Architectural Forum* 79 (October 1943): 33.

design. The idea played out at the Bauhaus, as well, where alliances with local industry in Dessau brought a certain relevancy and urgency to the pedagogy and, in theory, infused those industries with a constant stream of new ideas. The wartime advertising simply carried the idea through to the American scene and the fact of wartime anticipation. For instance, at the same time that Gropius expressed to Sigfried Giedion his sincere belief that all land would become public after the war, thus rendering the city a virtual tabula rasa for planners, he was designing a jewelry store and a drug store for Pittsburgh Plate Glass advertisements. The ads thus help us reconsider the postwar relationship between modernist architects and corporate clients like Lever, Seagram's, and General Motors. Was there ever a pure moment when modern architects would have looked askance at these sorts of partnerships? To the contrary, architects have always accommodated themselves to the prevailing system of patronage, and never more so than under corporate capitalism, when big business offered the greatest opportunity to practice, to build significant buildings, and to change the world through architecture.

Such patronage, beginning with the rich wartime advertising, popularized ideas that originated in the more obscure professional sphere. As they publicized products, they also publicized many of the key elements of progressive architecture and planning. In particular, Le Corbusier loomed large. The tall building in open space, the fifth façade, tabula rasa planning, separation of urban functions such as cars and pedestrians and commercial and residential areas—these all got played out repeatedly in the ads. While Le Corbusier had been translated and had long been acknowledged as a master of modern architecture, to have his ideas threaded through advertisements that ran in popular magazines enabled a wider cultural reception, placing his ideas in an American context and, importantly, in the context of consumer anticipation and the building boom. This gave them cohesion as a group, and in spite of the many different aesthetics and approaches expressed in the ads, their shared context may have lent coherence to modern design itself, situating it in a cultural milieu beyond the museum and the avant-garde.

The nature of the wartime ads as cultural products mediated the distance between progressive architects and the reader on the home front. They were populist, born of the needs of wartime propaganda. Yet they also aimed to swing public opinion in favor of big business. Captains of industry and admen assigned their visions to architects, and committees in corporate boardrooms filtered the responses, only to have them tweaked yet again by the sales techniques of advertising agencies and their artists. In order to create continuity within a given campaign, illustrators at the advertising firms reworked the ideas and drawings of the architects, essentially turning them into cartoons of modern architecture, a small but significant shift. This collaboration recast modernist ideas that originated in Europe into American terms, transformed them into a popular medium, and animated them with the aura of consumer culture. Understood in terms of patronage, the alliances fostered by these advertising campaigns parallel corporate sponsorship of art in the same period, a phenomenon Walter Abell noted as early as 1946. Abell wrote: "Government patronage was undoubtedly the dominant factor in the relationship between art and society during the 1930s. The present decade is witnessing an equally striking manifestation and one which, in certain respects, represents the opposite pole of social impulse: patronage by industry."[132] The alliances between art and industry have been well documented by James Sloan Allen and Michele Bogart, but the story for architecture, which is bound to industry like no other art, remains incomplete.[133] Such an account would clarify the important way architects contributed to design in industry, but it would also uncover the nexus between architectural practice and the production, merchandising, and distribution of building materials. Embedded in this nexus lies a multitude of answers to questions about the nature of stock materials, the absorption of a modernist aesthetic into the design of hardware, and the very process of design in a fully national economy, after, as Richard Neutra put it, *Sweet's Catalog* had become the modern quarry.[134]

The object of this essay has been more modest: to detail and interpret a significant encounter between architects, advertising agencies, and big business when the fate of all three seemed to hang in the balance. The ads invited people to "buy into" modern architecture in a way that simply did not happen in the 1930s, or after World War I, when the Modern Movement bloomed (mostly in Europe) out of a similar ethos. One of the most curious holes in the narrative of the "triumph" of modern architecture in the United States is the fact that it came to prominence in depression and war, when a strained building industry had little margin for error, private building lagged or was restricted under war provisions, and unemployed architects cast about for alternative means of survival: in other words, in a lull in building that lasted half a generation. Wartime advertisements transformed modern architecture, first obscuring its association with a mostly foreign movement associated with socialism and then binding it to native phenomena associated with period clichés such as "the American way of life," "better living," and the future itself—clichés that were instrumental in the revival of corporate America during and after the Depression. At the same time, ads tied the new architecture to the titanic struggles over which World War II was fought. It helped usher out a world that many people wished to leave behind, sloughing off the "old world ways" that skilled admen linked to the possibility of a clean material slate through postwar consumption. Architecture would be the reward for fifteen years of deprivation and sacrifice, the physical embodiment of moving on.

Any consideration of paper architecture should also acknowledge its status as distinct from the built environment. The architecture of 194X is fundamentally different from that of actual buildings, *but a claim can be made for the existence of a coherent "unbuilt environment."*[135] To begin with, the site, if you will, of the magazine page gave the anticipatory ads a kind of integrity as a group. One scarcely needs to invoke the idea of the memory theater to suggest that they all got "built," in some sense, on the same site, one on top of another, month by month, through the practice of reading. Much in the way readers get trained to look for regular features in magazines, the ad campaigns created monthly anticipation in readers. The overwhelming number of requests for Revere pamphlets is ample proof of this, but so is the nature of magazine reading in the period. Before other technologies of leisure and promotion intruded on the supremacy of the magazine, readers used their pages more actively, for instance, placing them in scrapbooks. So obvious was this active readership to magazine editors that *Parents Magazine* put an image of a scissors next to articles that readers would want to clip and paste into scrapbooks or save for after the war (Figure 3.41).[136] A scissors also appears in Williams Lescaze's Revere ad, a play on "sure surgery" (see Figure 2.3).[137] This active habit of reading made the ads internally referential to the set as well as to the anticipation of 194X. Yet there is something qualitatively different about the speculative architecture of the home front, as well. As a product—a word with important double meaning in this context—of architecture, advertising, and corporations, the unbuilt architecture of 194X offered something discursively richer than many professional dialogues and more accessible than buildings themselves, which are scattered over a large geographical area and which we often encounter when we are too harried to pay attention. Together the architects, admen, and

Figure 3.41. Idea file, *Parents' Magazine* (November 1943): 48.

captains of industry made architectural *images*, which they intended as a form of persuasion, convincing people to support the cause of fighting for a better way of life after the war. Modern architecture became visually paired with the war effort and with the forestalled dreams of the Depression and war. "Real" architecture could not have achieved this so easily. In short, 194X helped make modern architecture American, a vehicle through which the so-called American way of life might be attained.

　　And yet, the ads were not really about architecture. Their raison d'etre was publicity, and I don't mean this in the pejorative. Some of the bias in favor of monuments over paper architecture in architectural history derives from seeing them as architectural culminations, the end point of so much planning and design. The purest forms of modern architecture, however, are rarely, if ever, three-dimensional, as Ezra Stoller's photographs show and as these ads demonstrate. So many of the most cherished tenets of modern architecture—flexibility, universal space, functionalism—all become paradoxes the moment they leave the plane of the page. But what if we were to push the possibilities of this plane beyond its borders and consider the architecture of 194X as one building, the way Eugène Emmanuel Viollet-le-Duc considered the European cathedral as one building instantiated in different places over time. This would not only make the gerund "building" useful, but it would also imply a more conceptual development, not unlike the cathedrals of Europe, which culminate, according to this view, with the High Gothic of Amiens or Cologne Cathedrals. The point of historical arrival, rather than being a building, which is usually the object of the unbuilt, was modern architecture itself. This is, after all, what the cathedral evolution really maintains, the creation of a mature manner of building and thinking about architecture. With the architecture of 194X, instead of a *corpus mirabulus,* a church or *the* church, or the Gothic, we find an *annus mirabulus,* 194X, a temporal apotheosis, one worked out on paper and awaiting the pent-up energies of a war economy to be spent on the deferred dreams of more than a decade. As architecture manqué, a proxy for actual building opportunities, the ads must be understood as more than forecasts that we could match up with postwar architecture: they are the monuments of the war years. Yet as images they are not representations of a far-off building, which entails both erasure and invention. Rather, they are the thing itself in a different form: two-dimensional, but given mass over time, as part of a series, rather than in space, like a typical building. They were buildings pressed into the fold of the page, awaiting the postwar boom to blow them up.

4 The End of Planning
The Building Boom and the
Invention of Normalcy

"Are you *Doodling* or *Planning* for that Building Boom?" *Time* magazine posed the question to readers of *Architectural Forum* and other magazines in April 1943 as part of a new series of advertisements that threw much of the culture of planning into question (Figure 4.1).[1] The building boom loomed in the mythical future of 194X. Its promise inspired architectural and urban fantasies, mobilized big business and advertising agencies, roused politicians, and threw economists into rancorous debate. Everyone wanted a piece of it and, as much as any other social figure on the home front, it tied these various elements of society together. Like so much of the consumerist anticipation of the war years, the building boom figured to be the nation's natural compensation for years of waiting through the Depression and for the rationing and material deferments of war. Its central promise, houses stocked with new appliances for everyone, brought with it implications for the nation's economy and social structure. After World War I, the United States had mishandled reconversion, and a short advance of postwar activity retreated into depression. Big business watched vigilantly from the sidelines of World War II, nervous not to repeat the debacle of the early 1920s and ready to do whatever it could to prepare for the building boom. *Time* manipulated this instant but powerful myth in order to discredit the culture of planning, coupling its more visionary strains with doodling.

The image brought the point home: a drawing from 1882 by French caricaturist Albert Robida of an eighteen-story skyscraper made of "papier agglom é ré." If readers did not catch the reference to a paper skyscraper as a pun on paper architecture, they surely understood the parallel between chimeras of the past and contemporary visions of the postwar world. The new campaign declared a kind of cultural civil war, rooted in economic and political ideologies but fought out on the home front through cultural forms such as the ads. At the same time that Henry Luce used *Fortune* and *Architectural Forum* to advance the ideas of the National Resources Planning Board (NRPB) and to argue for social responsibility in the mass media and business, his flagship magazine, *Time*, sent out a chastening call for a no-nonsense approach to postwar planning. Real planning involved

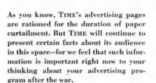

Figure 4.1. *Time* advertisement, "Are you doodling...?" *Architectural Forum* 78 (April 1943): 28.

"building Post-war Building markets." *Time*'s version of planning consisted of getting ready to make sales, stirring up prospects, forging a network of middlemen, and stimulating confidence. It had nothing to do with the built environment or urban transformation. In other words, *Time* co-opted the word planning for pure business, dismissing the visionary plans and architecture of 194X as frivolous.

The *Time* ads were part of a reaction to the culture of planning that began in 1943 and bloomed in 1944 and 1945. The background of the reaction was political and economic. In 1943, Congress cut the NRPB as part of a broader attack on New Deal agencies. In the wake of this blow to national planning, politicians, economists, and the building industry began to challenge the foundations of public planning and to assail the many cultural expressions that blossomed out of it. Classical economists mounted a stiff counterattack against the newfangled economics of pump priming, deficit spending, and full employment, meeting Alvin Hansen and the Keynesian basis of planning with a spirited defense of laissez-faire capitalism and the status quo. The change in ethos emboldened corporations and the ad firms that had embraced planning as a form of corporate social responsibility to reverse course. The politics and economics behind this shift have been explored elsewhere, but its cultural ramifications, especially for architecture and planning, remain unexamined.[2] The reaction in the building industry coupled modern architecture with planning, attacking the former in order to discredit the latter. Corporations had enlisted modern architecture as an important means of expressing a progressive and patriotic spirit. Preparations for the building boom turned this positive image upside down. By the end of 1945, most of the visionary campaigns had been canceled, others were altered, and some swung in the opposite direction. Architecture magazines, likewise, checked their commitments to planning. The inability of forward-thinking architects to forge a consistent and compelling agenda for postwar architecture and planning also threatened to dissipate the culture of planning. The Depression and war had shaken the foundations of architectural practice and confidence. With the NRPB dead, the International Congress of Modern Architecture (CIAM) suspended for the duration, native attempts to organize withering, the architectural magazines in retreat, and advertising opportunities drying up, architects faced the postwar period in a state of crisis.[3]

Reaction: The Death of the NRPB

The reaction began when a swing to the right in Congress after the 1942 elections shifted the balance of power in favor of the conservatives, who used the emergency of war to dismantle the New Deal.[4] The NRPB, one of the victims of this shift, was an easy target. It had become the government's primary attempt to organize a central planning agency. Its literature loudly trumpeted the cause of the sort of gestalt planning that so many architects had come to expect would be standard in 194X. Based loosely on the mature economy theory and the need for full employment, it favored carrying the war's strict control of resources into peacetime, which made it an object of Congressional ire. While its charter authorized a limited scope for the bureau, from the study of planning issues and the dissemination of its findings, its semiautonomous status irked Congress. Born out of executive order under the War Powers Act, Congress had no representation in it or authority over it. Lawmakers could neither amend the board nor demand special reports or studies. But Congress did have the power to curtail its activities to the point of making it irrelevant. In the first session of Congress after the 1942 elections in early 1943, the NRPB sustained injuries from which it would not recover.

The way the NRPB died is less important than the terms of the debate, which reveal a great deal about the culture of planning. Arguing over the fate of the NRPB on the floor of the Senate with Macy's president, Beardsley Ruml, Senator Frederick C. Smith of Ohio called the Board a "grave menace to society," indicative of the "dictatorial tactics of the federal bureaucracy."[5] Smith and his conservative colleagues in both the House of Representatives and the Senate feared that the NRPB, which they noted Roosevelt called "the planning arm of my Executive office," implied the "absorption by the state of all economic functions and the complete demolition of all free enterprise."[6] They argued that the loss of personal liberties would inevitably follow. While full of exaggerated claims and faulty arguments, this line of attack attracted support.

Smith saved particular venom for the urban planners, especially targeting many of the basic assumptions that progressive architects had begun to believe about postwar cities. The senator assaulted the strong laws of eminent domain on which postwar planning was predicated. Grandiose schemes of slum clearance and population migration drew heavy criticism from conservative senators. Such shifting of population, which Gropius casually had called "endangered production," and Saarinen insisted should rouse no moral dilemma, not only would have created the much-desired modernist tabula rasa for replanning and rebuilding but also would have required the socioeconomic analogue to architectural flexibility. Such cherished modernist ideals could easily become their own dogmas. In the same way that architectural flexibility guarded against the ossification of outdated cultural forms and behavior, a mobile population would counteract the regional and seasonal differences in the supply and demand of labor. Senator Smith was not so sanguine. Under the NRPB, Smith claimed, "labor is to be handled like chattel." Both urban and rural communities "are to be shifted from one locality to another, just as Mussolini, Hitler, and Stalin have been doing in their countries."[7] Quoting NRPB literature out of context, and using the concurrent anti-Communist fearmongering of the Dies Committee to great effect, Smith declared: "What duplicity and hypocrisy! It is planned to raze our cities and rebuild them . . . 'not by the square block,'" he added, quoting the NRPB, "'but by the square mile.'"[8] The obstreperous Smith and his conservative cohorts all but drowned out the anemic liberal response. Congress appropriated just enough money for the NRPB to shut down operations, and by August 1943 it was no more.

The fall of the NRPB mobilized architects and planners, who took the bureau's "demonstrations" as models, from *Fortune*'s Syracuse project to *Architectural Forum*'s *Planning with You*, Pittsburgh's *Civic Clinic for Better Living*, Stonorov and Kahn's *You*

and Your Neighborhood, and the work of the AIA's Committee on Postwar Reconstruction. Architects also rose to its defense, albeit ineffectually. Joseph Hudnut penned a
postmortem in the *Record*, martyring the defunct agency:

> Many people believe that the National Resources Planning Board died when a petu-
> lant Senate refused its annual appropriation. On the contrary, it was then that the
> NRPB came to life. From that time forth, the programs of this agency will live in poli-
> tics—to win and lose elections, to make and unmake the careers of Senators—and in
> the end the NRPB in some form or other will be reconstructed.[9]

Unfortunately for Hudnut, the NRPB had less chance of being reconstituted in another
form than the cities it aimed to rebuild. Only in piecemeal and partial efforts did planning
ever take place in the United States, in part because the NRPB met an untimely fate.
Rudolph Schindler, an infrequent writer, rued "the increasing conservatism of the
United States, as expressed in our Congress," as a setback for the already undervalued
architect and for the prospects of the city itself. "On this basis," he wrote, "optimistic
hopes for radically new city planning and government-sponsored housing will hardly
materialize."[10]

Architectural historian Talbot Hamlin weighed in on the issue, not from his isolated perch at *Pencil Points* but in a special issue of the *Antioch Review* devoted to the
NRPB's collapse. The critic couched the issue in grand terms: "The trend of New Deal
national planning, like that of the more enlightened local planning commissions, is to put
human values first; that of business and industrial planning is to put economic values
first. In the next few years the American people must decide which kind of planning they
want."[11] This was precisely the distinction that the *Time* magazine ad had made. The reaction in Congress, he wrote, was "symptomatic of a growing political revolt against governmental planning of any kind—a revolt not alone national, but on which bids fair to
hamper, if not to undo, the work of state and county and city planning commissions the
country over."[12] He thus fashioned the fall of the NRPB into a titanic conflict over the
nature of democracy that pitted the greatest forces in American society against one another. The episode in Congress continued the fundamental battle between laissez-faire
capitalism (which Hamlin called "the theory of the devil take the hindmost") and social
planning that lay beneath the disquieted surface of the New Deal—combatants that the
war had temporarily forced into a cease-fire. Not surprisingly, Hamlin framed his argument in terms of the mature economy theory, claiming that an unimpeded speculative
economy can only be democratic in a country with a frontier. But in a nation "where the
only frontier is the city slum or the hobo's jungle, *laissez faire* is merely a prettified term
for dog-eat-dog... the system by which the dogs who have eaten the most other dogs
achieve the right to do what planning is done."[13]

At the root of the entire conflict, Hamlin believed, lay a "confusion of the concepts
of democracy and laissez-faire capitalism."[14] Big business had managed to perpetuate a
"fallacy... that planning by the small boards of great corporations or of other financial

pressure groups over which the citizen has no control is somehow 'more American' than planning by governmental agencies over which he exerts more power than he realizes."[15] While much of his argument rehashed Progressive Era and New Deal contests over the role of government and the size and power of big business, the sharp-eyed architectural historian also understood that more modern forces were at work in causing "this popular apathy that is dooming humane planning to a slow death:"

> Primarily it is a result of the failure of the planners as a whole to show each citizen how his immediate future is bound up in the planning question, how intimately planning affects his living quarters, his working habits, his educational and recreational possibilities. It is a failure in salesmanship, in popular education. As a result, the great inarticulate public remains in abysmal ignorance, at the mercy of deep but unfounded prejudices, which are carefully stimulated by those who hate and fear the coming of a new and more equitable world.[16]

It was a failure, in other words, of promotion. For years, Hamlin had been listening to architects debate the virtues of public relations. Where its anemic application in architecture only impeded the growth of the profession, its failure in planning threatened the fabric of society.

Other writers in the liberal *Antioch Review* were equally enraged, seeing the cutting of the bureau as a sabotage of the visionary forces of change by reactionary forces that aimed to return to the conditions of the past. They charged that the actions of Congress amounted to an "attempt to shore up what is left of the nineteenth century," calling it the shortsighted policy that put "our heads into the jaws of fascism."[17] The hyperbolic attempt to volley totalitarianism back to the foe yielded to a measured defense of the NRPB's platform and of the economics behind it, including the ideas of Alvin Hansen. Raymond Walsh of the Congress of Industrial Organizations (CIO), an economist who worked alongside the author of the mature economy theory at Harvard, also condemned Congress, noting a swing in the political climate "toward a condition which is sometimes described as a state of 'normalcy.'" To stave this off, following Hamlin's plea for better salesmanship, he pleaded for "more mimeograph crankers and fewer utopians!"[18] Even progressives called for the tempering of visionary planning. By the end of 1943, D. K. Este Fisher, the AIA's "man in Washington," wrote confidentially that, while supporting their work, "I fully realize that there is considerable question of the wisdom of even mentioning the National Resources Planning Board."[19]

These renderings of the fate of the NRPB tapped into widespread concerns about the nature of information and politics in the United States. The skirmish in Congress erupted elsewhere, marking a larger political struggle to define the postwar world. The battle was especially pitched within the Office of War Information (OWI), between liberal New Dealers and writers, on the one hand, and conservatives and military officials, on the other hand, with a third branch of admen in charge of propaganda operating relatively free of the political turmoil. The writers, represented by Robert Sherwood and Alistair MacLeish, pushed a visionary agenda for the postwar world, brandishing a sincere if clichéd collection of appeals to democracy, individualism, and Christianity.[20] The second group, including Milton Eisenhower, Secretary of War Henry L. Simson, Secretary of the Navy Frank Knox, and Admiral Ernest J. King, adopted a more pragmatic approach, emphasizing the war over the postwar world. The visionaries in the OWI saw World War II as a war over values and the "American way of life," painting broad pictures about good and evil.[21] The writers, however, faint of heart and unschooled in bureaucratic matters, faded fast, first with MacLeish's resignation in early 1943 and then in waves of later resignations, firming up the conservative hold over the office. Finally, the same Congress that pulled the plug on the NRPB, slashed the OWI, silencing the already muffled voice of reform.[22]

The Road to Serfdom and the Bogey of the Mature Economy

While Congress uprooted the only centralized planning organization in the United States and purged the OWI of rabble-rousing reformists, the economist Friedrich Hayek supplied a rhetoric capable of eroding much of the goodwill generated for planning during the depression and war. A devout adherent to classical capitalism and an opponent of Keynes and Hansen, Hayek argued in *The Road to Serfdom* (1944) that the collective economy implicit in planning inevitably led to totalitarianism.[23] In contrast to the attacks in Congress, Hayek's criticism of planning, even if wrongheaded, was measured, working over historical examples that likened Germany in the 1920s to the United States in the 1930s, and he wrote cogently in a style accessible to the general public.[24] Hayek obliged architects like Stonorov and Kahn by bundling all forms of planning, acknowledging the culture of planning that had gained so much momentum during the war. But he did this in order to dismiss them all as part of an immoral system of social control. Planning on the model of the NRPB, or that advocated by most progressive architects, Hayek asserted, was tantamount to socialism and could be put into practice only through methods most planners abhorred.[25] The rhetoric of the mature economy had softened some of this resistance to methods of central control, making it seem not only desirable but also native and natural, part of a process of growth, decay, and rebirth. Hayek wrote persuasively against the inevitability of planning, upholding economic competition as the true "natural" economic system and dismissing the visionary planners with rhetorical flourishes such as: "From the saintly and single-minded idealist to the fanatic is often but a step."[26]

Charles Merriam, the former NRPB planner, laughed off Hayek's claims that planners demanded totalitarian control, calling it "one of the strange survivals of obscurantism in modern times. . . . Pessimism, defeatism, timidity—all the marks of Doubting Castle are sign posts on the *Road to Serfdom*."[27] Other economists and political scientists came to the defense of planning, most notably Herman Finer's rebuttal, *The Road to Reaction*, and Barbara Wootton's *Freedom under Planning*. Finer called the *Road to Serfdom* "the most sinister offensive against democracy to emerge from a democratic country for many decades."[28] Others declaimed Hayek as well. One reviewer excoriated his desire "to go back" as "jejune" nostalgia: "This well-worn sleight-of-hand, the identification of an abstract figment of the textbook with a lost Golden Age . . . remains wholly unhistorical."[29] Political scientist and theorist on totalitarianism, Carl J. Friedrich, countered Hayek using NRPB literature and his own wartime planning study of Boston.[30] Admonishing the Austrian economist for his lack of faith, he wrote: "Hayek shows little belief in the common man and his capacity for useful participation in the community's common concerns. . . . The road to serfdom lies through the timid disbelief in the capacity of the people to rule themselves."[31] But Hayek's desire to return to a golden age of free competition also had its adherents, including economist Joseph A. Schumpeter, who wrote an adulatory review.[32]

Hayek scarcely needed the demigods of economics and social science to buttress his cause. Closer to the building industry, Thomas S. Holden, the president of F.W. Dodge, which published *Architectural Record*, assaulted government spending for urban redevelopment. Using the pages of his magazine and other venues, he attacked planning and the forces behind it in more accessible terms than Hayek. F. W. Dodge was a pioneer in the publication of building statistics, publishing the *Dodge Report*, *Sweet's Catalog*, and the *Record*, among other magazines in the building industry. Even as his magazine published articles and ads that built up the culture of planning, Holden undermined its economic premise. In the sardonically titled "Who's Afraid of Prosperity," he wrote:

> The prospect of prosperity should please most of us. It may be somewhat upsetting to economic planners, who have come to the front as specialists in depression techniques, to well-meaning collectivists, to piecemeal collectivists, and to scheming collectivists, and to all those people selling fear of the future. . . . The postwar economy will be an enterprise-economy, not a dole economy.[33]

Holden's "specialists in depression techniques" referred to Alvin Hansen and those architects and planners who bought into the mature economy theory as a means of transforming American cities. He continued his diatribe through the end of the war and into the postwar period, in 1949 collecting his ideas in *The Great Illusion: An Inexhaustible Public Purse*, a polemic against the use of deficit spending, published, not surprisingly, by the National Association of Manufacturers.[34] Here was a key figure in the building industry contradicting everything that had been written in his magazine.

Waking Up Out of a Bad Dream House

The tenor of the ads in the *Record* and other magazines shifted in 1944 and 1945. Steeped in the classical capitalism of Hayek, rather than in the Keynesian economics of Hansen, and informed by the corresponding antiplanning sentiment in Congress, a number of corporations parted ways with planning, as well, dropping their anticipatory ad campaigns. In some cases, they replaced them with new campaigns that brazenly attacked modern architecture itself, saving special animus for the modern house.

In 1944 and 1945, advertising faced a new set of problems as the end of war grew increasingly apparent and rationed materials again became available. The war was won in stages, and the relaxation of priorities orders – those restrictions placed on vital materials by the government during the war – followed the unpredictable path to victory, altering the climate of the home front by degrees and determining the way companies prepared for postwar building. With the Allied invasion of France in June 1944 and the steady gains of the summer, culminating in the liberation of Paris in August, victory now seemed assured, and this changed the tone on the home front. Simultaneously, the war economy had pushed aside many of the fears of the mature economy theory, depriving planning of its economic justification. As production boomed, the public had money to spend, and waited for restrictions to be lifted.[35] The advertising firm Young & Rubicam took out an ad in *Fortune* magazine in January 1945 explaining how delicate issues arose with the release of civilian goods. Ads had to spur immediate sales, but not at the expense of alienating those who were still mired in the war effort.[36] With the overall image of a company at stake, the ad firm emphasized a larger conception of public relations. Overzealous ads would be taken as a sign of poor taste. Young & Rubicam promised ads that would tactfully negotiate the change in public sentiment accompanying the slow conversion to a peacetime economy.[37] The desire for a return to normalcy, in the form of business as usual, put consumption ahead of anticipation in the new ad campaigns of 1945.

The transition between war and peace was not only a problem for advertisers. After years of deferred desires, Americans were caught up in the frenzy of anticipating the postwar world. As V-Day, B-Day (Building Day), or 194X approached, unfounded futurism was met with skepticism. The more visionary strain of postwar thinking increasingly confronted a more sober response by some architects, architectural critics, and certain factions in the building industry. In some quarters, futurism was cause for alarm.[38] By the time the Allies had taken Paris in August 1944, a pragmatic mood had thoroughly set in on the home front, and the game of anticipation began to falter. Architectural and urban historian Paul Zucker, who had convened an important wartime symposium on planning and published *The New Architecture and City Planning* (1944), warned: "It is necessary here to protest energetically against one method of evading the issue, fostered by so many articles in popular magazines today, about the 'house of to-morrow,' the 'city of to-morrow.' There are very powerful vested interests more concerned in marketing a particular commodity than in promoting a really essential change."[39] Such criticism became common as the end of the war neared and visions of 194X came to seem less possible in the narrowing space between the present and the arrival of the "future." Richard Neutra wrote in response to the same intersection of advertising and planning: "[B]eing a consumer is not and, in fact, must not be a passive role. It spells often disaster to just 'drift into the market' and expose oneself to the high pressure salesmen who pounce on the unwary. No, what is needed . . . is to prepare and fortify oneself with a well studied master plan."[40] At first blush, Neutra applied the language of master planning to consumption, a typical rhetorical device at the time. But in fact he was writing about the "consumption" of local and state governments in planning postwar hospitals, schools, and other institutions and services, turning planning into an extrapolation of household management or home economics, a reversal of the strategy ads were then using. His was a warning about the dangers of allowing consumption and its devices, such as advertising, to drive planning, rather than having citizen action be the instrument. The mere fact that Zucker, Neutra, and others felt the need to warn against these developments in planning demonstrates the change in mood.

Criticism often took the form of parody. For instance, on October 31, 1945, New Jersey architect and expert on the Greenbelt Towns, O. Kline Fulmer, addressed the twenty-third annual convention of the American Institute of Steel Construction at French Lick, Indiana.[41] Before delivering a talk about the postwar plan of Toledo, Ohio, a wild, world's fair–style plan by Norman Bel Geddes (on which Fulmer assisted), he read a poem called "Postwar Dope":

> Listen my children, and you can hear
> Through the opium-laden atmosphere
> The voices of soothsayers, prophets and seers
> All fortune-telling the postwar years . . .
> How the world as we know it will suddenly cease
> 'ere the ink is dry on the Treaty of Peace.
> And presto! . . . a New World; Our Homes, our cars
> Will look like something fresh out of Mars
> And you'll casually step in your autogiro
> For 18 holes of golf in Cairo
> You'll live on pills.
> You'll carry your bride
> To a home made out of phenol-formaldehyde
> With electronic beams to do the chores
> Electric eyes to open the doors,
> And radar (that newest of trouble detectors)
> To warn of approaching bill collectors.
> Oh we won't have any homes . . . we'll live in trailers
> With six rooms furnished by Lord & Taylors
> And everyone, even in Winnepesaukee,
> Will own television and walk-talky [sic].
> And this, good friends—this prospect bright—
> Is to happen suddenly, quite overnight.
> Is it true, or false, or a glorious hoax?
> (It's just a lot of malarky, folks.)[42]

While Fulmer attacked the more theatrical visions of the postwar world as a whole, most critics focused at first on the miracle house idea. In December 1944, Boston architect Charles Maginnis gathered together a group of architects, planners, and housing specialists for a "Post-War Planning Conference" in Boston. He asked Nancy McClelland, an expert on furniture and the decorative arts, to join one of the panels and requested a title for her talk. McClelland responded that she might speak on "something about

'De-bunking the Dream House' – for I think that a great many people have a false idea that they are going to get 'All This and Heaven, too' in the new house."[43] The dream house was a media creation, generated by ads and articles in the architectural and popular press with so little restraint that they spurred comments from figures like Robert L. Davison, the director of research at the John B. Pierce Foundation, one of the leading venues for research on housing. Davison wrote that since priorities orders halted the building of permanent homes in 1942,

> the publicity men are hard at work, keeping alive the hope for some "wonder house" of the future. Maybe the publicity men are doing harm rather than good. They describe fairy tale dwellings preferably all plastic (plastic sounds modern) that will automatically wash your clothes, cook your meals, turn out ice or completely mixed cocktails, and indeed do almost everything for you except give birth to the baby. This keeps the whole problem in the realm of fantasy.[44]

By 1944, the "publicity men" – admen, corporate advertisers, and some branches of the print media – began trying to kill the dream house they had created. A Westinghouse ad, for instance, told readers to "Forget Miracle Houses."[45] The National Association of Home Builders (NAHB) was at the center of the reaction against the miracle house, using its journal, *American Builder and Building Age,* as a clearinghouse for advertisements from corporations that advocated a more practical approach to postwar America. It laced its pages with anti–dream house commentary. The earliest manifestation of the reaction came in April 1943 in the blurb "Post-War Delusions":

> There is no limit to the flights of fancy of an architect, industrial designer or clever artist in depicting the wonders of the post-war house, refrigerator, or what not. But production experts and the men who have to meet payrolls know that the world can't be changed over night and they feel that many of the day dreams are merely promising the public the impossible. . . . In the case of houses, we have been flooded with fantastic pencil dreams of structures which have never been built, using material and equipment which has not yet gone into production, let alone subjected to "on the job" testing.[46]

The houses featured in *American Builder* supported this point of view. As a mouthpiece for builders, the magazine advocated traditional architecture and established methods and materials. While an occasional modern house found its way in, the journal counted modernist architecture among the "fantastic pencil dreams" that were to be mistrusted.

Sharp criticism awaited any company or magazine that supported a form of modernism the NAHB deemed impractical. When Richard Pratt, architectural editor of the *Ladies' Home Journal,* began a wartime series that reviewed some of the best modern houses and ideas for postwar America, *American Builder* went on the offensive:

> The *Ladies' Home Journal* has joined the procession of magazines that seem to be carrying on a day dream campaign to mislead and confuse the public about what to expect in a post-war house. In the January issue it illustrates another "house of

Figure 4.2. Dailey/Kaiser House, in *Ladies' Home Journal* 61 (January 1944): 54–55. Reprinted with permission of Environmental Design Archives, University of California, Berkeley (Gardiner Dailey Papers).

the future" that is so preposterous that even though it is accompanied by a large picture of Henry Kaiser who seems to endorse it, the public will surely detect its impracticability.[47]

Kaiser's house was so large, according to *American Builder*, that it would "not fit one normal building site in 1,000. The 3-bedroom model has some 1,500 square feet of floor area, two baths, a prefabricated fireplace, also—all for $4,000! Will Daydreams never cease?"[48] One wonders, however, if it was the size and impossibly low price or something else that fueled the criticism. Kaiser's house, in fact, was built to expand flexibly with the needs of the family (Figure 4.2).[49] Only the largest versions, with prefabricated wings added several times over, matched the ungainly one that *American Builder* condemned. In fact, California architect Gardner Dailey designed the original core of the house to be modest. It was, however, thoroughly modern, and Dailey was a good target. He had done an ad for United States Gypsum Company, and his work had appeared in the *Forum*'s "New Houses in 194X" issue. The Kaiser-Dailey house used a three-foot module as the basis for a standardized, interchangeable system of parts. Standard panels made for flexible planning of rooms and rapid erection. The *Ladies' Home Journal* argued that through such standardization and the use of prefabricated kitchen and bathroom units, the house would require far fewer workmen to erect. *American Builder* may have rejected the house on stylistic grounds, but it also may have been protecting the domain of the traditional homebuilder from the threat of a novel assembly system.

Schemes like Kaiser's often came dressed in the exaggerated anticipatory language of the war years, rhetoric *American Builder* shunned. Despite the fact that some of the corporations that advertised in the magazine used the term 194X, it poked fun at the futurists in a parody, "The 204X House." The article reported the prognostications of "technologist," Dr. J. S. Thomas, who believed that people in 204X "will be 6 feet 3 inches tall, will live 125 years without gray hair . . . , live in a $1600 house containing unbreakable glass, plumbing, living rooms that redecorate themselves at the twist of a wrist, and filters that transform the outside city noise into inside classical symphonies."[50]

Such criticism won *American Builder* support in the building industry. As had happened with the architectural press, a number of ad campaigns reinforcing the NAHB's stance ran in the pages of the magazine. The Arkansas Soft Pine Bureau, for instance, ran an ad in the same January 1944 issue with the copy: "Take It Easy, Builders, About Miracle House Hoop-la!" "Vivid imaginations are predicting radical changes in design and construction of post-war homes," the ad claimed. "In the speed and short cuts of defense and war industry housing, they claim to see similar methods forecast in building the homes of 194?"[51] The Kaiser-Dailey house had been just this sort of thing, a timesaving system based on mass-production techniques derived from Kaiser's experience building military housing. According to the ad, women would not be interested in "pre-conceived factory-built" houses. Impersonal and alien, they ran against American individualism. "So builders," the ad continued, "take it easy when fantastic predictions are made that tomorrow's homes are going to be delivered at the site, practically ready to move into. A few may be, but mostly they'll be built by you, just as they always have." The description of the dream house exactly fits the portrait of the early Revere Copper and Brass ads, many of which were prefabricated, machine-built houses that could be delivered to the site and erected in hours. Prefabrication, and not modern architecture, per se, was the bugaboo of the Arkansas Soft Pine Bureau.

Other reactionary ads often connected new methods with modern architecture, understood in the reductive sense of a style. Dierks Lumber and Coal Company, for instance, launched a direct attack on modernist architecture in its ads, which ran in *American Builder* in 1945.[52] In its first ad of this kind in January 1945, a parody of a modern house serves as the foil for a conventional suburban house (Figure 4.3).[53] The modern one is built of glass block. Flat roofs serve as a landing pad for a helicopter, the ubiquitous symbol of futurism, and as leisure space with deck chairs and an umbrella, possibly making fun of the Barrett Division ads. A plate glass window of impossible dimensions spans one side of a room, allowing the world to peer in and discover that it is the bedroom, another joke: the only room with transparent glass is the bedroom, while the rest is highly concealed by the glass block. A metal spiral staircase provides access to the roof and anchors the image by connecting the two wings of the house where they form an "L." A brick chimney by contrast anchors the traditional house. Its prominent pitched roof

BRING YOUR POST-WAR PLANS

DOWN TO EARTH

Practical Plans Will Build Profits for You!

In spite of the starry-eyed visions of impractical promisers, the Home of Tomorrow will be the natural evolution of the homes of today. Your post-war home will not be made of star-dust ... it will continue to be *made of wood!*

An alarming number of prospective home-owners have been led to believe that within a few months after the war's end "Miracle Homes" of stratospheric design and construction .... push-button kitchens, elaborate electrical controls, plastic walls ... will be available at low cost. There is no sound basis for these architectural absurdities, say experienced builders ... The home of tomorrow will follow the conservative lines of tested worth, modified only by proved technical advancements.

FREE A Big Book of Practical Plans for Post-War Homes of *Tested* Value

BE READY FOR THE RUSH OF HOME CONSTRUCTION TO FOLLOW V-DAY!

Send NOW for the Dierks Plan Book of 25 Tested Homes, Free to Retail Lumber Dealers east of the Rockies. To sell *lumber,* you must sell gracious living and a lifetime of happiness in an attractive, efficient home. *You need plans to show*—tested plans with complete descriptions in a wide variety of types to suit every modern need and taste. Mail the coupon *today!*

Tested

DIERKS

LUMBER & COAL CO.

DIERKS BLDG.   **KANSAS CITY, MO.**

DIERKS LUMBER & COAL CO.
Dierks Bldg., Kansas City 6, Mo.

Please send my FREE sample copy of Dierks TESTED HOMES. Mail without obligation to:

Name ....

Address ....

City .... State ....

Figure 4.3. Advertisement for Dierks Lumber and Coal Company, *American Builder and Building Age* 67 (January 1945): 183.

and multiple gables shelter the house, while mullioned windows and shades create privacy. Wood replaces glass, and the branches of trees echo the blades of the helicopter. The copy curves in an arc springing from above the modern house ("Bring your post-war plans") to below the traditional one ("down to earth"). The modern house, moreover, floats on a cloud—it is literally a dream house—while the traditional house sits on an ample front yard.

Below the images, more substantial text explains the company's position: "In spite of the starry-eyed visions of impractical promisers, the Home of Tomorrow will be the natural evolution of the homes of today. Your post-war home will not be made of star-dust . . . it will continue to be *made of wood*!" After condemning the miracle home idea with "push-button kitchens, elaborate electrical controls, [and] plastic walls," the ad explains that "The home of tomorrow will follow the conservative lines of tested worth, modified only by proved technical advancements." The strange phrase "conservative lines of tested worth" implied that the lines of a house had a value that could be tested. Dierks Lumber and Coal willfully confused aesthetic appeal (the "lines") with value ("worth"), and moreover, with use-value ("tested worth"). And it associated all of this with newfangled materials and methods. Modern architecture, its "lines" untested, was too new to have achieved such a secure status.

A second Dierks ad of July 1945 went even further (Figure 4.4).[54] A rather mon-strous parody of a modern house, composed of arbitrary and awkward masses that float in different planes, clad in huge plate-glass windows, and a flat roof with the requisite heli-copter, rises out of the dark clouds of a young man's nightmare. "'Dream Homes' are no nightmares," the copy reads, "to wide-awake lumber dealers." The ad castigates "the fab-ulous and radical ideas that have been dreamed up by exponents of the 'Modern Miracle Homes.'" Dierks clearly intended to rouse the industry against the threat of new ideas. The dealer had a responsibility "to do the spade work for post-war profits by helping prospective builders plan their homes from the ground up, *instead of from the clouds down*." Like many ads of its kind, Dierks's publicized a pamphlet called *Tested Homes*, which had been in publication since before the war. *Tested Homes* featured twenty-five designs by Kansas City architect William S. Loth, all traditional suburban affairs, varying little in plan or elevation. It is in keeping with Dierks's message that it would offer a pam-phlet that was five years old as a model for postwar architecture.

Advertising Returns to Normalcy

By 1945, perhaps bowing to the pressures unleashed by the reactionary campaigns, Revere Copper and Brass and Stran-Steel had changed their campaigns, going in for ads that were heavy on text and short on atmosphere. Revere discontinued its pamphlets in late 1944 and turned to lighthearted animal parables. Stran-Steel left its aspirations for a Quonset hut civilization behind and churned out a series of ads that show buildings in the process of erection, their half-exposed frames being wrapped in relatively traditional skins (Figure 4.5).[55] The graphic method of a split image, similar to its earlier ads, now

"*Dream Homes*"

ARE NO NIGHTMARES

TO WIDE-AWAKE
LUMBER DEALERS

The fabulous and radical ideas that have been dreamed up by exponents of the "Modern Miracle Homes" may be confusing to prospective home-builders. But Lumber Dealers know that basically, post-war homes will be of time-tested design and construction—and that the majority will be built of wood.

Now is the time for the wide-awake dealer to do the spade work for post-war profits by helping prospective builders plan their homes from the ground up, *instead of from the clouds down.*

Free Your Copy of Dierks Practical
PLAN BOOK OF TESTED HOMES

Here's how you can crystalize the desire for post-war homes. An attractive book of 25 tested homes of advanced but sound design for modern living. These plans will sell lumber and building material for you. Each plan is fully described and illustrated. \

Send for your Sample Plan Book TODAY—it is FREE to lumber dealers east of the Rockies. (All others, please include 25c in coin or stamps to pay for cost of printing and postage.)

DIERKS

LUMBER & COAL CO.
DIERKS BLDG.   KANSAS CITY 6, MO.

DIERKS LUMBER & COAL CO.
Dierks Bldg., Kansas City 6, Mo.
   I am a Lumber Dealer. Please send my FREE sample copy of TESTED HOMES to:

Name ....

Address ....

Figure 4.4. Advertisement for Dierks Lumber and Coal Company, *American Builder and Building Age* 67 (July 1945): 160.

Figure 4.5. Advertisement for Stran-Steel, *Architectural Record* 97 (August 1945): 139.

served as a metaphor for all the construction that was beginning to happen, a visual pun on being partway out of the war economy. Instead of associating its steel with the clean, modern, new world anticipated for the postwar world, which was a play on surfaces, the ads associated the company's product with the "real" structure of the present.

U.S. Gypsum's publicity campaign followed a similar trajectory. After its more visionary advertising in 1941 and 1942, the company published pamphlets, two scrapbooks, and a magazine, *Popular Home,* all of which took a more moderate, inclusive view of architecture. The pamphlet, *Let's Be Sensible* (1944), typifies the reversal that occurred late in the war. With victory and the building boom seemingly around the corner, U.S. Gypsum advocated a less fanciful, more level way of approaching the postwar world. The pamphlet mockingly insisted that the predictions that homes of the future would "dust their own floors, cook their own meals and make their own beds, originate with those who have no direct connection with the building industry."[56] Of course, U.S. Gypsum's own ad campaign had fanned these futuristic flames in the first place. *Let's Be Sensible* predicted that things would be the same as before the war. Change would be gradual, both in process and style. This, it claimed, "is simply the 'American Way' of doing things: Never in the past has there been a period of progress so rapid that those in the business of building could not keep pace. It is folly to expect it now. The improvement of the old and the invention of the new will come through sound, sensible development—just as it always has—and America will be given more durable, livable and less costly homes."[57]

U.S. Gypsum followed up *Let's Be Sensible* with its two scrapbooks, *Pak of Ideas* and *Ideas Galore,* which encouraged consumers to collect ideas for their postwar houses, providing folders for scraps and instructions on how to design a house.[58] *Ideas Galore,* in particular, eschewed modern architecture. It came with twelve sets of floor plans and cutouts in scale for arranging furniture on those plans. The cover set the tone for the pamphlet (Figure 4.6), with twelve different rough renderings of the homes ranging from Victorian to Cape Cod. The most modern design on the cover was a split-level ranch house. With plans, elevations, and ideas for interiors in the form of a typical plan book, this scrapbook could not be misused to design modernist architecture. The closest model to the ranch house on the cover was a two-story house by Schweikher and Elting (Figure 4.7). In case the public thought it too risqué, U.S. Gypsum called it "Modified Modern," a kind of mollified modernism, at least in name. In spite of its pitched roof and traditional materials (brick and board-and-batten), progressive ideas substantially influenced the house. A free plan played itself out on the exterior, creating an artistic asymmetry for which U.S. Gypsum made excuses, claiming that the materials "combined to camouflage the unusual placement of doors and windows."[59] The pamphlet could not completely disguise the large casement windows, second-floor deck, built-ins, fluorescent lighting, and nontraditional fixtures and furniture. The house, a far cry from Paul Nelson's Suspended House or Walter Dorwin Teague's house for Revere Copper and Brass, saved most of the modernist moments for the interior, meaning a family could act modern and still look conventional on the outside. In fact, the scrapbook contained one or two other houses that were more contemporary than the ones on the cover, including

Figure 4.6. Cover, U.S. Gypsum Company, *Popular Home's Ideas Galore,* 1946.

a ranch house by Cliff May and a "pacific coast house" by John Deardorf, which U.S. Gypsum attempted to make socially acceptable by writing: "This clean-cut, informal approach to modern would challenge any die-hard traditionalist to give a nod of approval" (Figure 4.8).[60]

United States Gypsum Company's turnabout may have been a response to a new antimodern architecture campaign by the National Gypsum Company that ran in major magazines, including *Time* and *Newsweek,* as well as in the *Architectural Forum.* The

Figure 4.7. Schweikher and Elting House, U.S. Gypsum Company, *Popular Home's Ideas Galore,* 12.

most damning ad appeared in May 1944 (Figure 4.9).[61] A caricature of postwar planning, the ad depicts a doctor making a house call as the distressed wife of the "patient" looks on. As the doctor prods with his stethoscope, the husband stands with his shirt off, but barely pauses from his giddy activity of snipping cutouts for his latest model dream house—clearly not the sort of scraps one would put in the U.S. Gypsum scrapbook. The worried doctor can't seem to find anything wrong, but when he notices the models on the kitchen table, his brow furrows, and he offers a diagnosis: "It's called 'Post-War Dreamitis'... and it's catching!" The National Gypsum ad distinguished between planning and fantasy, urging practical planning: "[I]f you start now—today—with your planning you'll probably be living in your new house while the man with 'Post-War Dreamitis' will have nothing more tangible than his dreams."[62] The ad retold La Fontaine's fable of the ant and the cricket. The hard-working ant, like the practical postwar planner, used his summer to prepare for winter, while the cricket, like the man stricken with "dreamitis," lounged around daydreaming and enjoying himself, only to find that he had no food when the season turned. The moral is obvious: misguided anticipation could be a dangerous diversion, an indulgent form of leisure that might lead to mental instability, or worse, an unrealistic picture of postwar America. After all, the ultramodern models of architecture and not his physical health revealed this man's dementia, a wrongheaded form of planning.[63]

Figure 4.8. John Deardorf House, U.S. Gypsum Company, *Popular Home's Ideas Galore,* 16.

A writer for the *New Republic* noted the changes in advertising in 1944, connecting them to the larger reaction in Congress and elaborating the points that Talbot Hamlin had made in the *Antioch Review.* The withdrawal from visionary themes in advertising represented more than an innocent withering of enthusiasm; it ushered in an active disdain for the visionary itself. A Nash Kelvinator ad, which the author claimed was the most read ad of the year, featured a "lonesome soldier telling what kind of an America he wants when he returns home."[64] "Don't Change Anything!" implored the ad, a message the author read in political terms. Part of the desire in the waning months of the war for a return to "normalcy," "Don't Change a Thing" was a popular manifestation of Friedrich Hayek's romantic call for a return to a lost golden age. The phrase provided the counterpoint to the anticipatory advertisements. The *New Republic* commented:

> The idea is definitely not related to products. It does not mean unchanged car models, nor is it a plea to give us back the old baseburner and perish the thought of that electronically controlled heat conditioner. 'Don't Change Anything' excludes the wonderful world of tomorrow's mechanical devices. It deals, short and simple as it is, with vital political, social and economic factors. It commits the country to the status quo with what the economists call a base year of about 1928. In the face of this slogan, postwar conversion is to be without the benefit of government guidance.[65]

The success of the ad, the writer claimed, depended on "silencing other positive points of view. The first big success in this all-important direction was the elimination of the

It's called "Post-War Dreamitis" ... and it's catching!

IT'S a disease. And the funny thing about it is that you may have caught it and don't even realize the fact.

The symptoms sound more amusing than alarming. The patient thinks about post-war and the house he plans to build. He sees visions of partitions that appear and disappear as he touches a button. Houses that glitter with glass and plastics. Houses that revolve with the sun, where he lolls in comfort not equalled since the days of ancient Rome.

There are at least two alarming things about "Post-War Dreamitis", if you sincerely want to build a house some day soon:

1. You lose time worrying about impractical ideas, when there is no time to spare.

2. You get confused with dream ideas. And if you don't look out, you'll miss entirely the many new improvements in building and in materials that are ready and waiting.

For example, new "floating type" plaster walls and ceilings that reduce room-to-room noise and cut down on repair expense. Fire-proof gypsum sheathing at no more cost than old-style inflammable sheathing. High efficiency rock-wool insulation that brings year 'round comfort, and pays for itself even in the low-priced home by fuel savings. Washable wall finishes in colors, and noise-reducing materials for rooms where quiet is desired. These are just a few of the products which National Gypsum research has ready for your post-war home ... products that can be specified *now*.

START PLANNING NOW

You should start now if you want to avoid the rush later on. Most authorities predict 1,000,000 new homes a year in the 10 years after the war. So the man who begins planning today has the jump on the market. One of the best ways to begin is by seeing your nearby Gold Bond lumber or building material dealer, or a local contractor or architect. These men know building. They can tell you how to get the house you want and how to finance it up to 70% or 80%.

The main thing to remember is that if you start now—today—with your planning you'll probably be living in your new house while the man with "Post-War-Dreamitis" will have nothing more tangible than his dreams.

M. H. Baker

M. H. Baker, President
National Gypsum Company

TO ARCHITECTS!

Architects know better than anybody that it takes more than dreams to build houses. It takes definite plans and specifications. To avoid visionary dreaming by the public and encourage practical planning, National Gypsum is running this series of ads in National Magazines. Then, when building restrictions are lifted, the whole building industry—architects, manufacturers, dealers and builders—will be able to start right in building comfortable, efficient homes for the people of America. National Gypsum Company, Buffalo, New York.

BUILD BETTER WITH GOLD BOND

Wallboard · Lath · Plaster · Lime · Metal Products · Wallpaint · Insulation · Sound Control

Figure 4.9. Advertisement for National Gypsum Company, *Architectural Forum* 80 (May 1944): 54.

domestic program of the Office of War Information."[66] What seems at first to be a scurrilous claim based on faulty logic ends up driving to the heart of what happened to information during the war. In fact, Congress cut only parts of the OWI, but it continued to serve as an organ of military information, and it sheltered the ballyhoo of admen whose work contributed in a major way to wartime propaganda, and did so gratis. Wartime visions of postwar consumption and corporate ideologies of postwar America filtered through ads, while Alistair MacLeish's high-minded calls to a better postwar world were muzzled.[67]

The author admitted that the public had tired of a "plastic house in front of every two-car garage," "electric-eye door openers," "tear-drop motor cars," and other "pie in the sky" ideas, when it really wanted "radios and furnaces now."[68] Yet he forgave the exuberance of advertising, predicting that "in the three or four years following the war, industry will have those goods on the market."[69] The truly insidious advertising had turned its back on that future, offering up the "Don't Change Anything" motif: "Advertising in wartime has changed its character. No longer devoted to the promotion of products and services which it cannot currently deliver, it has become instead a primary weapon of the sale of social and economic ideas," and once the realities of postwar business set in, it turned to a "retrogressive" vision of America.[70] Part of the seduction of "Don't Change Anything" was precisely its opposition to "194X," its purported purchase on the past, on tradition, on American values, as opposed to a foolhardy romp into the unknown, untried, and, increasingly, un-American world of planning. As fears of Communism intensified late in the war, this last element streaked planning with the stain of something Soviet or foreign, redrawing the old target for a new round of arrows. The most emphatic critique of planning, however, came from *Time* magazine, the leading organ of Henry Luce's media empire, which had done so much to promote planning early in the war in *Fortune* and *Architectural Forum*.

Discrediting the Larger Culture of Planning: *Time* Magazine

The reaction against the Barnumesque techniques of some ad campaigns spread beyond the building industry, and beyond the house, to the entire culture of planning. The stakes were particularly high for publishers of variety magazines, which waged a battle through their own ad campaigns to entice advertisers from the building industry to buy space in their pages. *Saturday Evening Post, McCall's, Newsweek,* and *Time* all used the debate over postwar architecture and building to jockey for position in the postwar advertising market. Magazines paid close attention to news about the building industry, covering it in articles and inflecting their ad campaigns to suit public sentiment.

Time magazine's "Are You Doodling" campaign arose out of this context (see Figure 4.1). The magazine launched its satirical ads in the same months that Congress debated the fate of the NRPB, turning planning on its head in order to discredit the rampant futurism of other ad campaigns. *Time*'s ads made it clear that the visionary plans for postwar America were fantasy, the doodles of dreamers and cranks. Real planning involved "building Post-war Building markets." The repetition of the word *building* was important, a parallel to the NRPB's "plan for planning" that set up a further distinction between doodling or planning and building, the one a dreamy, useless activity, the other physical and "real." *Time*'s version of planning, as the text in the ads made clear, meant preparing for the postwar market. In other words, the magazine co-opted the word *planning* for business, dismissing the architecture of 194X as fantasy.

For the next fifteen months, *Time* ads treated readers to a history lesson of pipedreams from the past, each more ludicrous than the last. One featured a drawing of "A heavenly-haven-for-wandering-week-enders," a kind of dirigible that ferried wealthy pleasure seekers to various decadent destinations, in this case to the beach for a swim (Figure 4.10).[71] The ad casts the visionary mode as a self-indulgent fantasy of out-of-touch elites. In keeping with the whole series, it employed graphic tricks that reinforced the main point. In the background, behind the awkward balloon, which is anchored on the beach, a castle rises out of the sea. Instead of the typical "Are You Doodling" text, the ad inserted a photograph of the word *doodling* written in the sand. This dream, like the word *doodle* and the sandcastle behind it, would be washed away with the next tide. In the same vein, another ad featured Claude Nicolas Ledoux's House of the Agricultural Guards, part of his Revolutionary vision for reshaping French society, in the form of a celestial orb (Figure 4.11).[72] Poking fun at the design, the copy stated: "How the farmer got into this farmhouse after dark without breaking his neck was one of the many problems its designer, M. Le Doux [sic], left unsolved. Bigger problem was how to get this doodle down on a farm—to set this ball rolling off the blueprints into actual construction. M. Le Doux never solved that one either—so his golf-ball chalet for gentlemen farmers never got built."

In June 1944, *Time* sharpened its aim, targeting modern architecture explicitly with a new campaign. "Are you doodling . . ." changed to "Are you double-talking, or straight-thinking about that building boom?" The play on planning disappeared, and in its place the ads posited a more precise villain: the modern architect. By June 1944, "visionary" ads inundated the architectural press with the talking heads of architects and their ideas for postwar America. In any given issue of an architectural magazine, readers could see ads by Revere, Barrett, Celotex, Monsanto, and other companies, all with architect-experts offering postwar visions. Pittsburgh Plate Glass and General Electric had just begun their own campaigns in April 1944. Against this backdrop, with modern architects offered as authorities about planning the postwar world, *Time* ads featured two double-talking architects, flitting in paroxysms of joy about modern architecture and speaking nonsense. In the first of the series (Figure 4.12), a bow-tied architect kicks his heels together, wrings his fingers in uncontainable excitement, looks toward the heavens, and says: "Pre-fabilar houses on zilts? We'll build 10 million of 'em!"[73] In the next ad (Figure 4.13), the architect stands on a stool as if it were a soapbox, clenches his fist, thrusts a finger in the air, and says: "Snyflanked factories with frailbanks will sweep the country!"[74] In the third (Figure 4.14), an architect clasps his hands together above his head in a sign of triumph, and exclaims: "What's a home without a trefoil trellis and a zoot-proof stairway!"[75]

Figure 4.10. "Heavenly-haven-for-wandering-week-enders," *Time* advertisement, *Architectural Forum* 78 (April 1943): 28.

DOODLED IN 1847. How the farmer got into this farmhouse after dark without breaking his neck, was one of the many problems its designer, M. Le Doux, left unsolved. Bigger problem was how to get this doodle down on a farm—to set this ball rolling off the blueprints into actual construction. M. Le Doux never solved that one either—so his golf-ball chalet for gentlemen farmers never got built.

or planning for that building boom?

IN 1918 A LOT OF MEN in the building industry were dreaming beautiful dreams about a postwar industrial building boom. You heard statements like "More than 50% of our prewar plants are obsolete and need replacement"—"Hundreds of new products are clamoring for plants in which they can be made economically."

Well—here we are again. Nowadays many builders are echoing the words of 1918.

And maybe they're right. Maybe there will be a boom after this war. But somebody has to break ground for it—start the ball rolling.

How? One way is to show executives that the building industry can now have plants which will produce so much more efficiently and economically than outmoded ones that business simply can't afford not to build them.

And the most economical and effective way to tell this story to business is through the pages of TIME—the first-choice magazine of business executives, plant owners, and managers—the magazine they turn to for *information to help them think ahead and plan ahead and see the shape of things to come* . . . the magazine the employers of America believe in and vote their favorite over all the others they read*.

What's more, TIME is the magazine in which business and industry prefer to tell their own product stories!

*Among the subscribers to TIME (who altogether employ 33,000,000 people), are executives and engineers, Government officials, mayors, bankers, architects, and 22 other groups of leaders—all of whom recently voted "TIME is America's most important magazine."

TIME

THE GATEWAY

TO THE BUILDING MARKET

well—here we are again. Nowadays

*Among the subscribers to TIME (who

Figure 4.11. Planning or doodling? *Time* advertisement, *American Builder and Building Age* 65 (April 1943): 11.

Pre-fabilar houses on zilts ?
We'll build 10 million of em!

Are you double – talking...

Joe Kaufman

or straight-thinking about that building boom ?

TOP BUILDING MEN who ought to know say a lot of builders are just talking double-talk about that building boom.

"America will need billions of houses after the war," these dreamers babble, "so—whoosh! the houses will be built."

As if *need* alone ever built as much as a pup tent! The Chairman of the National Committee on Housing, Inc., Mrs. Dorothy Rosenman, puts it this way:

"Ballyhoo will bubble out and leave the soldier without a job, real-estate operators without a tenant, the builder without a buyer. We must have a plan that can work and that can obtain public support."

To make sure plans like these don't go up in pipe dreams, they must be sold to the kind of people (1) who can buy homes and the building materials that go into them and (2) who have a strong influence over what other people buy.

These are the people builders think of when they think of the readers of TIME—the million most influential family heads in America*—the people other people copy.

*Among the heads of these households are executives and engineers, government officials, mayors, bankers, architects, and 22 other groups of leaders who recently voted TIME "America's most important magazine."

THE **TIME** GATEWAY TO THE BUILDING MARKET

Figure 4.12. Pre-fabilar houses on zilts, *Time* advertisement, *Architectural Forum* 80 (June 1944): 193.

Are you double-talking or straight-thinking about the building-boom?

INDUSTRIAL building men in the know say: "Most postwar-building-boom talk is just double-talk!"

And, in a recent booklet, the staff of Architectural Forum sighs: "These are the days when anyone who discusses postwar markets has to get up in the stratosphere not to be a piker. The magazines have been full of fascinating ideas on houses, including such models as the disposable or Kleenex house, the all-glass or Gypsy Rose Lee house, the foxhole or World War III house, and the circular or Hamburger Heaven house, to say nothing of the fabulous factories some people have been dreaming about."

Buildings and booms never grow out of dreams. They grow out of an understanding of industrial needs and the formulation of plans that can work.

To make sure your down-to-earth plans show up in steel-and-stone plants, they must be *sold* to people who can help put them across: America's top industrial executives, plant owners and managers.

These are the businessmen that builders think of when they think of the readers of TIME.

For the readers of TIME are the top of the management market. Nearly half the businessmen who read TIME are executives or department heads, proprietors or partners.

And TIME is voted their first-choice magazine by the men who can directly do the most for building—by federal, state, and city planning commission members—by leading realtors in 60 cities—by architects—by members of the Mortgage Bank Association—by industrial research engineers.

What's more, advertising figures show that TIME, The Weekly Newsmagazine, is the medium in which business and industry prefer to tell their *own* product stories.

THE GATEWAY TO THE BUILDING MARKET

Figure 4.13. Snyflanked factories with frailbanks, *Time* advertisement, *Architectural Forum* (July 1944): 168.

Are you double-talking...
or straight-thinking about that building boom?

BUILDING MEN who know the score say: "Builders must stop double-talking and non-thinking about that postwar building boom."

FOR EXAMPLE, they are worried to find so many builders double-talking as if those 4,700,000 houses Americans hope to build after the war (according to The Architectural Forum) are as good as *built!*

But houses are never built just because they are *needed*—just because they are *hoped for.* Building booms seldom spring from *dreams.*

They grow out of plans that can work—out of plans that are sold. To make sure your plans really get across, they must be sold to the kind of people who can afford to start the ball rolling, to the kind of people who have a strong influence over what other people buy. These are the people builders think of when they think of the readers of TIME.

These are the people builders think of when they think of the readers of TIME

With twice the average U. S. income, TIME's million families can afford to own more homes and better homes, and to live in the best neighborhoods of their towns. And what's more, the readers of TIME are America's most influential families.

● Among the heads of these households are executives and engineers, government officials, mayors, bankers, architects, and 22 other groups of leaders who recently voted TIME "America's most important magazine."

THE **GATEWAY TO THE BUILDING MARKET**

Figure 4.14. Trefoil trellis, *Time* advertisement, *American Builder and Building Age* 66 (August 1944): 15.

Each of these ads manipulated the figure of the architect for the sake of parody, sending him up as a mad scientist, or worse, the mad artist-architect that so concerned Royal Barry Wills and Kenneth Reid. These were not Reid's "leaders of undeniable maleness." The architecture is equally insane, a physical manifestation of the nonsense jargon used to describe it. "Pre-fabilar" poked fun at the wartime interest in prefabrication, making it seem bizarre. "Zilts" probably played on stilts, and judging by the way they looked, pilotis. Some of the words were mere nonsense. A "trefoil trellis" seems to have been a light construction for helicopters to land on, a favorite subject of the futurists and an easy one to mock.

The images collected many of the strands of the heroic phase of the Modern Movement into a caricature of associations. In the "Pre-fabilar houses" ad of June 1944, a winding ramp of a stairway that leads from the ground to the raised first floor loosely quotes Le Corbusier's Villa Savoye (see Figure 4.12). Other elements were more generic, for instance, endless glass curtain walls, or curving glass that suggests a more moderne than modern aesthetic. In yet another ad, the delighted architect poetically predicts: "Lo the dawn of the plyfenallated plant with trifoil durgins!" (Figure 4.15).[76] The trifoil durgins recall the wings of an airplane, a fantasy of a building in flight, not unlike how art deco toasters appear to be very fast. Here the ad may be mocking the interest that a number of architects had in applying the lessons of the airplane industry during war to the production of houses after the war.[77] The plyfenallated plant itself recalls Erich Mendelsohn's Einstein Observatory, linking the fantasy of an entirely new architecture based on airplane technology with the discredited expressionist architecture of Germany—and the flights of fancy that came in the wake of the previous war. Taken together, the caricatures create a picture of an alien architecture threatening to invade the country. The xenophobia created a free association between the foreign architecture, "double-talk," and enemy propaganda. As everyone on the home front knew, "Loose Lips Sink Ships," a phrase invented by the War Advertising Council and presumably passed by the OWI. Considering the virulence of anti-German sentiment, such "foreign" architecture and the "double-talk" of their designers could come to stand for an alien force that Americans should resist.

The foil to (and defense against) this foreign architecture was "straight-thinking," the verbal equivalent to Dierks Lumber and Coal Company's "lines of tested worth."[78] Each ad gave an example, usually quoting an official from the Producers' Council, Inc., or a member of the NAHB. "Building booms seldom spring from *dreams*" one ad asserted: "They grow out of plans that can work—out of plans that are *sold*. To make sure your plans really get across, they must be sold to the kind of people who can afford to start the ball rolling, to the kind of people who have a strong influence over what other people buy. These are the people builders think of when they think of readers of TIME."[79] Straight-thinking was really an economic idea, a vote of faith in classical capitalism as opposed to the planned "pipedreams" of wartime advertising and foreign systems, among which might be included mature economy remedies like full employment and New Deal economic planning.

Figure 4.15. Plyfenallated plant, *Time* advertisement, *American Builder and Building Age* 66 (October 1944): 55.

Time's straight-thinking echoed broader sentiments. As if in step with the Normandy invasion, in June 1944 Robert Moses dismissed what he famously called the "long-haired planners" with a chastening call for common sense in the *New York Times Magazine*.[80] Municipal planning had to choose, he argued, "between the subsidized lamas in their remote mountain temples and those who must work in the market place."[81] Moses aimed his tirade directly at *Fortune* magazine, Eliel Saarinen, Erich Mendelsohn, Walter Gropius, and other "Beiunskis," which he defined as a "refugee whose critical faculties outrun his gratitude to the country which has given him a home."[82] Xenophobic, anti-intellectual, and opposed to the visionary anticipation of 194X, his article amounted to a premortem dissection of the culture of planning. It set off a battle over postwar planning, the response to which we have already seen in the writing of Guy Greer. Moses would have found support in unexpected places, at least for his interest in practical matters. In "Planning Is Politics, but Are Planners Politicians?" housing expert Catherine Bauer Wurster lauded the "earnest sincerity" of the British planners and obliquely warned against American exuberance: "I have some sympathy with the caustic sneers of Sir Gwilym Gibbon for the 'Utopian planners.' He does at least understand that it is not only useless but irresponsible to make radical proposals without recognizing their revolutionary political implications."[83] Albert Mayer and Julian Whittlesey, important architect-planners associated with the Regional Planning Association of America who were busy with major projects in the Pacific theater, wrote a two-part article in *Architectural Forum* in November 1943 and January 1944 calling for "horse sense planning."[84] Moses was hardly a lone voice, and the *Time* ads amplified these larger concerns with *Time*'s own caustic humor.

In February 1945, when many of the architectural advertising campaigns had already ended, *Time* again changed its campaign. Each month until the end of the war, its ads featured "Show-Room Homes of the Nation," recently constructed houses that *Architectural Forum* believed were "most likely to influence new trends."[85] As the war wound down, the polemic of its previous campaigns was no longer necessary. Other companies had joined the fray against the more overwrought visions of the future. Most advertising now toed a more moderate line, showing modern architecture as one of many options. *Time* did the same. The company reduced the sharp antimodernism of its previous ads, and a more catholic range of styles took their place. A Gropius and Breuer house at Cohasset Beach, Massachusetts, was the first in the series (Figure 4.16).[86] While the ad credited the architects, the point was to show houses of "the kind of people who can afford to start the ball rolling" after the war. Style was subordinated to class: "Of course *all* TIME-readers don't own homes like Mrs. Hagerty's. But by and large the more than a million readers of TIME *do* own the modern or traditional, sumptuous or simple, *show-room homes of the nation!*" *Time* knew that the building boom would play (and pay) out through the pages of national magazines. All three of its campaigns competed to make *Time* a standard space for building industry ads. Only this last series recognized the strategic advantage of stylistic neutrality. The alternation from modern to traditional followed the logic of the campaign, but it was also prescient. In contrast to the ads of 1942

Figure 4.16. Walter Gropius and Marcel Breuer, house in Cohasset Beach, *Time* advertisement, *American Builder and Building Age* 67 (March 1945): 5.

to 1944, the building boom would not carry with it a stylistic mandate for modernist architecture. Like a lot of other corporations, *Time* circumvented the whole issue by appealing to a lifestyle rather than to an architectural style.

Conclusions

In the summer of 1945, the European war well in hand, an article in the *American Scholar*, the magazine of the Phi Beta Kappa Society, lampooned the absurd overuse of planning on the home front. In "The War-in-Peace Plan," Paul Bushnell wrote: "Men require peace, but they must *also* have their danger and destruction. So if the accustomed perils and calamities which have served this latter purpose are ever removed by science and a planned social order, there can be no escape from the need to provide planned danger and destruction."[87] Bushnell proposed a ludicrous blending of war and peace, complete with a plan for official Public Adversaries (instead of Defenders) appointed to foment discord. The critique goes to the heart of social planning and its penchant for schematizing human nature to fit it into utopian ideals. Bushnell revealed the emperor's new clothes. His parody also insinuates something about the unpredictability of social change in cataclysmic moments. Uncertainty fueled the call for a return to normalcy that lay behind the reaction against planning, even among the scholars and intellectuals who formed the readership for this journal.

The return to normalcy, metaphorically, if not literally, was a return home — of troops, displaced families, and war workers. Put another way, home (and by association, domesticity) provided the most ready conceptual framework for understanding the resumption of peace after the break of war and depression, a reconversion of the home front back to the home. Even if the remembered prewar home sprang from an imagined past, its illusion offered the comforts of undisrupted conventions, a restoration of all that had been eroded by the displacements of war. It is why, perhaps, Norman Rockwell's covers for the *Saturday Evening Post* struck such a chord during the war, and it explains why the miracle house came under attack. The visionary architecture and planning of 194X threatened to resist this return to normalcy: wild visions of change ran counter to the shifting mood in the last months of the war. It is why Stonorov and Kahn put the family and their home at the center of their diagram, precisely to guard against this sort of reaction. The failure of the NRPB, too, speaks to this complicated context of planning on the home front. Set up strictly as a forum for research and coordination in planning, the bureau had no power to enact any of its ideas. Yet when its "actions" threatened to bring planning to fruition, even indirectly, Congress clamped down on it. A virtually powerless agency was seen as a menace to the American Way, a Trojan horse opening the door to an invasion of totalitarian or Communist thought. For opponents of the NRPB in Congress, planning had become a visceral threat. Such is the power of a well-played, or even overworked, metaphor.

It is impossible to assess how these representations of architecture and their designers altered the course of American architecture and culture. As some ads pumped up progressive architecture, the reactionary campaigns (and possibly to a greater degree, the more moderate ones) deflated it, in effect negating its social mission by reducing it to a mere consumer choice, or pulling it into the increasingly fraught culture of planning. At the beginning of the war, the most contemporary of architectural ideas and images had been the ideal complement to the ad. The purported honesty of clean lines posed a visual rebuttal to the dubious claims many ads offered, if not to the essential artifice of advertising itself. The reactionary campaigns turned the unsavoriness of ballyhoo against modernist architecture, singling it out as the symbolic form on which outrageous claims for postwar America hinged. The great promises of the early ad campaigns dissolved as companies altered their tack to secure the best position in the postwar market. Postwar expediency silenced the visionary tone of the home front. These visions warped under the pressures of actual consumption and the political sea change as the United States made the transition from World War II to the Cold War. With the end of the advertising campaigns and the waning of New Deal liberalism, the architects' hopes of leading the multitudes also ended. Planning, of course, did take place in the postwar era. Planners cleared slums, erected projects, and planned cities, but never approaching the extent envisioned during the war—and the architect would never become the master planner that so many architects on the home front imagined at the helm of a vast public bureaucracy, commanding builders, engineers, and real estate men, lawyers, economists, and sociologists.

An ad for Janitrol Gas-Fired Heating Equipment sums up this shift. The image played on the metaphor of the architect as citizen-leader and world planner in order to argue against visionary architecture and planning (Figure 4.17).[88] The illustration shows a sharply dressed architect, blueprint in hand, leading the multitudes away from a curvaceous modern building. The image is rife with mixed metaphors. He is a kind of Pied Piper, the blueprint his pipe, and the entranced public the children he has saved from the "dream world" of the headline, which is to say, the fate of visionary architecture. Alternatively, he is a Moses figure, leading the "chosen people" from their Egyptian captivity, in this case the slavish adherence to foreign European modernism.[89] In fact, the followers traverse an ill-defined "red sea" between the past and the future. The building he leads them away from suggests not just modernism but German expressionism, a xenophobic twist on an already confused narrative. The postwar architect-cum-Moses would be neither a Howard Roark showing the people to the promised land of 194X nor Giedion's idealized planner, tracing the plan with tactile perceptiveness, but rather a businessman leading them back to the sane, tried approaches of the past, back to normalcy.

Ads had made a cliché of the Modern Movement and the visionary planning for 194X. While clichés gain density and power through repetition, the same process can make them a liability. What made planning a powerful cliché—what made it stand in for careful, deliberate debate or reasoning on the home front—also undermined it. When planning took on the characteristics of a slogan, it forfeited some of its complexity, making it susceptible, like all slogans, to quick political attack. The context of the culture of planning, the conditions that made it a cliché on the home front, were vanishing even

You can help lead the public out of a DREAM WORLD!

THE postwar world is going to see some mighty fine advancements in every phase of human living. But it isn't going to be the *dream world* lots of people are seriously expecting. Progress will pick up where it left off . . . and then go on from there. That isn't reactionary. It's plain common sense.

You, as a home designer and builder, can do more than any other single group in convincing the public that home building and household equipment isn't going to be so very different from that which was on the market before the war.

Sure, improvements are continually being made. But no honest manufacturer will be offering new and untried equipment which has not been *thoroughly proven in actual use.*

What will Janitrol have to offer?

Janitrol tomorrow, just as before the war, will offer the finest gas-fired heating equipment available . . . equipment which has been thoroughly laboratory-tested, completely proved in actual field installations . . . equipment that reflects the newest refinements and the most advanced designs . . . results of never ending research and development programs.

So, the public doesn't have to drift into a dream world of pink-hued fantasy to find their "ideal" in heating equipment. Janitrol already has made a dream of warmth and comfort a happy reality for thousands of satisfied home owners.

Even before equipment is again available, you can help lead thousands more out of a dream world into *real heating comfort* and *long lasting liveability* by specifying Janitrol, the most modern heating equipment already proven in actual service. Be sure you have all the facts, write today for complete descriptive literature. Surface Combustion, Toledo 1, Ohio.

Janitrol GAS-FIRED HEATING EQUIPMENT

Figure 4.17. Ad for Janitrol, *Architectural Forum* (November 1945): 45.

before the war ended. Its conceptual and metaphorical frame, moreover, was rehearsed during the Depression and war. The culture of planning was structured, understood, and performed in terms of Depression and war. It even shows up as war manqué, and the international crisis gave it its moral, social, economic, and nationalistic authority. Consequently, the rhetorical basis of planning in an era of abundance was set in a moment of scarcity. The earlier frame did not fit the conditions of the later period. One might object that war created full employment and established the United States as the most powerful world economy, but the Depression and the home front are continuous in being moments of scarcity, the latter being of special interest because it was imposed from above as part of a strategic use of resources—a form of national planning. The new economic realities of the building boom presented a set of conditions that the language of planning could not address and still has not. Planning has often argued from the position, or assumption, of scarcity, and so is tinged with pessimism, which historically plays poorly among Americans. On the level of metaphor, planning called forth associations of austerity and want at precisely that moment when Americans dreamed of abundance and were about to have unprecedented access to it.

Other forces complicated the picture. What of 1946 and beyond, or the realities of European reconstruction under U.S. guidance? By then, the terms that gave planning its meaning, its metaphorical framework, had collapsed, and the very different metaphor of the Cold War began to exert its pull. The rise of the military–industrial complex upset the traditional balance of collective thought and American capitalism. Local planning could scarcely argue with the Pentagon and its corporate contractors, or the highway program and its corporate sponsors such as General Motors, any more than local communities now can successfully argue against the incursion of Wal-Mart and other forms of development. Some communities pull together the collective will and find the language to argue it out among themselves and ultimately in court, but most fail. This is not a matter of mere words: "Metaphors as linguistic expressions are possible precisely because they are metaphors in a person's conceptual system."[90] Planning failed, in part, because its advocates failed to find a metaphorical frame that would make its wartime coherence last beyond the war. Returning veterans and civilians starting new lives after the war opted instead for a monumental lawnmower on a sublime plot of grass, with a subtle icon reminding of the war bonds that underwrote their abundant lives (see Plate 12).

Afterword

Planning, the vivid word used to narrate the world of 194X, today may well seem to be a dead word, or at least dated, representing a failed mission. But I believe this mission rests dormant in American culture, awaiting the right conditions to reassert itself. Planning emerged as a specialized field in the first place in the Progressive Era out of the conditions of nineteenth-century capitalism and urbanism. The Depression focused it and made it a matter of national and federal concern. In turn, war briefly made planning ubiquitous, as paradigmatic as engineering had been earlier in the century. War also Americanized planning. Postwar bounty and the return to laissez-faire stymied its progress, and the failures of urban renewal and the Great Society put it into remission. Blinded by abundance and dispersed by contemporary land-use patterns, Americans have few clear models for collective behavior. Yet the battle between laissez-faire and a planned society, between individualism and collectivism—though it is rarely so starkly drawn—is far from over, and not just in our cities. The environmental crisis threatens the survival of the species, if not all species, if we do not find ways of acting collectively for the greater good: acting, in other words, in precisely those ways that the postwar period rejected by choosing a world of national highways and private cars, overdevelopment, agribusiness, and corporate hegemony—by choosing a less planned world. Clearly, the culture of planning still has things to teach us.

Recent elections and events, moreover, including resistance to election reform and corporate scandals, have made clear how implicated in politics corporations are, how self-interest rather than collective interest guides the national agenda. Simultaneously, the push to privatize Social Security, health care, and public education demonstrates the utter retreat from the ideals of the New Deal and the Great Society. The continued dominance of developers over the built environment, with the resulting sprawl of subdivisions, strip malls, and highway networks, and the persistent morbidity of the neglected parts of our cities (and more recently, suburbs) are the material manifestations of these *choices.* Equally so is the fate of urban renewal in the postwar decades, the closest Americans came to the comprehensive planning born of depression and war. These are the geographical, ecological, and architectural outcomes of a lost battle.

In spite of my resistance to "presentist" history, these events have juxtaposed 194X to a present that has made me feel increasingly alienated from my country. The themes of this book have become more personal over time, bound up in a crisis of personal identity vis-à-vis national identity. This crisis resonates eerily with T. S. Eliot's response to the events leading up to World War II, set down in his "The Idea of a Christian Society."[1] Paraphrasing Eliot, it is not a failure to comprehend the turn of events, none of which are surprising. Nor is my distress strictly about a disagreement with current policy or the behavior of the moment. The feeling is one of humiliation, as Eliot put it, which demands some form of action. What is happening implicates us all and demands we take responsibility: for war, and moreover for the nation's bellicosity; for the state of the environment, and moreover for the nation's disregard for the world's resources; for the stunning gulf between haves and have-nots, and moreover for the carefully constructed system that widens this gulf and calls it freedom or supply-side economics, or worse, celebrates it as individualism and "the American Way." We are tracing a tangent that will soon touch Ayn Rand's objectivism, a philosophy of hyperindividualism articulated in *The Fountainhead* in the same years that gave us Eliot's essay (and World War II), and one painstakingly framed in terms of architecture. Now more than ever we might gain from studying Stonorov and Kahn's planning diagram (see Figure I.1), onto which we might draw a final layer representing global planning.

The current problem is not, as Eliot wrote of England on the cusp of the war, "a criticism of the government, but a doubt of the validity of a civilization."[2] Americans might pose similar generalizations about the United States today. Is our society, which continues to presume its superiority and rightness, "assembled around anything more permanent than a congeries of banks, insurance companies and industries," or updating Eliot, oil companies, war contractors, Wal-Marts, and developers?[3] Has it any beliefs more essential than an unexamined belief in economic success? What, in other words, will Americans pursue as their mythic Fountainhead, the individual inviolable, beloved community, or some compromise between the two? Eliot searched for the "unified religious-social code of behaviour" he believed, with some nostalgia, Christianity once supplied to the West, a code lost to the upheavals of modernity. At the same time that he wrote, the architect-planners of World War II addressed the same dilemma and found in planning a secular means of setting down such a unified code of behavior, one in which, to quote Eliot again, "the natural end of man—virtue and well-being in community—is acknowledged for all."[4]

As a means of stimulating collective identity, planning failed. In its place, Americans have lived under the organizing principles, if not the social codes, of a military–industrial–corporate complex that formed to win World War II, grew fat on the Cold War and globalization, and supplied the postwar middle classes with their abundance. More than ever, Americans and their leaders have lost sight of the bigger picture, of a unified but flexible code of behavior that might give depth to this abundance, or provide succor as it dwindles. This is not to discredit individualism in toto: self-interest, and the competitive instincts unleashed by it, drive people and society forward, but its base is, and always has been, collective interest. Without a sense of the collective, self-interest is tantamount to self-destruction. Just observe any sandbox in a playground. *194X* looks back to a moment when people thought deeply about the relationship between self-interest and community, the same moment that split the two and pushed them on their path to the present.

Appendix: Wartime Advertising Campaigns

This appendix lists many of the advertising campaigns in which architects or industrial designers presented their designs. I endeavored to include every advertisement in each series. Because of the inconsistency of binding practices, the bound volumes of magazines do not always retain the advertising sections; as a consequence, I cited the examples that I was able to find, regardless of the magazine, in an attempt to furnish a full list of citations for future researchers.

Alexander Smith and Sons Carpet Company

Architectural Record 85 (January 1939): 113. Raymond Anthony Court.
Architectural Record 85 (April 1939): 129. Ely Jacques Kahn.
Architectural Record 85 (June 1939): third cover. Harvey Wiley Corbett.
Architectural Record 86 (August 1939): 31. James W. O'Conner.
Architectural Record 86 (October 1939): 133. David Supowitz.
Architectural Record 87 (June 1940): fourth cover. William Lescaze.
Architectural Record 88 (October 1940): 17. Walter Scholar.
Architectural Record 88 (December 1940). Robert von Ezdorf of Cross and Cross.
Architectural Record 89 (March 1941): 33. Hal Pereira.
Architectural Record 89 (April 1941): 37. John Eberson.
Architectural Record 89 (June 1941): 147. Thomas Stapleton.
Architectural Record 90 (July 1941): 2–3. Corbett, Lescaze, Pereira, Ely Jacques Kahn.
Architectural Record 90 (December 1941): 123. John Ullmann Jr.

Barrett Division: Allied Chemical and Dye Corporation

This series ran in *Architectural Forum* and *Pencil Points*.

Pencil Points (May 1943): 89. George Nelson, Department Store in 194X.

Architectural Forum (July 1943): 121. Richard Bennett, Factory in 194X.

Architectural Forum (September 1943): 26. Harwell Hamilton Harris, Multiple Dwelling in 194X.

Architectural Forum (October 1943): 38. J. Stanley Sharp (architect) and Jedd S. Reisner, School in 194X.

Architectural Forum (February 1944): 127. Hugh Stubbins Jr., Hotel in 194X.

Pencil Points (June 1944): 19. Carl Koch, Dwelling in 194X.

Architectural Forum (July 1944): 41. Ely Jacques Kahn and Alan Jacobs, Recreation Center in 194X.

Architectural Record (August 1944): 62. Caleb Hornbostel, Shuttle Airport in 194X.

Architectural Forum (October 1944): 228. Charles Platt, Public Housing in 194X.

Architectural Forum (December 1944): 62. J. Floyd Yewell, Theater in 194X.

Architectural Forum (March 1945): 223. Charles Warner Jr. (Columbia University), Residence Roof in 194X.

Architectural Forum (June 1945): 179. Kahn and Stonorov, Business Neighborhood in 194X.

Architectural Forum (September 1945): 73. Simon Breines (Pomerance and Breines), Hotel in 194X.

Architectural Forum (December 1945): 144. Torquato De Felice, Office Building in 194X.

Celotex

This series ran in *Saturday Evening Post, Collier's, American Home,* and *Pencil Points.*

Saturday Evening Post (February 27, 1943): 81. Antonin Raymond.

American Home 29 (February 1943): 41. Skidmore, Owings and Merrill.

American Home 29 (March 1943): 43. George Fred Keck.

Saturday Evening Post (May 15, 1943): 107. Pierre and Wright.

Saturday Evening Post (July 10, 1943): 89. Arnold Southwell, Modulok, Inc.

Collier's (August 7, 1943): 41. John B. Pierce Foundation House.

Collier's (October 20, 1943): 59. Andrew N. Rebori.

Douglas Fir Plywood

Architectural Forum 68 (March 1938): 25. John Fugard.

Architectural Forum 68 (June 1938): 27. William Wurster.

Architectural Forum 69 (August 1938): 26. Richard Neutra.

Architectural Forum 70 (June 1939): 88. A. Lawrence Kocher.

Architectural Forum 71 (November 1939): 18. George Wellington Stoddard.

General Electric

This series ran in *Architectural Forum, Pencil Points, Architectural Record,* and *Interiors.*

Architectural Forum (April 1944): 28–29. Morris Sanders.
Architectural Forum (May 1944): 20–21. J. Gordon Lippincott.
Architectural Forum (June 1944): 180–81. Egmont Arens.
Architectural Forum (July 1944): 176–77. Nathaniel A. Owings.
Architectural Forum (August 1944): 46–47. Graham, Anderson, Probst and White.
Architectural Forum (September 1944): 20–21. Helmuth Bartsch of Holabird and Root.
Architectural Forum (October 1944): 212–13. G. McStay Jackson.
Architectural Forum (November 1944): 196–97. Walter Wurdeman and Welton Becket.
Architectural Forum (December 1944): 66–67. G. McStay Jackson.
Architectural Forum (January 1945): 24–25. Theodore Criley.
Architectural Forum (March 1945): 228–29. Donald Deskey.
Pencil Points (April 1945): 2–3. Ketchum, Gina and Sharp.
Architectural Forum (May 1945): 22–23. George Cooper Rudolph.
Architectural Forum (July 1945): 196–97. Louis E. McAllister.
Pencil Points (August 1945): 108–9. Silverman and Levy.
Architectural Forum (September 1945). John Gordon Rideout and Ernst Payer.
Pencil Points (October 1945): 24–25. Lawrence Perkins.
Pencil Points (December 1945): 2–3. E. Post Tooker of Tooker and Marsh.
Architectural Record (January 1946): 46–47. J. Gordon Carr, Office.

Monsanto

This series ran in *Architectural Record* and *Architectural Forum* and included both architects and industrial designers.

Architectural Record (May 1943): 13. Philip Will.
Architectural Record (June 1943): 15. Egmont Arens.
Architectural Record (July 1943): 25. Morris Ketchum.
Architectural Record (August 1943): 13. Harris Armstrong.
Architectural Record (September 1943): 13. George Nelson.
Architectural Record (October 1943): 31. Marcel Breuer.
Architectural Record (November 1943): 25. William Lescaze.
Architectural Record (December 1943): 29. Richard Bennett.
Architectural Record (January 1944): 21. George Fred Keck.
Architectural Record (March 1944): 11. Carl Sundberg.

Pittsburgh Plate Glass

This series ran in *Architectural Forum, Pencil Points,* and *Architectural Record.*

Architectural Forum (April 1943): 135. W. H. Cassebeer, Store.

Pencil Points (April 1944): 31. William Lescaze, Florist.

Pencil Points (May 1944): 113. Robert Alan Jacobs and Ely Jacques Kahn, Department Store.

Pencil Points (June 1944): 19. Carl Koch, Dwelling.

Pencil Points (July 1944): 27. Holabird and Root, Hardware Store.

Architectural Forum (August 1944): 41. Pietro Belluschi, Shoes and Leather Shop.

Architectural Forum (October 1944): 62. Silverman and Levy, General Store.

Architectural Forum (November 1944): 162. Krummeck and Gruen, Haberdashery.

Architectural Forum (March 1945): 173. Louis Skidmore, Grocery.

Architectural Forum (April 1945): 148. Samuel Glaser and Ladislav Rado, Women's Apparel.

Architectural Forum (July 1945): 169. Amadeo Leone of Smith, Hinchman and Grylls, Drug Store.

Architectural Forum (September 1945): 48–49. Thalheimer and Weitz.

Architectural Forum (September 1945): 85. José A. Fernandes, Jewelry Store.

Architectural Forum (November 1945): 195. Hervey Parke Clark, Bakery.

Architectural Forum (January 1946): 133. Amadeo Leone, Auto Salesroom.

Progressive Architecture (April 1946): 119. Alfred Shaw.

Progressive Architecture (June 1946): 5. Perkins and Little.

Architectural Forum (August 1946): 2. Robert Alan Jacobs, Service Station.

Architectural Forum (October 1946): 85. Pietro Belluschi, Shoe Store.

Architectural Forum (December 1946): 21. William Lescaze, Theater.

Pittsburgh Plate Glass (Portfolio)

Forty-one designs were created by these architects for Pittsburgh Plate Glass during or immediately after the war. Not all of these designs ran as advertisements, but they were available as a portfolio from Pittsburgh Plate Glass, *There Is a New Trend in Store Design,* 1945.

Smith, Hinchman and Grylls, Automobile Sales Room.

Hervey Parke Clark, Bakery.

Holabird and Root, Bar.

Shaw, Naess and Murphy, Bar.

Pietro Belluschi, Beauty Shop.

Gruen and Krummeck, Candy Store.

Glaser and Rado, Cosmetic Shop.

Robert Allan Jacobs, Department Store.

Rowland H. Crawford, Drug Store.

Walter Gropius, Drug Store.

Smith, Hinchman and Grylls, Drug Store.

William Lescaze, Florist Shop.
Morris Sanders, Florist Shop.
Stonorov and Kahn, Furniture Store.
Skidmore, Owings and Merrill, Furniture Store.
Silverman and Levy, General Store.
Saarinen and Swanson, Gift Shop.
Skidmore, Owings and Merrill, Grocery Store.
Gruen and Krummeck, Haberdashery Store.
Holabird and Root, Hardware Store.
Perkins and Little, Hardware Store.
Shaw, Naess and Murphy, Hardware Store.
Silverman and Levy, Hardware Store.
José A. Fernandez, Jewelry Store.
Walter Gropius, Jewelry Store.
Igor B. Polevitzky, Jewelry Store.
Gardner A. Dailey, Market.
Morris Lapidus, Men's Shop.
Rowland H. Crawford, Restaurant.
Saarinen and Swanson, Restaurant.
Igor B. Polevitzky, Restaurant.
Robert Allan Jacobs, Service Station.
Pietro Belluschi, Shoe Store.
Thalheimer and Weitz, Shoe Store.
Stonorov and Kahn, Shoe Store.
William Lescaze, Theater.
Perkins and Little, Theater.
Thalheimer and Weitz, Theater.
José A. Fernandez, Women's Apparel Shop.
Glaser and Rado, Women's Apparel Shop.
Morris Lapidus, Women's Apparel Shop.

Revere Copper and Brass in *Architectural Forum*

Architectural Forum (October 1941): 42–43. Norman Bel Geddes.
Architectural Forum (November 1941): 48–49. Paul Nelson.
Architectural Forum (December 1941): 36–37. William Hamby.
Architectural Forum (January 1942): 58–59. Walter Dorwin Teague.
Architectural Forum (February 1942): 56–57. R. Buckminster Fuller.
Architectural Forum (March 1942): 20–21. Cass Gilbert Jr.
Architectural Forum (April 1942): 50–51. Walter B. Sanders.
Architectural Forum (May 1942): 42–43. George F. Keck.
Architectural Forum (July 1942): 10–11. A. Lawrence Kocher.

Architectural Forum (October 1942): 106–7. Lawrence B. Perkins.
Architectural Forum (December 1942): 108–9. H. H. Harris.
Architectural Forum (February 1943): 13. Carl F. Boester.
Architectural Forum (March 1943): 26. George Nelson.
Architectural Forum (May 1943): 50–51. Robert Alexander.
Architectural Forum (June 1943): 130–31. William Wurster.
Architectural Forum (July 1943): 29. William Lescaze.
Architectural Forum (August 1943): 122–23. Stonorov and Kahn.
Architectural Forum (September 1943): 14–15. Antonin Raymond.
Architectural Forum (October 1943): 154–55. Simon Breines.
Architectural Forum (December 1943): 14–15. Serge Chermayeff.
Architectural Forum (February 1944): 134–35. Fritz Burns.
Architectural Forum (April 1944): 8–9. Rosenfield and Breines.
Architectural Forum (May 1944): 143. John E. Dinwiddie.
Architectural Forum (July 1944): 56–57. Preview of Postwar America, an ad for its series.
Architectural Forum (September 1944): 56–57. J. Gordon Lippincott.
Architectural Forum (October 1944): 46–47. William Lescaze.
Architectural Forum (November 1944): 44–45. Stonorov and Kahn.

Revere in *Saturday Evening Post*

Saturday Evening Post (January 17, 1942): 69. R. Buckminster Fuller.
Saturday Evening Post (February 21, 1942): 69. Cass Gilbert Jr.
Saturday Evening Post (March 14, 1942): 64. Walter B. Sanders.
Saturday Evening Post (May 9, 1942): 68. George Fred Keck.
Saturday Evening Post (July 11, 1942): 37. A. Lawrence Kocher.
Saturday Evening Post (October 17, 1942): 53. Lawrence B. Perkins.
Saturday Evening Post (December 12, 1942): 45. Harwell Hamilton Harris.
Saturday Evening Post (January 16, 1943): 61. Carl F. Boester.
Saturday Evening Post (February 13, 1943): 58. George Nelson.
Saturday Evening Post (May 1, 1943): 47. Robert Alexander.
Saturday Evening Post (June 19, 1943): 64. William Lescaze.
Saturday Evening Post (July 3, 1943): 57. Stonorov and Kahn.
Saturday Evening Post (August 7, 1943): 66. Antonin Raymond.
Saturday Evening Post (September 25, 1943): 45. Simon Breines.
Saturday Evening Post (November 20, 1943): 76–77. Chermayeff.
Saturday Evening Post (January 22, 1944): 56–57. Fritz Burns.
Saturday Evening Post (March 4, 1944): 64–65. Rosenfield and Breines.
Saturday Evening Post (April 15, 1944): 42–43. John Ekin Dinwiddie.
Saturday Evening Post (August 19, 1944): 54–55. J. Gordon Lippincott.
Saturday Evening Post (September 16, 1944): 66–67. William Lescaze.
Saturday Evening Post (October 14, 1944): 70–71. Stonorov and Kahn.

Norman Bel Geddes, Paul Nelson, William Hamby, and Walter Dorwin Teague did pamphlets for Revere, but I could not find their ads in *Saturday Evening Post*.

Time Magazine

Several different series of *Time* advertisements ran during the war in *Architectural Forum, American Builder and Building Age, Printers' Ink,* and *Electrical Merchandising.* This list was generated by combining advertisements found in the Time, Inc., Archives (identified by advertisement number rather than page number) with those found in the magazines.

Are You Doodling . . . ?

Robida Skyscraper of Papier Aggloméré: *Architectural Forum* (April 1943), *American Builder and Building Age* (April 1943).

George Cruikshank, Hot Air Balloon: *Architectural Forum* (May 6, 1943), *American Builder and Building Age* (May 1, 1943), ad 31.

Robida Elfin Penthouse: *Architectural Forum* (June 8, 1943), *American Builder and Building Age* (June 1, 1943), ad 88.

Shaving System 1745: *Architectural Forum* (July 6, 1943), *American Builder and Building Age* (June 1, 1943), ad 98.

Heavenly Haven: *Architectural Forum* (August 6, 1943), *American Builder and Building Age* (August 1, 1943), ad 106.

Dream City under One Roof: *Architectural Forum* (September 8, 1943), *American Builder and Building Age* (September 1, 1943), ad 119.

Agricola Air Conditioning Engine: *Architectural Forum* (October 8, 1943), *American Builder and Building Age* (October 1, 1943), ad 124.

Rube Goldberg in 1661: *Architectural Forum* (November 8, 1943), *American Builder and Building Age* (November 1, 1943), ad 146.

Robida-Air Bike Garages: *Architectural Forum* (January 8, 1944), *American Builder and Building Age* (January 1, 1944).

Ledoux: *Architectural Forum* (February 8, 1944), *American Builder and Building Age* (February 1944).

Athanasius Kircher Eavesdropping Machine: *American Builder and Building Age* (March 8, 1944), *American Builder and Building Age* (March 1, 1944).

Superterranean Roads: *Architectural Forum* (April 8, 1944), *American Builder and Building Age* (April 1, 1944).

Puck in 1886—glass box: *Architectural Forum* (May 8, 1944), *American Builder and Building Age* (May 1, 1944), *Printers' Ink* (April 21, 1944), ad 252.

Double-Talking

Zilts: *Architectural Forum* and *American Builder and Building Age* (June 1944), *Printers' Ink* (June 16, 1944).

Snyflanked: *Architectural Forum* and *American Builder and Building Age* (July 1944), *Printers' Ink* (June 23, 1944).

Trefoil Trellis: *Architectural Forum* and *American Builder and Building Age* (September 1944), *Printers' Ink* (September 9, 1944).

Plyfenallated Plant: *Architectural Forum* and *American Builder and Building Age* (October 1944), *Printers' Ink* (October 6, 1944).

Portisans with Double Flories: *Architectural Forum* and *American Builder and Building Age* (November 1944), *Printers' Ink* (November 3, 1944).

The Show-Room Homes of the Nation

This ran in *Electrical Merchandising* as "The Show-Place for Home Appliances."

Gropius/Breuer, Cohasset: *American Builder and Building Age* (March 1945), *Printers' Ink* (February 9, 1945).

Burke's Home: *Building Homes* (March 30, 1945), "Leading National Advertisers" (March 1945).

Otter House: *Pencil Points* (May 1945), *American Builder and Building Age* (May 1945), *Printers' Ink* (May 6, 1945).

Riefler, Princeton: *Pencil Points* (June 1945), *American Builder and Building Age* (June 1945), *Printers' Ink* (June 1, 1945).

Elgin Robertson: *Building Homes* (July 15, 1945).

Voorhees and Everhard: *Architectural Forum* (August 1945), *American Builder and Building Age* (August 1945).

Otter House, Chestnut Hill: *Electrical Merchandising* (August 1945).

Riefler Home: *Electrical Merchandising* (September 1945).

Burke's Home: *Electrical Merchandising* (November 1945).

Herbert de Staebler's Home: *Architectural Forum* and *Building Homes* (November 1945) and (October 1945).

Winston-Salem House: *Electrical Merchandising* (December 1945).

Show-Room Plants of the Nation

Sperry Gyroscope Company, Great Neck: *Architectural Forum* (March 1945), *American Builder and Building Age* (March 1945), *Advertising Age* (September 10, 1945).

Johnson and Johnson, New Brunswick: *Architectural Forum* (November 1945), *Building Industrial* (November 1945).

United States Gypsum

This series ran in *Architectural Forum* only, although United States Gypsum also advertised in *Life, Better Homes and Gardens, American Home,* and *Good Housekeeping.*

Architectural Forum (March 1941): 37–40. Richard Boring Snow, Solution to a Defense Housing Project.

Architectural Forum (May 1941): 60–63. Cameron Clark, Small Home Community Project.

Architectural Forum (July 1941): 84–87. Gardner Dailey, Study for a California Supermarket.

Architectural Forum (August 1941): 35–38. E. D. Stone, Study for an Avenue of the Americas.

Architectural Forum (October 1941): 54–57. George Keck, Trans-Duo House.

Architectural Forum (January 1942): 38–40. Perkins, Wheeler and Will, School.

Architectural Forum (March 1942): 50–53. Eero Saarinen, Demountable Space.

Architectural Forum (May 1942): 58–61. Don Hatch, A Study for Durationsville.

Notes

Preface

1. For my contribution to this debate, see Shanken, "Planning Memory: Living Memorials in the United States during World War II," 130–47.

Introduction

1. Louis I. Kahn Archives, Box 68, Folder: G.H. Appointment, University of Pennsylvania. See Shanken, "The Uncharted Kahn: The Visuality of Planning and Promotion in the 1930s and 1940s," 310–27. The architects probably created the unpublished diagram as part of a pamphlet they made for Revere Copper and Brass, which is discussed in more detail in chapter 3. While the image in Figure I.1 comes from Kahn's papers, a manuscript with the diagram was deposited in the Oscar Stonorov Papers (hereafter cited as Stonorov Papers), American Heritage Center, Box 6, Folder: Faith for Living.

2. Alexander, *Preview of a New Way of Life.*

3. William Lescaze, untitled lecture at the AIA Annual Meeting in Detroit (June 22, 1942): 3. William Lescaze Papers (hereafter cited as Lescaze Papers), Syracuse University Archives, Box 65, Folder: Writings: William Lescaze Lectures 1940–43.

4. Burnett, "Getting Down to Business," 606.

5. Shreve, "The Outlook of the Profession," 3–4. For a mid-Depression assessment of the work of these agencies and their effect on architects, see "Architecture and Government."

6. When Henry Morganthau Jr. took over the Treasury from Harold L. Ickes in 1934, he instituted a new policy that worked against the hiring of private architects for public work. See Lee, *Architects to the Nation: The Rise and Decline of the Supervising Architect's Office,* 253–57.

7. Hamlin, "Can We Plan Action in Crisis, or Are We Doomed to Muddle Through?" 748.

8. Raskin, "Out on a Limb: Horoscope for Architects after the War," 759.

9. Brownlee and De Long, *Louis I. Kahn: In the Realm of Architecture,* 25.

10. Bannister and Bellamy, *The Architect at Mid-Century: Evolution and Achievement,* 78.

11. Ibid., 78–79.

12. Maginnis, "Musings on the Morrow," 10.

13. Brooks, "These Dolorous Architects," 182.

14. Ibid.

15. Myers, "Was the Architect of Tomorrow Here Yesterday?" 14.

16. Statement by D. K. Este Fisher Jr. in the Session "The Architectural Profession and War Service" at the Cincinnati meeting of the AIA, May 26, 1943, 3. Archives of the American Institute of Architects (hereafter cited as AIA Archives), Box 131035983, Folder 4–4.2b: Special Representative in Washington.

17. Ibid., 4. Ironically, before hiring him for the job, Shreve expressed these exact concerns about Fisher himself. Shreve wrote confidentially to G. Corner Fenhagen: "The one point with respect to Fisher which has been made and on which you and Jim Edmunds might give me comment is that he 'dresses too well.'" The worry was that "Fisher is not a 'mixer' or a 'slap-you-on-the-back' man. Those who know him recognize his abilities and his qualities as a first-rate representative to the Institute. The thing they question is his ability to sit down with the representative of the steel industry or the plumbing fixtures, or the cement manufacturers and talk with them on a basis of trading drinks or meals or figures in a way to win their collaboration and their 'tip-offs.'" Architects clearly had not worked through their own self-doubt. Shreve to Fenhagen (August 7, 1942), AIA Archives, Box 131035983, Folder 4–4.2 (b), Special Representative in Washington (D. K. Este Fisher Jr.) (Part III).

18. Fisher, *Bulletin of the AIA.*

19. Reid, "New Beginnings," 242.

20. Wills, Cartoon of "Architectural Man."

21. Rand, *The Fountainhead.*

22. For a rich discussion of these ideas, see Haskell, ed., *The Authority of Experts: Studies in History and Theory.* Also, the following ideas were first addressed in Shanken, "Between Brotherhood and Bureaucracy: Joseph Hudnut, Louis I. Kahn and the American Society of Planners and Architects," 147–75.

23. The outline of this argument depends on Bender, "The Erosion of Public Culture: Cities, Discourses, and Professional Disciplines," 86.

24. Cohen, "Building a Discipline: Early Institutional Settings for Architectural Education in Philadelphia, 1804–1890," 139–83. Also, see Woods, *From Craft to Profession: The Practice of Architecture in Nineteenth-Century America.*

25. Bender, "The Erosion of Public Culture," 89.

26. Ibid.

27. Shanken, "From the Gospel of Efficiency to Modernism: A History of Sweet's Catalog, 1906–1947."

28. Bannister and Bellamy, *The Architect at Mid-Century,* 73; and U.S. Bureau of the Census, Sixteenth Census of the United States.

29. See Peterson, *The Birth of City Planning in the United States, 1840–1917, Creating the North American Landscape.*

30. See Krueckeberg, ed., *The American Planner: Biographies and Recollections,* 15, 29–30. According to Krueckeberg, some six firms produced 70 percent of the comprehensive urban plans until 1926.

31. Ibid., 29.

32. Ibid.

33. From *A.I.A. Bulletin: Official Notices to Members* 2 (April 1944): cover.

34. Anne Tyng, who worked in Louis Kahn's office after the war, confirmed this view, asserting that many architects in this period saw architecture and planning as part of one indivisible pursuit. Author's interview with Tyng, January 21, 2005.

35. "What's in a Name," 32.

36. Ibid.

37. Reid, "Plan," facing 18.

38. Edmund R. Purves to R. H. Shreve (February 25, 1942), AIA Archives, Box 131035983, Folder 4–4.2b: Special Representative in Washington.

39. See the introduction to Hartman and Cigliano, eds., *Pencil Points Reader: A Journal for the Drafting Room, 1920–1943.*

40. Guilbaut, *How New York Stole the Idea of Modern Art: Abstract Expressionism, Freedom, and the Cold War.*

41. Shanken, "Between Brotherhood and Bureaucracy."

42. See Samuel E. Lunden to James T. Grady (August 12, 1943), AIA Archives, Box 131040288, Folder 4–4.32 Post-War Reconstruction Committee and General 1943 part II.

43. Sitte, *The Art of Building Cities: City Building According to Its Artistic Fundamentals,* with an introduction by Ralph Walker and a note by Eliel Saarinen.

44. Lesser known is Justement's *New Cities for Old: City Building in Terms of Space, Time and Money,* a Keynesian account of planning efforts in Washington, D.C., by the architect who ran the AIA's local committee on urban reconstruction; Creighton's *Planning to Build;* and Leipziger-Pearce's *The Architectonic City in the Americas: Significant Forms, Origins and Prospects.* Neutra's *Survival through Design* was also written in part during the war, which lent it the title, as did the war's continuation in the form of the Cold War. Neutra wrote some of it while he taught at Bennington College. See Hines, *Richard Neutra and the Search for Modern Architecture: A Biography and History,* 193–94, 220.

45. To be sure, the 1930s gave rise to books on social and economic planning, but in far smaller numbers and with a narrower focus than the gestalt planning under consideration here. See, for example, Beard, *America Faces the Future,* especially Beard's "A 'Five-Year Plan' for America," 117–40; and Soule, *A Planned Society.*

46. Similar cultural shifts occurred among historians. David Noble has written about a paradigm shift during the same period in how historians "organized their narratives." They moved from the perspective of Frederick Turner and Charles Beard, seeing history as a conflict between the people and the interests, a progressive narrative of good versus evil, democracy versus monopoly, and the ideal Republic versus laissez-faire, to a notion of "progress guided by experts" and the development of a consensus history. Beard explicitly called on planning as a counter to laissez-faire in *The Future Comes* (1933) and *Toward Civilization* (1930). See Noble, "The Reconstruction of Progress: Charles Beard, Richard Hofstadter, and Postwar Historical Thought," 61.

47. Scholars have now filled in many of the gaps of the culture of the home front, from histories of race, class, and gender to advertising and consumption, film, photography, and art. Some of the key sources include Polenberg, *America at War: The Home Front, 1941–1945* and *War and Society: The United States, 1941–1945;* Fox, *Madison Avenue Goes to War: The Strange Military Career of American Advertising, 1941–45;* Blum, *V Was for Victory: Politics and American Culture during World War II;* Hartmann, *Home Front and Beyond: American Women in the 1940s;* Honey, *Creating Rosie the Riveter: Class, Gender, and Propaganda during World War II;* Winkler, *Home Front U.S.A.: America during World War II;* Koppes and Black, *Hollywood Goes to War: How Politics, Profits, and Propaganda Shaped World War II Movies;* and Cohen, *A Consumer's Republic: The Politics of Mass Consumption in Postwar America.*

48. Kennedy, *Freedom from Fear: The American People in Depression and War, 1929–1945.* The exceptions are Brinkley, *The End of Reform: New Deal Liberalism in Recession and War;* Rosenof, *Economics in the Long Run: New Deal Theorists and Their Legacies;* and Reagan, *Designing a New America: The Origins of New Deal Planning, 1890–1943.* None of these authors is an architectural or planning historian.

49. Fussell, *Wartime: Understanding and Behavior in the Second World War.*

1. The Culture of Planning

1. Polanyi, *The Great Transformation,* 3; Huizinga, *Homo Ludens: A Study of the Play Element in Culture,* especially chapters 5, on play and war, and 12, where he advances his darkest assertions; Giedion, *Space, Time and Architecture: The Growth of a New Tradition;* Eliot, *The Idea of a Christian Society.*

2. Lakoff and Johnson, *Metaphors We Live By,* 3–6.

3. See Graham, *Toward a Planned Society: From Roosevelt to Nixon.* The FHA guaranteed loans for prospective homebuyers and promoted both new house construction and modernization projects. See Shanken, "Architectural Competitions and Bureaucracy, 1934–1945." The Resettlement Administration

built mostly agricultural communities for immigrant workers. The Bureau of Reclamation built the Grand Coulee Dam and Boulder Dam, partly with PWA money. The TVA, a range of improvement projects in the South, was an important testing ground for regional planning. The CCC constructed camps, barns, bathhouses, lookout towers, museums, and dwellings, some of which were designed by private architects.

4. The best account of the NRPB is Reagan's *Designing a New America*. Reagan treats the contributions of individual members of the NRPB, including Charles E. Merriam, Wesley Clair Mitchell, and Frederic A. Delano. For the ideological battles over planning, see pp. 196–223. See also Clawson, *New Deal Planning: The National Resources Planning Board*. For a specific study of the urban focus of the NRPB, see Funigiello, *The Challenge to Urban Liberalism: Federal–City Relations during World War II*, especially 163–86. Also see Graham's terse synopsis of the NRPB in *Toward a Planned Society*.

5. In their attention to the political and urban history, respectively, both Patrick D. Reagan and Philip J. Funigiello underestimate the importance of the NRPB for urban planning.

6. The number of planners listed in the proceedings of the 1942 National Conference on Planning of the American Society of Planning Officials who also played a role at the NRPB or its predecessors shows to what extent the bureau created a nexus for urban planners. They include Frederic A. Delano, Walter H. Blucher, Charles E. Merriam, Hugh R. Pomeroy, Ralph J. Watkins, Glenn E. McLaughlin, Guy Greer, Robert B. Mitchell, Louis Wirth, Philip H. Elwood, Ben H. Kizer, Baldwin M. Woods, Charles S. Ascher, John M. Picton, and V. B. Stanbery.

7. Reagan, *Designing a New America*, 2.

8. National Planning Board, *Final Report, 1933–34*, 15. I have not found circulation figures on this pamphlet, and a reception is equally difficult to reconstruct, but given that the organization saw itself primarily as a disseminator of information and agent of agitation, it seems likely that the report was widely distributed.

9. Ibid., 30.

10. M. Christine Boyer traces the emergence of planning as an important cultural idea in *Dreaming the Rational City: The Myth of American City Planning*.

11. National Planning Board, *Final Report, 1933–34*, 30.

12. Ibid.

13. Ibid.

14. Ibid., 31.

15. Ibid.

16. It is in this regard that Alan Brinkley wrote of planning in this period being something akin to a religion. See *The End of Reform*, 47.

17. National Planning Board, *Final Report, 1933–34*, 31.

18. Ibid., 18.

19. Ibid., 66.

20. Ibid., 67.

21. Ibid., 22.

22. Ibid.

23. Reagan, *Designing a New America*, 191. Roosevelt's idea for making the NRPB part of the executive branch may have come from a much earlier suggestion by Clarence S. Stein, who had proposed a broad planning agency to Governor Roosevelt in 1931 that would function under the New York executive branch. Stein outlined a set of ideas for such an organization with close parallels to those that the NRPB later took up. See "Memorandum to Governor Franklin D. Roosevelt Suggesting a Regional Planning Board in the Executive Department," in Stein, *The Writings of Clarence S. Stein: Architect of the Planned Community*.

24. Reagan has shown how this new status proved to be a mixed blessing, in the end forcing Roosevelt to expend more political capital than he wanted on the bureau and ultimately contributing to its demise. See *Designing a New America*, 224–46.

25. Funigiello has pointed out that the planning statutes of several states in the 1940s and Title I of the Housing Act of 1949 have their origins in the wartime work of the NRPB's Urban Section. See *The Challenge to Urban Liberalism*, 180.

26. Ibid., 163–86. The work of the Urban Section needs to be updated in light of more recent work in urban planning and the history of architecture.

27. Ibid., 165.

28. Bacon is well known for his book *The Design of Cities*, which has been a standard text in the field for several decades.

29. The Corpus Christi plan received some attention in architectural circles: see "Organization of the City: From Corpus Christi Newspapers."

30. Funigiello, *The Challenge to Urban Liberalism*, 173–76. For Tacoma, see Shaffer, "Tacoma Looks Forward." *Pencil Points* also reported on their general effort in "Genesis of the NRPB Demonstrations." See also *City Plan*.

31. *Action for Cities: A Guide for Community Planning*. Curiously, the guide was not published by the NRPB through the U.S. Government Printing Office, as most of its documents were published, but under the auspices of the American Municipal Association, the American Society of Planning Officials, and the International City Managers' Association. One wonders if the NRPB, already under intense pressure from Congress, found sponsors in order to assure that *Action for Cities* was not thwarted if the bureau were to be cut.

32. Ibid., 1.

33. Ibid., 4.

34. Moses, "Mr. Moses Dissects the 'Long-Haired Planners,'" 16.

35. *Action for Cities*, 33.

36. See "Organization of the City" for descriptions of the three demonstrations, and accompanying visual material.

37. *Action for Cities*, 57.

38. Ibid., 57.

39. Hudnut, "The Political Art of Planning," 185.

40. U.S. Housing Authority, *What the Housing Act Can Do for Your City*, 8.

41. Pai, *The Portfolio and the Diagram: Architecture, Discourse, and Modernity in America*.

42. Shanken, "The Uncharted Kahn," 310–27.

43. Ibid.

44. Modley, "Pictographs Today and Tomorrow," 659–64. See also Cartwright, *Otto Neurath: Philosophy between Science and Politics*. Neurath was president of the Central Planning Office in Munich in 1919 and founded the Museum of Housing and Town Planning in Vienna in 1923.

45. U.S. Housing Authority, *What the Housing Act Can Do for Your City*, 7.

46. The influence of this system in the United States has not been fully explored, even though isotypes have become ubiquitous since the 1930s, painted on restroom doors and used in traffic signage.

47. Neurath, "Visual Representation of Architectural Problems."

48. *Pencil Points* cover 26 (March 1945). Stamo Papadaki Papers. Manuscripts Division. Department of Rare Books and Special Collections. Princeton University.

49. See Carter and Goldfinger, *The County of London Plan*, and Davison, *Social Security: The Story of British Social Progress and the Beveridge Plan*, 26–27, 32–33. For an account of the importance of the Beveridge Report on American planning, see Rodgers, *Atlantic Crossings: Social Politics in the Progressive Age*, 488–501.

50. Walker and Colley, *Sketch Plan for the Development of Metropolitan Corpus Christi*.

51. "The right angle is lawful, it is a part of our determinism, it is obligatory." Le Corbusier, *The City of To-Morrow and Its Planning*, 21.

52. Beveridge, *Social Insurance and Allied Services*.

53. Giedion, *Space, Time and Architecture*, 542.

54. Quoted in Schapiro, "Nature of Abstract Art," 93. Originally in *Cahiers d'Art VI* (1931), 353. Kandinsky wrote: *"Qu'il nous suffice ici de dire qu'elle est liée à cette faculté en apparence nouvelle la peau de la Nature son essence, son 'contenu'."*

55. Giedion, *Space, Time and Architecture*, 357.

56. Portions of the next three paragraphs first appeared in Shanken, "Uncharted Kahn."

57. The phrasing of abstraction as the *"cri de guerre"* of modernism is from Irving Lavin of the Institute for Advanced Study, 2004.

58. Schapiro, "Nature of Abstract Art," 77.

59. Ibid.

60. Ibid., 78.

61. Le Corbusier, *The City of To-Morrow and Its Planning*.

62. For an early expression of this attitude, see Stein, "Dinosaur Cities."

63. Greer began as a mining expert, wrote a dissertation on industry in the Ruhr Valley after World War I, in which he fought, played a minor role in the peace negotiations at Paris and Versailles, and was an international official of the Reparation Commission. He was at the Brookings Institution in the mid-1920s and spent the late 1920s in Europe as a representative of a U.S. banking house. He later worked for the Federal Housing Administration, where he worked with Miles Colean. See *Harper's Magazine* 181 (November 1940), back pages; and Greer, *The Ruhr-Lorraine Industrial Problem: A Study of the Economic Interdependence of Two Regions and Their Relationship to the Reparation Question*.

64. This pamphlet had multiple iterations and was published several times by different publishers. Greer and Hansen, *Urban Redevelopment and Housing. Planning Pamphlets No. 10.*

65. See Reagan's discussion of Hansen's economic theories and their role in NRPB reports. *Designing a New America*, 221–22.

66. The Thomas and Wagner bills, both proposed in various forms in the early to mid-1940s, promised to provide the first advanced legislation in "housing and urban redevelopment," a name that elided the already maligned word *planning*. These bills created a vehicle for federal aid to local planning efforts, easing land acquisition laws and setting up a structure for cooperation in planning at different levels of government. Hansen had played a central role in drafting the bills with Alfred Bettman, a major planner based in Cincinnati. Hansen and Bettman's drafts for the Urban Redevelopment Bill can be found in the Alvin Harvey Hansen Papers, Box 2 E-L, Folder Four Proposed Plans for Financing Urban Redevelopment. Also Box 1, A-D, Folder A Bill-1945. The main congressional discussion of the Hansen-Bettman work came in connection with S 953 in the 78th Congress, 1st session, and the 78th Congress, 2nd session, Report no. 539, part 4: Post-War Economic Policy and Planning, Report of the Special Committee on Post-War Economic Policy and Planning June 12 (legislative day, May 9, 1944).

67. An incomplete list of his publications on postwar planning include Greer and Hansen, "The Federal Debt and the Future"; Greer, "The Future of Urban Real Estate"; "A Plan for Post-War Urban Rebuilding" (July 11, 1942, and July 18, 1942); "City Replanning and Rebuilding"; "Getting Ready for Federal Aid in Urban Redevelopment: The Hansen-Greer Plan"; "Must Our Cities Continue to Decay?"; and even after the war: "Layman to Architect—A Sermon."

68. Augspurger, *An Economy of Abundant Beauty: Fortune Magazine and Depression America*, 196–99.

69. Galbraith, "Transition to Peace: Business in A.D. 194Q."

70. Hansen and Greer, "Toward Full Use of Our Resources."

71. Baughman, *Henry R. Luce and the Rise of the American News Media*. Baughman accounts for none of Luce's wartime activities in any detail and neglects to link the larger idea of the American Century to comparable efforts in American industry. For this context, see Bird, *"Better Living": Advertising, Media and the New Vocabulary of Business Leadership, 1935–1955*.

72. For the larger context of Luce's interest in planning, see Augspurger, *An Economy of Abundant Beauty*, especially 191–223.

73. See "Planning with You," "New Building for 194X," and "Syracuse Tackles Its Future." See also Memo, Roy E. Larsen to The Staff (May 15, 1944), under "Arch Forum-Org," Time Archives; and Howard Myers, et al., to *Architectural Forum* Staff (May 15, 1944), under "Arch Forum-Org," Time Archives.

74. Russell Van Nest Black and Mary Hedges Black had just published *Planning for the Small American City: An Outline of Principles and Procedure Especially Applicable to the City of Fifty Thousand or Less*, and Pomeroy was the president of the American Institute of Planners.

75. See Isaacs, "How Mr. Grimm's Fairy Tale Came True" (December 8, 1949), manuscript in the Loeb Library, Harvard University. Isaacs makes clear that the NRPB was directly involved.

76. "Syracuse Tackles Its Future," 121.

77. The article compared the Syracuse plan to the "vast Dutch program," which segregated residential blocks in open green spaces away from traffic. The author also drew attention to an earlier Dutch model of 1901 in which Holland conducted studies and drew up plans for every town with a population of 10,000 or greater. This, however, required the "strong controlling authority" of "the democratic town unit itself." Ibid., 158.

78. "New Buildings for 194X," 71.

79. Ibid., 70.

80. Greer wrote about the Syracuse plan elsewhere, too. See "Applied Plans as Seen in Syracuse."

81. Greer revised the articles into a book after the war, including two unsigned articles from May and November 1943. See Greer, *Your City Tomorrow*. The final chapter, "A Program for Action," borrows explicitly from the language of the NRPB's "Action for Cities."

82. Greer, ed., *The Problem of the Cities and Towns: Report of the Conference on Urbanism, Harvard, March 5–6, 1942*.

83. Greer, "City Planning: Battle of the Approach," 164. The attack predated Moses's famous criticism of "long-haired planners" in "Mr. Moses Dissects the 'Long-Haired Planners,'" 16–17, 38–39.

84. Greer, "City Planning," 165.

85. Ibid.

86. Ibid.

87. Ibid., 168, 183, 224.

88. Ibid., 183.

89. From Greer, "So You're Going to Plan a City," 122.

90. Saarinen's ideas are set forth in his book *The City: Its Growth, Its Decay, Its Future*.

91. J. Davidson Stephen Papers, Archives of American Art, Smithsonian Institution (hereafter cited as Stephen Papers).

92. See his résumé, Stephen Papers.

93. Greer, "So You're Going to Plan a City," 123.

94. Stephen claimed that his studies of downtown Detroit had inspired Vardo. See Stephen's résumé, Stephen Papers.

95. Greer, "After the Plans, What?" The original image appeared in Forshaw and Abercombie, *County of London Plan. Fortune* published a slightly different version. Neither remains in the LCC Archives or in the Time Archives.

96. For the MARS Group, see Gold, *The Experience of Modernism: Modern Architects and the Future City, 1928–1953*.

97. The comparison may have come from Hermann Herrey, an Austrian architect who trained under Josef Hoffmann in Vienna (where the painting is) and whom Gropius helped bring to the United States. Herrey had published the same comparison in Herrey, Herrey, and Pertzoff, "An Organic Theory of City Planning."

98. Gropius, *Rebuilding Our Communities.*

99. The comparison impressed Sigfried Giedion enough that he repeated it years later. *A Decade of New Architecture.*

100. Greer, "New Start for the Cities," 195. See, for instance, the so-called Beveridge Report of November 1942. Beveridge, *Social Insurance and Allied Services.*

101. As Christina Cogdell's work on Norman Bel Geddes demonstrates, eugenics strongly influenced industrial design, giving a theoretical underpinning to the idea of streamlining. Cogdell, "The Futurama Recontextualized: Norman Bel Geddes's Eugenic 'World of Tomorrow.'"

102. McGovern, "Sold American: Inventing the Consumer, 1890–1940."

103. A national referendum on the name took place in April 1941. See National Referendum on the Name, Planned Parenthood Federation of America (PPFA), Box 25, Folder 16, Sophia Smith Collection, Smith College.

104. Planned Parenthood Federation of America, *Planned Parenthood: Its Contribution to Family, Community, and Nation.*

105. The leveling off of population was a key element of Hansen's theory of secular stagnation, which is detailed in chapter 2. Critic Lewis Mumford corresponded with Hansen when the latter worked at the Federal Reserve and adopted even more stringent ideas on planning based on the decline in the birth rate. See his analysis of the London County Council plan in *City Development: Studies in Disintegration and Renewal.* Mumford may have built his case on the much earlier work of Clough Williams-Ellis, whose *England and the Octopus* had forcefully addressed the issue of birth control as a function of planning. See Mumford, *City Development,* 42.

106. Israeli, "The Psychology of Planning" and "Originality in Planning"; Merrifield, "Morale and the Planning Society"; Chapin, "The Relation of Sociometry to Planning in an Expanding Social Universe"; and Caprio, "Postwar Planning in Mental Hygiene." See Doob, *The Plans of Men,* an early study of the relationship between the social sciences and planning, especially regional planning.

107. Seward, "Sex Roles in Postwar Planning," 177.

108. Ibid., 181.

109. Rosenfield, "Planning for Shock Treatment."

110. See Erikson, *A Way of Looking at Things,* 366–74.

111. "Report of a Conference on Germany after the War." The group included a range of eminent social scientists, including physicians; educators; philosophers; psychoanalysts and psychologists such as Erich Fromm and Kurt Lewin; sociologists such as Geoffrey Gorer and Talcott Parsons, who had just won a competition for the planning of Boston (The Boston Contest); and Lewis Lorwin, formerly of the NRPB, who was also a founder of the National Planning Association and adviser to the first U.S. Delegation to the United Nations.

112. Erikson, *A Way of Looking at Things,* 368.

113. Ibid.

114. This phrase comes from my colleague, Arthur Denner, from a conversation on January 25, 1997.

115. For another example, see Eliasberg, "Facing Post-War Germany," in which the writer argues for the internment of all Germans as workers in nations against which they fought both as a form of reparation and as a method of psychological retraining. Eliasberg placed such psychological reconditioning at the center of postwar planning in Europe. Unreconstructed Nazis, by contrast, would be quarantined in a virtually empty Germany.

116. Mumford, *The Social Foundations of Post-War Building,* 154–97.

117. Ibid., 181.

118. The collaborative nature of the New Deal anticipated the vogue of interdisciplinary studies in the 1960s and after, but it also provides a great analogue for the swelling interest at the same time among modern architects in collaboration and interaction with the sciences and social sciences.

119. Wolman, "Sociometric Planning of a New Community." Wolman calls the town "Centerville," but the project was probably Greenhills near Cincinnati, designed by Roland A. Wank. See Moreno and Jennings, *Who Shall Survive? A New Approach to the Problem of Human Interrelations*, 335–60.

120. Fox, *Madison Avenue Goes to War*. More might be done comparing the respective situations of admen and architects in making the transition from depression to war. Both suffered from the economic depression of the 1930s and from New Deal policies, and both tried to use the war to improve their situations.

121. Advertisement for Brasco Modern Store Fronts, *Architectural Forum* 76 (March 1942): 49.

122. Lawrence B. Perkins, advertisement for Revere Copper and Brass, *Architectural Forum* 77 (October 1942): 106–7.

123. Advertisement for Swans Down Cake Flour, *Ladies' Home Journal* (March 1943): 78.

124. The absurdity of the ad was noticed and written about by Neider in "Advertise for Victory," 772.

125. Boester, *Home . . . for a Nation on Wings*, 4. Michael C. C. Adams gives another good example: "An elderly gentleman on a bus in Viola, Kentucky, home of a munitions plant, hit a female passenger with his umbrella when she said she hoped the war wouldn't end until she had worked long enough to buy a refrigerator." *The Best War Ever: America and World War II*, 8.

126. Alexander, *Preview of a New Way of Life (Revere's Part in Better Living)*, 12.

127. Advertisement for General Electric, *Architectural Forum* 81 (December 1944): 66–67.

128. Westbrook, "Fighting for the American Family," 195–222.

129. Advertisement for Alcoa Aluminum, *Architectural Forum* 80 (January 1944): 133, and *Pencil Points* (January 1944): 93.

130. While we do not know exactly where Alcoa ran the ad, many companies associated with the building industry blanketed the press, running their campaigns in a variety of magazines such as *Time*, *Ladies' Home Journal*, *Parents Magazine*, and *Saturday Evening Post*, as well as in architecture and building magazines.

131. Advertisement for the Associated General Contractors of America, *Architectural Forum* (April 1944): 182.

132. I have not found circulation figures on J. A. Zurn Manufacturing's pamphlet *A New Era of Building Is Only Marking Time*, but judging by similar efforts by Revere Copper and Brass (see chapter 3), it may have reached tens of thousands of people, including professionals in design and building, as well as laypeople.

133. The design for the airport was created by Ludo Zimmer, but the company went to the expense of having Hugh Ferriss render Zimmer's conception, which shows up in Ferriss's job book as "Zimmer Air Colony," 1942, suggesting that the image belonged to a larger project. Hugh Ferriss Job Book, Avery Archives, Columbia University.

134. For a comparative analysis of Depression-era attempts in industry, academia, and journalism to back planning, see Graham's discussion of historian Charles A. Beard, economic writer Stuart Chase, and Gerard Swope of General Electric in Graham, *Toward a Planned Society*, 13–17.

135. Advertisement for Duraglass, *American Perfumer* (March 1944): 74. J. Walter Thompson Archives at Duke University: Domestic Advertising Collection, Owen and Illinois Glass, 1944, Box 1.

136. Advertisement for Coyne and Delany Plumbing, *Architectural Forum* (September 1944): 191.

137. Advertisement for Mueller Climatrol, *Architectural Forum* (August 1944): opposite 16.

138. Another example of planning for comfort is the National Radiator Company's advertisement in *American Home* 34 (November 1945): 70. The ad copy stated: "Plan to be comfortable." It advertised a larger pamphlet of the same name. "We've written a booklet to help you plan comfort into that home you've dreamed about for so long." See also the advertisement for Emerson Electric in *Architectural Forum*. The use of planning in relation to states of being, such as comfort, can be found as early as the late 1930s, when ads for products such as air conditioners first appealed to architects to include them in their specifications.

139. Advertisement for Bruce Streamline Floors, *Architectural Forum* (February 1945): 64–65.

140. See Lears, *Fables of Abundance: A Cultural History of Advertising in America*.

141. Leuchtenburg, "The New Deal and the Analogue of War."

142. The sense of 194X as an afterlife comes from a conversation with architectural historian Janet Temos of Princeton University.

2. Old Cities, New Frontiers

1. Walter Gropius to Sigfried Giedion (March 10, 1942). Reginald Isaacs Papers (hereafter cited as Isaacs Papers), Archives of American Art, Smithsonian Institution, Box 5, Folder: Research Material: S. Giedion.

2. Ibid.

3. Other organizers included Frederick J. Adams, Joseph Hudnut, Morris B. Lambie, and Martin Wagner. While architects had a large role in organizing the conference, economists and planners dominated the proceedings. The conference was held March 5–6, 1942, and produced a published report edited by Greer. See Greer, ed., *The Problem of the Cities and Towns.*

4. Bettman collaborated with Hansen in drafting a proposed congressional bill on postwar planning. Various drafts of this proposed bill can be found among the Alvin Harvey Hansen Papers at the Harvard University Archives. See "A Bill" (February 1, 1945), Hug (FP)–3.42 Alvin Harvey Hansen, Research Notes, MSS, Typescripts, etc., Box 1, A-D, Folder: A Bill-1945.

5. Hansen, Foreword to *The Problem of the Cities and Towns,* ix.

6. Ibid. Le Corbusier's *The City of Tomorrow and Its Planning* is rife with biological words such as skeleton, "tentacular," organism, cell, sickness, metaphors he easily could have borrowed from E. E. Viollet-le-Duc or Patrick Geddes. See especially chapter 14, "Physic or Surgery."

7. Gropius and Wagner, "The New City Pattern for the People and by the People," 101.

8. The literature on the body politic is vast. For example, Harris, *Foreign Bodies and the Body Politic: Discourses of Social Pathology in Early Modern England;* and Nast and Pile, eds., *Places through the Body.* Also, see Casillo, "Mumford and the Organicist Concept in Social Thought." Gropius paid particular attention to the work of the German Darwinian Ernst Haeckel, going so far as to use some of his images in *Rebuilding Our Communities.* For Viollet-le-Duc, see Bressani, "The Life of Stone: Viollet-le-Duc's Physiology of Architecture."

9. Gropius and Wagner, "The New City Pattern," 101. This is almost certainly Gropius's writing. In a lecture he gave in February 1945 in Chicago, he repeated himself almost verbatim, ending with "Freed of dead weight, the reopened areas of the dying cities could then be returned to their proper functions as integral parts of an organic social structure for the whole region." See Gropius, *Rebuilding Our Communities,* 49–50.

10. Gropius, Letter to Sigfried Giedion (March 10, 1942), Isaacs Papers, Box 5, Folder: Research Material: S. Giedion.

11. See the section on flexibility in Forty, *Words and Buildings: A Vocabulary of Modern Architecture,* 142–48.

12. Katherine Solomonson suggested this last interpretation.

13. Gropius and Wagner, "The New City Pattern," 114, 116. For a similar line of investigation in the NRPB, see Ascher and United States National Resources Planning Board, *Better Cities.*

14. Le Corbusier provocatively ended *The City of Tomorrow* with an "homage to the great town planner" (302), illustrated with an image of Louis XIV commanding the building of the Invalides.

15. Letter Walter Gropius to Maxwell Fry (January 6, 1943): 1, Isaacs Papers, Box 5, Research Material: E. Maxwell Fry. Also in 1942, Gropius had launched into a comprehensive plan for metropolitan Boston with Martin Wagner, based on building self-contained town units for about five thousand people, distributed along superhighways, with the aim of combating the congestion of urban Boston. Along with the plan for the decentralization of Boston, Gropius and Wagner planned what he called in his letter to Fry a "reconceptu-

alization of the old town." See Gropius and Wagner, "A Program for City Reconstruction." The final chapter of Greer's *The Problem of the Cities and Towns* elaborates on Gropius and Wagner's theories of planning (95–116).

16. See Mumford, *The CIAM Discourse on Urbanism, 1928–1960.*

17. For good explanations of the mature economy, see Gilbert, *An Economic Program for American Democracy;* Swanson and Schmidt, *Economic Stagnation or Progress: A Critique of Recent Doctrines on the Mature Economy, Oversavings, and Deficit Spending.* Also Terborgh, *The Bogey of the Mature Economy.* Terborgh's piece is a polemic against Hansen's theories, but it explains the theory well.

18. "Testimony of Alvin H. Hansen," May 1939, in "Hearings before the Temporary National Economic Committee," 3503. See Rosenof, *Economics in the Long Run,* 57.

19. Hansen, *Fiscal Policy and Business Cycles,* 297. I am indebted to Rosenof for this citation (*Economics in the Long Run,* 54).

20. For a history of Hansen's contribution to fiscal policy and his legacy, see Salant, "Alvin Hansen and the Fiscal Policy Seminar."

21. Mumford, *City Development,* 198–240. See Alvin H. Hansen and Guy Greer to Lewis Mumford, Letters, 1941–1942, Folder 1527, Lewis Mumford Papers, Special Collections, University of Pennsylvania. For an account of how Keynesian ideas became fashionable and why, see Lekachman, *The Age of Keynes: A Biographical Study.* Incidentally, Sigfried Giedion was giving his seminal Charles Eliot Norton lectures at Harvard in the same moment, which led to the publication of *Space, Time and Architecture,* a book that was published shortly before the Harvard Conference on Urbanism.

22. Mumford, *The Social Foundations of Post-War Building.*

23. Churchill, *The City Is the People;* Justement, *New Cities for Old.*

24. See Justement, *New Cities for Old.*

25. Brinkley, *The End of Reform,* 132–35. See also Kennedy, *Freedom from Fear,* 122–23, 373–74, 785–86. Kennedy calls the mature economy part of an "unexcavated layer" of assumptions about economics (122).

26. Terborgh, *The Bogey of Economic Maturity,* 4–6.

27. Hayek, *The Road to Serfdom;* Terborgh's refutation of Hansen's theories came only after the high production levels of war made the theory seem improbable. Hansen responded in "Some Notes on Terborgh's 'The Bogey of Economic Maturity.'"

28. Gallup, *The Gallup Poll: Public Opinion 1935–1971,* 594. Only 20 percent disagreed.

29. See Keyserling, "Deficiencies of Past Programs and Nature of New Needs," 82. See also Swanson and Schmidt, *Economic Stagnation or Progress.* For the economic context of New Deal economic theories, see Rosenof, *Economics in the Long Run.*

30. Both theory and metaphor continued for decades in Kinnard, ed., *The New England Region: Problems of a Mature Economy;* and Ranis, ed., *Taiwan: From Developing to Mature Economy.* In fact, the mature city has continued to be a normative model for urban planning. See New York State Financial Control Board, *The Mature City Model: An Econometric Model for New York City in the 1980s;* and Dayton Department of Planning, *Planning in the Mature City—Dayton, Ohio.*

31. Sert credited the rest of CIAM as authors, so it is unclear how much of *Can Our Cities Survive?* might have come from some of the other members. According to Josep M. Rovira i Gimeno, CIAM commissioned it while Sert was still in Europe. See Rovira i Gimeno, ed., *Sert: Half a Century of Architecture: 1928–1979, A Complete Work,* 112–13.

32. Sert, *Can Our Cities Survive? An ABC of Urban Problems, Their Analysis, Their Solutions,* 4. He followed other writers in thinking of cities in these terms. Shortly after the turn of the century, Patrick Geddes wrote of the city in terms strongly derived from his roots as a biologist. In the 1920s and 1930s, Robert Park of the Chicago School of Sociology wrote of "human ecology" and imagined the city in biological and ecological terms, likely picking up on Progressive Era rhetoric. Although Geddes and Park frequently fell under

the spell of their own metaphors, unlike Sert, they understood that they were using metaphors as a way of analyzing the city. Serge Chermayeff linked Sert's book with Geddes' in a wartime article on planning, "Four Viewpoints on Architecture and Planning: Planning Urns or Urbanism," 74. See Geddes, *Cities in Evolution: An Introduction to the Town Planning Movement and to the Study of Civics,* and Park, "Human Ecology," for an earlier use of similar metaphors.

33. Sert, *Can Our Cities Survive?* 4.

34. Ibid., 12.

35. Sert based *Can Our Cities Survive?* on the Athens Charter of 1933 (x). The earlier document curiously contains few rhetorical flourishes and none of the sustained metaphorical qualities of Sert's book. Sert dressed up the provisions of the Charter in the metaphors of the mature economy.

36. Sontag, *Illness as Metaphor.* This sort of thinking suffuses Sontag's book. See in particular 57–58.

37. Sert, *Can Our Cities Survive?* 2.

38. Ibid., 24.

39. Ibid., 41.

40. Ibid., 144.

41. Ibid., 154.

42. Ibid., 79.

43. Saarinen, *The City,* 293.

44. Ibid. Housing expert Miles Colean criticized Saarinen's use of biological metaphors: "The penchant of planners to discuss urban enlargement, dispersion and contraction in the biological terms of growth and decay, cell structure, and so forth, is not only unscientific . . . but leads directly to the concept of our existing cities as diseased organisms." Colean suggested physics instead. See "Parturition or Physics?" 34.

45. William Lescaze, advertisement for Revere Copper and Brass, *Saturday Evening Post* (September 16, 1944): 66–67.

46. The Allegheny Conference, which is still in existence, led directly to Renaissance One in Pittsburgh. For a history of the organization, see Mershon, "Corporate Social Responsibility and Urban Revitalization: The Allegheny Conference on Community Development, 1943–1968." I also benefited from the research of Adam Pobiak, a student of mine at Oberlin College.

47. Allegheny Conference on Community Development, *A Civic Clinic for Better Living.*

48. Ibid.

49. Ibid.

50. McLaughlin and Watkins, "The Problem of Industrial Growth in a Mature Economy," 4.

51. Allegheny Conference on Community Development, *A Civic Clinic for Better Living,* unpaginated [2].

52. Wright, *Frank Lloyd Wright Collected Writings, Vol. 4, 1939–1949,* 61.

53. "Planning Progress," *The Bulletin Index* (July 11, 1940), in the Pittsburgh City Planning Files, Carnegie Library, Pittsburgh.

54. Klein, *Frontiers of Historical Imagination: Narrating the European Conquest of Native America, 1890–1990,* 13. I have leaned on Klein's explanation for its attention to Turner's rhetoric. Turner, "The Significance of the Frontier in American History."

55. Klein, *Frontiers of Historical Imagination,* 13–14.

56. Slotkin, *Gunfighter Nation: The Myth of the Frontier in Twentieth-Century America,* 255–312.

57. Ibid., 5.

58. Myers, "Was the Architect of Tomorrow Here Yesterday?" 14. It would not be surprising if his words came directly from Hansen. Myers's managing editor, George Nelson, worked with Hansen's partner, Guy Greer, at *Fortune.*

59. Klein, *Frontiers of Historical Imagination,* 13–20.

60. McLaughlin and Watkins, "The Problem of Industrial Growth," 1.

61. Myers, "Was the Architect of Tomorrow Here Yesterday?" 14.

62. Walker, "Planning for Peace," 41.

63. Ibid., 42.

64. Historian Charles Beard embraced planning in the 1930s through a Marxist teleology not unrelated to this logic. Beard, ed., *Toward Civilization*. See Beard's final chapter, "The Planning of Civilization," especially 297–301.

65. The language continued to permeate planning literature in the postwar decades. See, for instance, Abrams, *The City Is the Frontier*; Cook, *The New Urban Frontier: New Metropolises for America*; and Musselman, *The Church on the Urban Frontier*. John F. Kennedy's "New Frontier" built on this earlier language and further tied it to cities as well as to the space race.

66. Wallace, *New Frontiers*, 3. Wallace and Hansen carried on an extensive correspondence beginning in the early 1930s and extending beyond the war years.

67. Ibid., 4–5.

68. Ibid., 6.

69. Ibid., 10; for his sketch of the mature economy theory, see 271–72.

70. Ibid., 274.

71. Ibid., 286.

72. Kahn worked on Jersey Homesteads in Roosevelt, New Jersey, with Alfred Kastner, 1935–37. See Brownlee and De Long, *Louis I. Kahn*, 12–13. J. L. Moreno applied his theories of sociometry, discussed in chapter 1, in a Resettlement Administration project. See Moreno and Jennings, *Who Shall Survive?* especially 335–60.

73. Nettels, "Frederick Jackson Turner and the New Deal," 263.

74. Ibid., 262.

75. Quoted in Nettels, "Frederick Jackson Turner and the New Deal," 263.

76. Hansen, "Mr. Keynes on Underemployment Equilibrium," 681.

77. Hansen, "Some Notes on Terborgh's 'The Bogey of Economic Maturity,'" 15.

78. Hansen, "Social Planning for Tomorrow."

79. The New Deal revisited the idea of "natural rights," the NRPB going so far as to create a "Second Bill of Rights" inspired in part by Roosevelt's "Four Freedoms." It created a wide net for social security, including the right to work, leisure, food, clothing, shelter, and medical care. National Resources Planning Board, *National Resources Development Report for 1943*. See Reagan, *Designing a New America*, 218–19.

80. Ely is also associated with Thorstein Veblen as one of the leading economists of the American Institutionalists, a school of economics of the early twentieth century that preceded Keynes in challenging the precepts of classical economics. He also taught Wesley C. Mitchell, a key economist with the NRPB, and organized the American Economics Association, which Hansen later served as President.

81. Nelson, *Researching for a New Standard of Living*. Nelson wrote a piece for the *New York Times* as well: "Home Owner of the Future Held Likely to Give More Study to Interior Plan." Nelson had studied under Auguste Perret in Paris, absorbing European modernism firsthand. When the war began, he fled Paris, destitute and urgently in need of work. Riley and Abram, eds., *The Filter of Reason: The Work of Paul Nelson*. Nelson, who wrote a desperate plea for help to Lewis Mumford in 1942, likely jumped at the opportunity to do an advertisement for Revere. See Letter Paul Nelson to Lewis Mumford (July 29, 1940), Mumford Archives, University of Pennsylvania.

82. Riley and Abram, eds., *The Filter of Reason*, 13, 28–31.

83. Nelson, *Researching for a New Standard of Living*, 6.

84. Ibid., 8. Nelson referred to "plug-in" rooms, bringing ideas from Le Corbusier to a wide American public and anticipating Archigram ideas by twenty years.

85. Ibid., 8.

86. Ibid., 5.

87. Ibid., 8.

88. Ibid., 10. Lewis Mumford coined the term *Neotechnic* to refer to a future phase of civilization when the machine would be tamed and made the servant of mankind, freeing people for higher pursuits than labor. See Mumford, "The Neotechnic Phase," in *Technics and Civilization.*

89. Nelson, *Researching for a New Standard of Living,* 9.

90. Ibid., 8.

91. Carl Boester, advertisement for Revere Copper and Brass, *Architectural Forum* (February 1943): 12–13.

92. Boester, *Home . . . For a Nation on Wings,* 4.

93. Boester, a researcher in housing at the Purdue Research Center in Chicago, had easy access to Wright's ideas. This suggests a kind of regionalist approach to 194X, with Midwesterners like Wright, Wallace, and Boester proposing solutions tied directly to the character of the land.

94. Boester, *Home . . . For a Nation on Wings,* 6.

95. For a brief analysis of how this economic shift affected the art world, see Mamiya, *Pop Art and Consumer Culture: American Super Market,* 2.

96. Boester, *Home . . . For a Nation on Wings,* 8.

97. "Planning with You," *Architectural Forum* 81 (August 1944): 79–81. The *Forum* published the pamphlet in full in *Architectural Forum* (August 1943): 63–80.

98. Architectural Forum, advertisement for *Planning with You, Architectural Forum* 79 (August 1943): 81.

99. Architectural Forum, advertisement for *Planning with You, Architectural Forum* 79 (September 1943): 64.

100. Architectural Forum, *Planning with You,* 72.

101. In fact, Saarinen's *The City* was reviewed in the same issue of the *Forum* in which *Planning with You* first appeared.

102. George Nelson, who was instrumental to the Syracuse Project and who wrote a pamphlet for Revere Copper and Brass (see chapter 3), probably wrote the pamphlet.

103. Architectural Forum, advertisement for *Planning With You, New York Times* (May 19, 1943): 19.

104. Ibid.

105. Ibid.

106. Howard Myers to Messrs. Larsen and Black (June 1, 1943), Time Archives.

107. Architectural Forum, advertisement for *Planning with You, Architectural Forum* 78 (June 1943): 157.

108. The condensed comments were published in the August 1943 issue of *Architectural Forum;* see also Howard Myers to Luce, Larsen, Stillman, Black, Barnes and Pratt (May 24, 1943), Time Archives.

109. Architectural Forum, advertisement for *Architectural Forum* 79 (August 1943): 82.

110. "First in the 'Forum,' Then on the Ground" (September 12, 1944), an interoffice memorandum from Howard Myers to Time, Inc., detailing the Forum's contribution to architecture and postwar planning. Also, Architectural Forum, "A Flood of Checks Is Carrying 'Planning with You' Out of the Grass Roots."

111. Architectural Forum, "A Flood of Checks," 64.

112. Architectural Forum, advertisement for *Planning with You, Architectural Forum* 80 (May 1944): 70.

113. Robert D. Kohn to Myers, excerpted in Myers to Luce, et. al., Time Archives.

114. Robert Armstrong to Myers, excerpted in Myers to Luce, et. al., Time Archives.

115. See "A Personal Invitation to Every Reader of the Architectural Forum," 63; and Architectural Forum, advertisement for *Planning with You, Architectural Forum* 79 (August 1943): 81.

116. "A Personal Invitation," 65.

117. Advertisement for Herman Nelson Co., *Pencil Points* (July 1944): 50–51.

118. Finished in 1954, the sprawling complex of over thirty buildings became emblematic of the failure of modern architecture when it was torn down less than twenty years later in the early 1970s. For more on Pruitt-Igoe, see Comerio, "Pruitt-Igoe and Other Stories," "The Experiment That Failed," and "The

Tragedy of Pruitt-Igoe." For a more critical view that dubs the Pruitt-Igoe debacle a myth, see Bristol, "The Pruitt-Igoe Myth."

119. "Slum Surgery for St. Louis," 128.

120. Rosenof, *Economics in the Long Run.*

121. Leven, ed., *The Mature Metropolis;* Hanten, Kasoff, and Redburn, *New Directions for the Mature Metropolis: Policies and Strategies for Change.*

122. Committee on Banking, Finance, and Urban Affairs, *How Cities Can Grow Old Gracefully,* prepared for the Subcommittee on the City, House of Representatives, 95th Congress, First Session.

3. Advertising Nothing, Anticipating Nowhere

1. Lizabeth Cohen writes of the shaping of the citizen-consumer in this period. See Cohen, *A Consumers' Republic: The Politics of Mass Consumption in Postwar America.* See also Fox and Lears, *The Culture of Consumption: Critical Essays in American History 1880–1980;* and Susan Strasser, McGovern, and Judt, eds., *Getting and Spending: European and American Consumer Societies in the Twentieth Century.* For the basic sense of consumer culture, see Fox and Lears, eds., *The Power of Culture.*

2. Shanken, "Better Living: Toward a Cultural History of a Business Slogan."

3. Throughout the war, the advertising industry debated the merits of advertising for products that were unavailable. Advertising revenues boomed in 1942 and continued at high levels throughout the war. For interesting commentary on the pros and cons of advertising during wartime, see "Faith in Advertising Pays Rich Dividends"; "These Advertisers, Now Great, Began in 1915–1918"; and "Advertising during Two World Wars."

4. Alexander Smith and Sons Carpet Company had run a series of ads between 1939 and 1941, but without original, visionary designs and the cast of leading progressive architects. See Appendix.

5. Woods, *From Craft to Profession,* 168–69.

6. Boyd, "Public Relations." Kenneth Reid introduced the new section as a form of service to the profession that filled the void of AIA inaction. Reid, "Here, There, This and That."

7. AIA President Richmond Shreve first relaxed the AIA's stance against advertising after an ad campaign by Alexander Smith and Sons Carpet Company was brought up as a violation of the AIA Code of Ethics because it featured a photograph of an architect next to his work. See AIA Board of Directors, Minutes July 31, August 1, 1941, Box RG509 SR2 AIA, Board of Directors Minutes Miscellaneous 194191943, Box 5, AIA Archives.

8. Fox, *Madison Avenue Goes to War.*

9. The Vinson and Voorhis Bills are two examples. The latter attempted to curb all advertising during the war. See Fox, *Madison Avenue Goes to War,* 25–28.

10. For a good historical assessment of the conflict between admen and New Deal policy, see Fox, *Madison Avenue Goes to War,* 10–43.

11. Lears, *Fables of Abundance,* 247–49, and Fox, *Madison Avenue Goes to War,* 92–93.

12. Fox, *Madison Avenue Goes to War,* 92.

13. Neider, "Advertise for Victory," 770.

14. Fox, *Madison Avenue Goes to War,* 93.

15. Neider, "Advertise for Victory," 771.

16. For a specific history of the War Advertising Council, see Griffith, "The Selling of America: The Advertising Council and American Politics, 1942–1960."

17. Fox, *Madison Avenue Goes to War,* 11.

18. See Repplier, "Advertising Dons Long Pants."

19. Richard Boring Snow, advertisement for U.S. Gypsum, *Architectural Forum* 74 (March 1941): 37–40.

20. The graphics were so convincing that the *Avery Index to Architectural Periodicals* indexed two of the ads as if they were articles. See George Keck, "Solution to an Architectural Problem for the United States Gypsum Company: George Fred Keck Plans the Trans-Duo," *Architectural Forum* 75 (October 1941): 54–57; and Don E. Hatch, Dick Bennett, Jedd Resiner, and Florence Schust, "United States Gypsum Company Presents a Study for Durationville," *Architectural Forum* 76 (May 1942): 58–61.

21. Edward D. Stone, advertisement for U.S. Gypsum, "Study for an Avenue for the Americas," *Architectural Forum* 75 (August 1941): 35–39. It appeared a month after the *Forum* published a portfolio of Stone's work. See "A Portfolio of Work by Edward D. Stone."

22. La France, "Rebirth of an Avenue," 11.

23. Mumford, "The Sky Line: Cloud over Sixth Avenue: Home on the Park," 78.

24. Ibid. The exhibition was held in the basement showrooms of the American Radiator Building and Standard Sanitary Corporation at 50 West Fortieth Street. The echoes of contemporary debates over the fate of the World Trade Center site are uncanny. Over sixty years later, Herbert Muschamp offered a startlingly similar message after the first round of designs for the World Trade Center site were published.

25. Stone credited the students and architects in his firm in the advertisement. Notably, these included Ernest Rapp and Stanley Sharp.

26. "Sixth Avenue to Help Hemisphere Trade," 5.

27. "Blueprint for an Avenue: Plans of Manhattan's Sixth Avenue Association," 70.

28. Stone, "Study for an Avenue for the Americas," 35.

29. Ferriss's original drawings seem to be lost. New York University, where Stone taught, has no record of the course. A record of the drawing appears in Ferriss's project book in the Avery Archives.

30. "Building's Post-War Pattern," 73–78.

31. Stone, "Study for an Avenue of the Americas," 35–38.

32. Ibid., 35.

33. Eero Saarinen, Ad for U.S. Gypsum, "Demountable Space," *Architectural Forum* 76 (March 1942): 50–53. It was also Saarinen's first published project for a complete building without his father. It was republished alongside Fuller's work and Paul Nelson's Suspended House in "The Prefabricated House." Fuller popularized the idea of mast-erection for houses, but the idea had currency for other projects that may have been more direct sources for Saarinen. Mumford had written about a German experiment in mast apart-ments. See Mumford, "Mass-Production and the Modern House," 13; and a project by Carlos Le Duc for a Mexican theater erected by mast, in "Proposed Building," 46.

34. Meyer, *Journey through Chaos*. See Crawford, "Daily Life on the Home Front: Women, Blacks, and the Struggle for Public Housing." For the race riots, see "Storm over New Housing in Detroit."

35. "Housing Problem Confronts Detroit," 30.

36. "Detroiters in Riot on Negro Project," 40.

37. Saarinen, "Demountable Space," 50.

38. The emphasis on mobility also recalls an article by the young I. M. Pei for "Standardized Propa-ganda Units for the Chinese Government."

39. The general idea that architecture moved from an architecture of mass, in which the wall was the primary site of invention and expression, to volume, in which space became the primary focus, comes from a lecture by David Brownlee, "Making Time for Architecture," at the University of Pennsylvania in 2000.

40. See "Magazine Advertising."

41. Time-Advertising Promotion 1943. Time Archives.

42. For example, see "Bel Geddes Sees Wider Use of Prefabrication in Homes," and Hamby, "More Labor-Saving Devices Predicted for Future Homes."

43. Simon Breines, for instance, was approached by St. Georges and Keyes, which had read about his idea for a house with an insulating layer of water on the roof (from an interview with Breines, July 18, 2003). Breines was the last living architect to have worked on a Revere Copper and Brass advertisement. The author owes a great debt to him for his accounts of the process.

44. Brownlee and De Long, *Louis I. Kahn,* 33.

45. Bannister and Bellamy, *The Architect at Mid-Century,* 52.

46. Revere Copper and Brass, advertisement, *Architectural Forum* 81 (July 1944): 57.

47. Revere Copper and Brass, advertisement, *Architectural Forum* (January 1942): 58–59.

48. Walter B. Sanders, advertisement for Revere Copper and Brass, *Architectural Forum* (April 1942): 50–51. Sanders was a Michigan architect who had tested a Buckminster Fuller Dymaxion Deployment Unit in 1941, worked as a consultant for Albert Kahn, and was one of the few American members of CIAM.

49. Sanders, *Apartment Homes for Tomorrow's Better Living.*

50. Lawrence B. Perkins, advertisement for Revere Copper and Brass, *Architectural Forum* (October 1942): 106–7.

51. Fox, *Madison Avenue Goes to War,* 93.

52. Lawrence B. Perkins, advertisement for Revere Copper and Brass, *Architectural Forum* 77 (October 1942): 106–7; and *Saturday Evening Post* (October 17, 1942): 53.

53. Perkins, *After Total War Can Come Total Living,* back cover. This was in the Revere pamphlet series.

54. This is Robert Westbrook's compelling thesis in his article "Fighting for the American Family."

55. Lawrence B. Perkins, advertisement for Revere Copper and Brass, *Architectural Forum* 77 (October 1942): 106–7.

56. Ibid., 107.

57. Perkins, *After Total War Can Come Total Living,* 3.

58. Ibid.

59. Ibid.

60. Perkins's community center may have had its roots in a minor utopia that Claude F. Bragdon outlined during World War I in *Architecture and Democracy.* See especially the material on Camp Sherman Community Club House near Cleveland.

61. Nelson, advertisement for Revere Copper and Brass, *Architectural Forum* (March 1943): 26.

62. George Nelson, *Your Children Could Romp Here While You Shop,* 1.

63. A similar approach was then being tried in Rye, New York, a site that the New York–based Nelson would have known. Baker and Funaro, *Shopping Centers: Design and Operation,* 14–15.

64. Gruen, *The Heart of Our Cities: The Urban Crisis, Diagnosis and Cure.* Also see Gabrielle Esperdy's *Modernizing Main Street: Architecture and Consumer Culture in the New Deal.*

65. Nelson, *Your Children Could Romp Here,* 6.

66. Hudnut, "Architecture after the Peace."

67. Ibid., 126.

68. Alexander, *Preview of a New Way of Life.* For a good analysis of Baldwin Hills Village, see Hines, "Housing, Baseball, and Creeping Socialism: The Battle of Chavez Ravine, Los Angeles, 1949–1959."

69. Letter Robert E. Alexander to Richard K. Snively (October 28, 1942), in the Robert Alexander Papers, Collection 30872, Cornell University, Rare and Manuscript Collections.

70. Alexander, *Preview of a New Way of Life,* 5. Alexander even proposed that the demountable house would be so flexible that he would pack it up and take it on vacation, trailing the entire house behind his personal plane as he traveled.

71. Ibid. See also Wright, "The New Frontier: Broadacre City."

72. Alexander, *Preview of a New Way of Life,* 11.

73. Ibid., 13.

74. Alexander, *Preview of a New Way of Life,* 12.

75. Walter B. Sanders, advertisement for Revere Copper and Brass, *Architectural Forum* (April 1942): 50–51.

76. See "A Plan for Harlem's Redevelopment."

77. Lescaze, *Uplifting the Downtrodden,* 7.

78. Ibid., 13.

79. Lescaze, *A Citizens Country Club or Leisure Center.* Henry S. Churchill echoed the idea in his book *The City Is the People,* 177. Churchill referred to the school as a "common mans' club." Esther Da Costa Meyer has pointed out that the community center also bears a formal resemblance to Le Corbusier's scheme for the League of Nations in Geneva of 1927. See Le Corbusier and Brooks, *The Le Corbusier Archive,* 258.

80. Lescaze had worked on the Williamsburg Houses (1934–38) with Shreve, Lamb, and Harmon. They were an important precedent for his Revere design. See Stern, Gilmartin, and Mellins, *New York 1930: Architecture and Urbanism between the Two Wars,* 495. Also see Richard Plunz for the larger context of "slab block" housing, *A History of Housing in New York City: Dwelling Type and Social Change in the American Metropolis,* 165–206.

81. Lescaze, *A Citizens Country Club,* 6.

82. William Lescaze, "Planning—for Whom, How, and When," Lecture at the Worcester Art Museum (February 16, 1943): 10. Lescaze Papers, Box 65, Folder: Writing, Lectures, 1940–43.

83. Marchand, *Advertising the American Dream: Making Way for Modernity, 1920–1940,* 130.

84. Ibid., 138.

85. Stonorov and Kahn, *Why City Planning Is Your Responsibility,* 4.

86. Ibid., 4–8.

87. Brownlee and De Long argue that Kahn had learned the lesson that "neighborhoods ought to be preserved and strengthened rather than demolished and rebuilt" from his work on Old Swedes, "where he had discovered to his surprise that residents did not want to leave their old houses." *Louis I. Kahn,* 25–27.

88. Stonorov and Kahn, *Why City Planning Is Your Responsibility,* 3.

89. Brownlee and De Long, *Louis I. Kahn,* 33. See also Donald Haggerty to Stonorov and Kahn (August 10, 1943), Stonorov Papers, Box 40, Folder: Correspondence July–September 1943.

90. Alexander Crosby to Stonorov (August 5, 1943); Bryn J. Hovde to C. Donald Dallas (August 6, 1943); and C. Donald Dallas to Bryn J. Hovde (August 12, 1943), Stonorov Papers, Box 40, Folder: Correspondence July–September 1943.

91. Alexander Crosby to Edmund Bacon (September 7, 1943), Stonorov Papers, Box 40, Folder: Correspondence July–September 1943.

92. Alexander Crosby to Stonorov and Kahn (September 22, 1943), Stonorov Papers, Box 40, Folder: Correspondence July–September 1943.

93. Stonorov and Kahn, *You and Your Neighborhood;* Brownlee and De Long, *Louis I. Kahn,* 24–25, 48.

94. Stonorov and Kahn, *You and Your Neighborhood.*

95. Stonorov to Edward Carter (March 15, 1944), Stonorov Papers, Box 40, Folder: Correspondence January–March 1944.

96. See various letters in the Stonorov Papers, Box 41, Folder: Correspondence January–March 1945.

97. Stonorov and Kahn to M. St. Georges (December 31, 1943), Stonorov Papers, Box 40, Folder: Correspondence October–December 1943.

98. Stonorov and Kahn, advertisement for Revere Copper and Brass, *Architectural Forum* 81 (November 1944): 45.

99. This Quonset hut community center suggests some link with Stran-Steel, which advanced its Quonset hut as a possible building block for the modern city.

100. The same ad also appeared in the July 3, 1943, *Saturday Evening Post.* For Kahn's urbanism, see Reed, "Toward Form: Louis I. Kahn's Urban Designs for Philadelphia, 1939–1962."

101. In addition to Barrett, Monsanto Plastics, Durez Plastics, and Celotex ran campaigns that used visions of postwar architecture and products designed by well-known architects or industrial designs. See Appendix.

102. George Nelson, advertisement for Barrett Roofing, *Architectural Forum* 78 (May 1943): 53.

103. In fact, ten of the fourteen Barrett architects had appeared in one of the first two 194X issues. Four had done Revere Copper and Brass ads.

104. Charles Platt, advertisement for Barrett Roofing, *Architectural Forum* (October 1944): 228.

105. Stonorov and Kahn, advertisement for Barrett Roofing, *Architectural Forum* (June 1945): 179.

106. Walker, "Planning for Peace"; Giedion, "The Need for Monumentality."

107. "Store Designers Don't Suffer from Traditional Fixations—Thank God," 42.

108. Longstreth, *City Center to Regional Mall: Architecture, the Automobile, and Retailing in Los Angeles, 1920–1950;* Gillette, "The Evolution of the Planned Shopping Center in Suburb and City."

109. "Store Designers Don't Suffer from Traditional Fixations," 42.

110. Lescaze, advertisement for Pittsburgh Plate Glass, *Architectural Forum* 80 (April 1944): 221; and *Pencil Points* 25 (April 1944): 31.

111. Lescaze, Florist Shop, *Pencil Points* 25 (August 1944): 50.

112. *Pencil Points* 25 (August 1944): cover.

113. Advertisement for *Pencil Points, Pencil Points* 25 (November 1944): 109.

114. The two-page ads ran in the architectural magazines, *Interiors,* and the trade press. Variations on the ads also ran in *American Home* and General Electric's own *Magazine of Light.*

115. Lawrence B. Perkins, advertisement for General Electric, *Progressive Architecture* 26 (October 1945): 24–25.

116. "Crow Island School, Winnetka, Ill.: Eliel and Eero Saarinen, Perkins, Wheeler and Will, Architects."

117. Perkins, advertisement for General Electric, *Progressive Architecture* 26 (October 1945): 25.

118. Le Corbusier, *Towards a New Architecture,* 289.

119. Forty, *Words and Buildings,* 142–48. See the entry on flexibility.

120. Tobey, *Technology as Freedom: The New Deal and the Electrical Modernization of the American Home.*

121. Advertisement for Stran-Steel, *Architectural Forum* 80 (April 1944): 160.

122. Advertisement for Stran-Steel, *Architectural Forum* 80 (March 1944): 47.

123. Advertisement for Stran-Steel, *Pencil Points* 25 (February 1944): 25.

124. "A Satellite Town for the Detroit Area," 91–99.

125. Advertisement for Bohn Aluminum, *Fortune* (May 1945): 173.

126. Marchand, *Advertising the American Dream,* 206–83.

127. Marion Harper and V. M. Epes Harper, *4500 Newspaper Pictures and Their Significance for Advertisers* (McCann Erickson [1943]). Warshaw Collection of the Archives Center, Smithsonian Institution, Advertising Industry, Box 9.

128. Marchand, *Advertising the American Dream,* 112.

129. Marberry, "Leg Art?"

130. From an interview with architect Simon Breines, August 10, 2003.

131. Blake, *Form Follows Fiasco: Why Modern Architecture Hasn't Worked.*

132. Abell, "Industry and Painting," 82.

133. Allen, *The Romance of Commerce and Culture: Capitalism, Modernism, and the Chicago-Aspen Crusade for Cultural Reform;* and Bogart, *Artists, Advertising, and the Borders of Art.*

134. Shanken, "From the Gospel of Efficiency to Modernism." See also Neutra, *Survival through Design,* 51.

135. This discussion profited from participation in Barry Bergdoll and Clare Zimmerman's session at the 2002 Society of Architectural Historians Conference in Richmond, "The Unbuilt."

136. *Parents Magazine* (November 1943): 48.

137. See also Wright, "Bathrooms for the Future." Incidentally, Henry Wright worked alongside George Nelson at *Architectural Forum.*

4. The End of Planning

1. The ads ran in *American Builder and Building Age, Architectural Forum, Printers' Ink, Electrical Merchandising,* and possibly elsewhere.

2. Theodore Rosenof provides a clear economic history of the rise and fall (and subsequent return) of Hansen's theories and more broadly of Keynesian economics in this period. *Economics in the Long Run.*

3. For the failure of the a wartime attempt to organize modernists as planners, see Shanken, "Between Brotherhood and Bureaucracy," 147–75.

4. Brinkley, *The End of Reform,* 141–46.

5. *Congressional Record* 89, 1 (February 8, 1943): 717.

6. Ibid. Similar references can be found throughout the *Congressional Record* in 1943. A group of vocal Republicans added to Smith's attack, equating the NRPB with German, Russian, and Italian forms of totalitarianism. See, for instance, Noah M. Mason (Ill.), *Congressional Record Appendix* 89, 9 (March 15, 1943): A1183. On the NRPB leading inevitably to regimentation and authoritarianism, see Gerald W. Landis (Ind.), *Congressional Record Appendix* 89, 10 (April 5, 1943): A1612; and John E. Rankin (Miss.), *Congressional Record Appendix* 89, 9 (March 11, 1943): A1146. Senator Robert A. Taft of Ohio, Senator Millard E. Tydings of Maryland, and Joseph P. Kennedy all spoke against the NRPB. See "Editorial: Program for Progress," 147–48.

7. Smith, *Congressional Record* 89, 1 (February 8, 1943): 719.

8. Ibid.

9. See Hudnut, "The Political Art of Planning," 194–95.

10. Schindler, "The Architect—Postwar-Post Everybody" (October and November 1944).

11. Talbot Hamlin, "A Public Opinion for Planning," 183.

12. Ibid., 182.

13. Ibid., 189.

14. Ibid., 187.

15. Ibid., 186.

16. Ibid., 184.

17. "Editorial: Program for Progress," 147.

18. Walsh, "Action for Postwar Planning," 157.

19. D. K. Este Fisher to George T. Seabury (December 28, 1943), AIA Archives, Box 131036046, Folder 4–4.2 (b): Washington Representative.

20. Winkler, *The Politics of Propaganda: The Office of War Information 1942–1945,* 55.

21. Ibid., 76.

22. Ibid., 66.

23. Hayek, *The Road to Serfdom.* All citations are taken from the 1994 edition published by the University of Chicago Press.

24. In fact, *The Road to Serfdom* may be the best-selling book on economics ever. After its first few limited wartime printings, *Reader's Digest* distributed more than six hundred thousand copies of a condensed version in 1945. Subsequently, the Book-of-the-Month Club picked it up. By 1994, over a quarter of a million more copies had been sold, in addition to over twenty authorized translations. See Milton Friedman's introduction to the 1994 edition.

25. *The Road to Serfdom,* 151.

26. Ibid., 63. For Hayek's attack on the inevitability of planning leading to totalitarianism, see especially 54–63.

27. Merriam, "Book Review and Notices," 135.

28. Finer, *Road to Reaction.*

29. Roll, Review of *The Road to Serfdom,* 179.

30. Friedrich, Review of *The Road to Serfdom.* See his entry in the "Boston Contest," in *The Boston Contest of 1944.*

31. Friedrich, Review of *The Road to Serfdom,* 579.

32. Schumpeter, Review of *The Road to Serfdom.* See also Director, Review of *The Road to Serfdom.*

33. Holden, "Who's Afraid of Prosperity?"

34. Holden, *The Great Illusion: An Inexhaustible Public Purse.* Holden deserves more attention because of his relatively high profile. He was an oft-quoted authority on the building industry in the *New*

York Times, and he also was popular on the lecture circuit, spreading his bias against the necessity of public spending on urban rehabilitation. See, for instance, "Postwar Urban Redevelopment," a talk he gave to the Conference on Urban Problems of the United States Chamber of Commerce (September 29, 1943), AIA Archives, Box 131040288, Folder: Post-War Reconstruction Committee and General 1943, Part II.

35. For a good account of how the war quickly altered the Depression-era attitudes about spending, see Blum, *V Was for Victory.*

36. Advertisement for Young and Rubicam, Inc., *Fortune* 31, no. 1 (January 1945): 169.

37. The position attracted Time, Inc., which chose Young and Rubican, although much of Time's advertising remained in-house.

38. Mennel, "'Miracle House Hoop-La': Corporate Rhetoric and the Construction of the Postwar American House."

39. Zucker, "The Role of Architecture in Future Civilization," 36.

40. Richard Neutra, "The Insurance of Planning" (January 3, 1945), Richard Neutra Papers, Syracuse University Archives, Box 2, Folder: Writings D-J.

41. Little information is available on Otis Fulmer, although it appears that he knew Mumford, who wrote the introduction to his book, *Greenbelt.*

42. Fulmer, "Toledo Tomorrow," 22. Fulmer was reading a poem by an unnamed architect, whom he thought was from Michigan. Norman Bel Geddes, one of the icons of futurism in the 1930s and 1940s, authored an urban plan for Toledo in 1945. See Geddes, *Toledo Tomorrow.*

43. Nancy McClelland to Charles D. Maginnis (December 6, 1944). Archives of American Art, Smithsonian Institution, Charles Maginnis Papers: 1451; 432.

44. Robert L. Davison, "When Science Takes Over the Home" (undated). From an unpublished manuscript in the Douglas Putnam Haskell Papers, Avery Drawings and Archives, Columbia University, Box 88.

45. Advertisement for Westinghouse Corporation, *American Builder and Building Age* (February 1945): 13.

46. "Post-War Delusions," 18.

47. "More Daydreams," 26.

48. Ibid.

49. "The House Planned for Peace," 54–55. Two months after the *American Builder* article, *Architectural Forum* wrote its "Omnibus" issue, praising the efforts of various popular magazines to publicize advanced ideas on housing ("House Omnibus," 89–145). While Pratt's series fed the public a steady diet of Frank Lloyd Wright, Carl Koch, George Fred Keck, Lawrence Kocher, and others, the article singled out Dailey's house for *Ladies' Home Journal* as exemplary. Countering *American Builders'* criticism with praise, the *Forum* described Richard Pratt as having "no peer as an effective crusader for the best contemporary design. . . . During Pratt's tenure," the article went on to say, "no JOURNAL house has ever blushed beneath a gabled roof" (109).

50. "The 204X House," 26.

51. Advertisement for Arkansas Soft Pine Bureau, *American Builder and Building Age* 65 (January 1944): 30. The ad publicized the Bureau's pamphlet, *Arkansas Soft Pine: A Handbook for Builders.*

52. Dierks began in the Midwest and by the 1940s had a vast lumber and coal business that spanned Kansas, Nebraska, Iowa, and Arkansas. Weyerhaeuser took it over in 1969.

53. Advertisement for Dierks Lumber & Coal Company, *American Builder and Building Age* 67 (January 1945): 183.

54. Advertisement for Dierks Lumber & Coal Company, *American Builder and Building Age* 67 (July 1945): 160.

55. Advertisement for Stran-Steel, *Architectural Record* 97 (August 1945): 139. See also the August 1945 issue of *Architectural Forum* (201).

56. U.S. Gypsum Company, *Let's Be Sensible about Post-War Building: A Practical Forecast of Residential Building Immediately Following the End of the War,* preface.

57. Ibid., 58.

58. U.S. Gypsum Company, *Popular Home's Ideas Galore: How to Build . . . Buy . . . Modernize and Decorate,* and *Pak of Ideas.*

59. U.S. Gypsum Company, *Popular Home's Ideas Galore,* 12.

60. Ibid., 16.

61. Advertisement for National Gypsum Company, *Architectural Forum* 80 (May 1944): 54. The company's campaign caused some consternation among architects; see "Gypsum Men Discredit 'Dream House.'"

62. Ibid.

63. Other National Gypsum Company ads that took a stance against the visionary strain appeared in the January and March 1944 issues of *Architectural Forum* and in the March 13, 1944, issue of *Time.*

64. "Advertising in Wartime" (advertisement), *The New Republic* 110 (February 21, 1944): 233–36.

65. Ibid.

66. Ibid.

67. Ibid.

68. Ibid., 236.

69. Ibid.

70. Ibid., 236.

71. Advertisement for *Time* magazine, *Architectural Forum* 78 (April 1943): 28.

72. Advertisement for *Time* magazine, *American Builder and Building Age* 65 (April 1943): 11. The same ad appeared in the August 1943 and February 1944 issues of *Architectural Forum.* For Ledoux's design, see his *L'Architecture considérée sous le rapport de l'art des Moeurs et de la Législation,* 254.

73. Advertisement for *Time* magazine, *Architectural Forum* 80 (June 1944): 193. "Ten million new houses" was a common refrain during the war, referring to how many houses some experts thought the United States needed to avoid a serious housing shortage. See Rosenman, *A Million Homes a Year.* Rosenman was a housing expert who strongly favored public housing projects.

74. Advertisement for *Time* magazine, *Architectural Forum* 81 (July 1944): 168.

75. Advertisement for *Time* magazine, *American Builder and Building Age* 66 (August 1944): 15.

76. Advertisement for *Time* magazine, *American Builder and Building Age* 66 (October 1944): 55.

77. Robert Alexander was especially interested in this sort of conversion and appealed to Lockheed, where he worked as a production manager during the war, to develop itself into a house manufacturer and distributor. For more on Alexander, see the Robert Alexander Papers, Cornell University, Rare and Manuscript Collections, Collection 3087. Several pamphlets in the Revere series, including those by Alexander and Simon Breines, based the postwar house on airplane technology from the war.

78. Adding one more possible level of interpretation, the *Oxford English Dictionary* dates the first use of "straight" to mean heterosexual as 1941, casting the maleness of these double-talking architects further in doubt. The source is an American book, George W. Henry's *Sex Variants: A Study of Homosexual Patterns.*

79. Advertisement for *Time* magazine, *American Builder and Building Age* 66 (August 1944): 15.

80. Moses, "Mr. Moses Dissects the 'Long-Haired Planners,'" 16.

81. Ibid., 16.

82. Ibid.

83. Wurster, "Planning Is Politics . . . But Are Planners Politicians?" 68.

84. Mayer and Whittlesey, "Horse Sense Planning," Parts I and II.

85. Advertisement for *Time* magazine, *American Builder and Building Age* 67 (February 1945): 5.

86. Advertisement for *Time* magazine, *American Builder and Building Age* 67 (February 1945): 5; and *Pencil Points* (March 1945): 139.

87. Bushnell, "The War-in-Peace Plan," 343.

88. Advertisement for Janitrol, *Architectural Forum* 83 (November 1945): 45.

89. I am indebted to Hugo Meyer of Princeton University for the reading of the architect as Moses.

90. Lakoff and Johnson, *Metaphors We Live By,* 6.

Afterword

1. T. S. Eliot, *The Idea of a Christian Society.*

2. Eliot, 65.

3. Ibid.

4. Ibid.

Bibliography

"The 204X House." *American Builder and Building Age* 66 (1944): 26.

Abell, Walter. "Industry and Painting." *Magazine of Art* 39 (March 1946): 83–93, 114–18.

Abrams, Charles. *The City Is the Frontier.* New York: Harper & Row, 1965.

Action for Cities: A Guide for Community Planning. Chicago: Public Administration Service, 1943.

Adams, Michael C. C. *The Best War Ever: America and World War II, the American Moment.* Baltimore: Johns Hopkins University Press, 1994.

"Advertising during Two World Wars." *Printers' Ink* 203 (June 25, 1943): 16–17.

Alexander, Robert Evans. *Preview of a New Way of Life (Revere's Part in Better Living).* New York: Revere Copper and Brass, 1943.

Allegheny Conference on Community Development. *A Civic Clinic for Better Living.* Pittsburgh, Pa.: The Conference, 1945.

Allen, James Sloan. *The Romance of Commerce and Culture: Capitalism, Modernism, and the Chicago-Aspen Crusade for Cultural Reform.* Chicago: University of Chicago Press, 1983.

Architectural Forum. "A Flood of Checks Is Carrying 'Planning with You' Out of the Grass Roots." *Architectural Forum* 79 (October 1943): 63–64.

——. *Planning with You. Architectural Forum* 79 (August 1943): 63–80.

"Architecture and Government." *American Architect and Architecture* 150 (January 1937): 22–28.

Ascher, Charles S., and United States National Resources Planning Board. *Better Cities.* Washington, D.C.: U.S. Government Printing Office, 1942.

Augspurger, Michael. *An Economy of Abundant Beauty: Fortune Magazine and Depression America.* Ithaca, N.Y.: Cornell University Press, 2004.

Bacon, Edmund N. *The Design of Cities.* New York: Viking Press, 1967.

Baker, Geoffrey Harold, and Bruno Funaro. *Shopping Centers: Design and Operation.* New York: Reinhold, 1951.

Bannister, Turpin C., and Francis Rufus Bellamy. *The Architect at Mid-Century: Evolution and Achievement.* New York: Reinhold, 1954.

Baughman, James L. *Henry R. Luce and the Rise of the American News Media.* Boston: Twayne Publishers, 1987.

Beard, Charles Austin. *America Faces the Future.* Cambridge, Mass.: Riverside Press, 1933.

——, ed. *Toward Civilization.* London: Longmans Green, 1930.

Beard, Charles Austin, and George H. E. Smith. *The Future Comes.* New York: Macmillan, 1933.

"Bel Geddes Sees Wider Use of Prefabrication in Homes." *New York Times,* March 15, 1942, RE1.

Bender, Thomas. "The Erosion of Public Culture: Cities, Discourses, and Professional Disciplines." In *The Authority of Experts: Studies in History and Theory,* edited by Thomas L. Haskell, 84–106. Bloomington: Indiana University Press, 1984.

Beveridge, William Henry. *Social Insurance and Allied Services.* New York: Macmillan, 1942.

Bird, William L. *"Better Living": Advertising, Media and the New Vocabulary of Business Leadership, 1935–1955, Media Topographies.* Evanston, Ill.: Northwestern University Press, 1999.

Black, Russell Van Nest, and Mary Hedges Black. *Planning for the Small American City: An Outline of Principles and Procedure Especially Applicable to the City of Fifty Thousand or Less.* Chicago: Public Administration Service, 1944.

Blake, Peter. *Form Follows Fiasco: Why Modern Architecture Hasn't Worked.* Boston: Little, Brown, 1977.

"Blueprint for an Avenue: Plans of Manhattan's Sixth Avenue Association." *Time,* June 23, 1941, 70.

Blum, John Morton. *V Was for Victory: Politics and American Culture During World War II.* New York: Harcourt Brace Jovanovich, 1976.

Boester, Carl. *Home . . . For a Nation on Wings.* New York: Revere Copper and Brass, 1943.

Bogart, Michele Helene. *Artists, Advertising, and the Borders of Art.* Chicago: University of Chicago Press, 1995.

The Boston Contest of 1944, Prize Winning Programs. Boston: The Boston University, 1945.

Boyd, David Knickerbacker. "Public Relations." *Pencil Points* 22 (January 1941): 35–38.

Boyer, M. Christine. *Dreaming the Rational City: The Myth of American City Planning.* Cambridge, Mass.: MIT Press, 1983.

Bragdon, Claude Fayette. *Architecture and Democracy.* New York: Alfred A. Knopf, 1918.

Bressani, Martin. "The Life of Stone: Viollet-Le-Duc's Physiology of Architecture." *ANY* 14 (1996): 22–27.

Brinkley, Alan. *The End of Reform: New Deal Liberalism in Recession and War.* New York: Vintage Books, 1996.

Bristol, Katharine G. "The Pruitt-Igoe Myth." *Journal of Architectural Education* 44, no. 3 (May 1991): 163–71.

Brooks, J. Woolson. "These Dolorous Architects." *Journal of the American Institute of Architects* 1 (April 1944): 182–85.

Brownlee, David Bruce, and David G. De Long. *Louis I. Kahn: In the Realm of Architecture.* Los Angeles: Museum of Contemporary Art; New York: Rizzoli, 1991.

"Building's Post-War Pattern." *Architectural Forum* 75 (September 1941): 139–51.

Burnett, Hal. "Getting Down to Business." *Pencil Points* 22 (September 1941): 606–8.

Bushnell, Paul Palmer. "War-in-Peace Plan." *The American Scholar* 3 (Summer 1945): 342–50.

Caprio, F. S. "Postwar Planning in Mental Hygiene." *Medical Record* 157 (1944): 93–95.

Carter, E. J., and Ernö Goldfinger. *The County of London Plan.* West Drayton, Middlesex, Eng.: Penguin Books, 1945.

Cartwright, Nancy. *Otto Neurath: Philosophy between Science and Politics.* New York: Cambridge University Press, 1996.

Casillo, R. "Lewis Mumford and the Organicist Concept in Social Thought." *Journal of the History of Ideas* 53, no. 1 (1992): 91–116.

Chapin, F. S. "The Relation of Sociometry to Planning in an Expanding Social Universe." *Sociometry* 6 (1943): 234–40.

Chermayeff, Serge Ivan. "Four Viewpoints on Architecture and Planning. Planning: Urns or Urbanism?" *New Pencil Points* 24 (February 1943): 72–77.

Churchill, Henry Stern. *The City Is the People.* New York: Reynal & Hitchcock, 1945.

City Plan. Salt Lake City: The City, 1943.

Clawson, Marion. *New Deal Planning: The National Resources Planning Board.* Baltimore: Johns Hopkins University Press, 1981.

Cogdell, Christina. "The Futurama Recontextualized: Norman Bel Geddes's Eugenic 'World of Tomorrow.'" *American Quarterly* 52, no. 2 (June 2000): 193–245.

Cohen, Jeff A. "Building a Discipline: Early Institutional Settings for Architectural Education in Philadelphia, 1804–1890." *Journal of the Society of Architectural Historians* 53 (June 1994): 139–83.

Cohen, Lizabeth. *A Consumer's Republic: The Politics of Mass Consumption in Postwar America.* 1st Vintage Books ed. New York: Vintage Books, 2004.

Colean, Miles. "Parturition or Physics?" *Architectural Forum* 79 (September 1943): 34.

Comerio, Mary C. "The Experiment That Failed." *Architecture Plus* 1 (October 1973): 17–18.

———. "Pruitt Igoe and Other Stories." *Journal of Architectural Education* 34, no. 4 (Summer 1981): 26–31.

———. "The Tragedy of Pruitt-Igoe." *Time* (October 27, 1971): 38.

Committee on Banking, Finance, and Urban Affairs. *How Cities Can Grow Old Gracefully.* Washington: U.S. Government Printing Office, 1977.

Cook, Daniel W. *The New Urban Frontier: New Metropolises for America. Design for Dream Cities, 'Cosmopolitas.'* Berkeley: University of California Press, 1964.

Crawford, Margaret. "Daily Life on the Home Front: Women, Blacks, and the Struggle for Public Housing." In *World War II and the American Dream,* edited by Donald Albrecht, 90–143. Washington, D.C., Cambridge, Mass.: National Building Museum; MIT Press, 1995.

Creighton, Thomas H. *Planning to Build.* Garden City, N.Y.: Doubleday, Doran & Co., 1945.

"Crow Island School, Winnetka, Ill.: Eliel and Eero Saarinen, Perkins, Wheeler and Will, Architects." *Architectural Forum* 75 (August 1941): 79–92.

Davison, Ronald C. *Social Security: The Story of British Social Progress and the Beveridge Plan.* London: G. G. Harrap, 1943.

Dayton Department of Planning. *Planning in the Mature City—Dayton, Ohio.* Dayton: Dayton Department of Planning, 1979.

"Detroiters in Riot on Negro Project." *New York Times,* March 1, 1942, 40.

Director, Aaron. Review of *The Road to Serfdom. The American Economic Review* 35, no. 1 (March 1945): 173–75.

Doob, Leonard William. *The Plans of Men.* New Haven: Yale University Press, 1940.

"Editorial: Program for Progress." *The Antioch Review* 3 (June 1943): 147–52.

Eliasberg, W. G. "Facing Post-War Germany." *Journal of Social Psychology* 20, no. 2 (November 1944): 301–11.

Eliot, T. S. *The Idea of a Christian Society.* London: Faber & Faber, 1939.

Erikson, Erik H. *A Way of Looking at Things: Selected Papers from 1930 to 1980.* Edited by Stephen Schlein. 1st ed. New York: Norton, 1987.

Esperdy, Gabrielle. *Modernizing Main Street: Architecture and Consumer Culture in the New Deal.* Chicago: University of Chicago Press, 2008.

"The Experiment That Failed." *Architecture Plus* 1, no. 9 (October 1973): 17–18.

"Faith in Advertising Pays Rich Dividends." *Printers' Ink* 197 (August 22, 1941): 82–94.

Finer, Herman. *Road to Reaction.* Boston: Little, Brown, 1945.

Fisher, D. K. Este, Jr. *Bulletin of the AIA* 18 (December 30, 1942): unpaginated.

Forshaw, J. H., and P. Abercombie. *County of London Plan.* London: Macmillan, 1943.

Forty, Adrian. *Words and Buildings: A Vocabulary of Modern Architecture.* New York: Thames & Hudson, 2000.

Fox, Frank W. *Madison Avenue Goes to War: The Strange Military Career of American Advertising, 1941–45.* Charles E. Merrill Monograph Series in the Humanities and Social Sciences. Vol. 4, No.1. Provo, Utah: Brigham Young University Press, 1975.

Fox, Richard Wightman, and T. J. Jackson Lears. *The Culture of Consumption: Critical Essays in American History, 1880–1980.* 1st ed. New York: Pantheon Books, 1983.

——. *The Power of Culture: Critical Essays in American History.* Chicago: University of Chicago Press, 1993.

Friedman, Milton. "Introduction." In *The Road to Serfdom,* by Friedrich A. von Hayek, ix–xx. Chicago: University of Chicago Press, 1994.

Friedrich, Carl J. Review of *The Road to Serfdom. The American Political Science Review* 39, no. 3 (June 1945): 575–79.

Fulmer, Otis Kline. *Greenbelt.* Washington, D.C.: American Council on Public Affairs, 1941.

——. "Toledo Tomorrow." In *Proceedings of the Twenty-Third Annual Convention.* American Institute of Steel Construction, Inc., 1945.

Funigiello, Philip J. *The Challenge to Urban Liberalism: Federal–City Relations during World War II.* 1st ed. Knoxville: University of Tennessee Press, 1978.

Fussell, Paul. *Wartime: Understanding and Behavior in the Second World War.* New York: Oxford University Press, 1989.

Galbraith, John Kenneth. "Transition to Peace: Business in A.D. 194Q." *Fortune* 29 (January 1944): 84–87.

Gallup, George Horace. *The Gallup Poll: Public Opinion, 1935–1971.* 1st ed. Vol. 1. New York: Random House, 1972.

Geddes, Norman Bel. *Toledo Tomorrow.* Toledo, Oh.: Toledo Blade, 1945.

Geddes, Patrick. *Cities in Evolution: An Introduction to the Town Planning Movement and to the Study of Civics.* London,: Williams & Norgate, 1915.

"Genesis of the NRPB Demonstrations." *Pencil Points* 24 (August 1943): 32–33.

Giedion, Sigfried. *A Decade of New Architecture.* Zürich: Girsberger, 1951.

——. "The Need for New Monumentality." In *New Architecture and City Planning: A Symposium,* edited by Paul Zucker, 549–68. New York: Philosophical Library, 1944.

——. *Space, Time and Architecture: The Growth of a New Tradition.* Cambridge: Harvard University Press, 1941.

Gilbert, Richard Vincent. *An Economic Program for American Democracy.* New York: Vanguard Press, 1938.

Gillette, Howard, Jr. "The Evolution of the Planned Shopping Center in Suburb and City." *Journal of the American Planning Association* 51, no. 4 (Autumn 1985): 449–60.

Gold, John Robert. *The Experience of Modernism: Modern Architects and the Future City, 1928–53.* 1st ed. London: E & FN Spon, 1997.

Graham, Otis L. *Toward a Planned Society: From Roosevelt to Nixon.* New York: Oxford University Press, 1976.

Greer, Guy. "After the Plans, What?" *Fortune* 30 (July 1944): 168–72.

——. "Applied Plans as Seen in Syracuse." *American Planning and Civic Annual* (1944): 156–62.

——. "City Planning: Battle of the Approach." *Fortune* 28 (November 1943): 164–68, 183, 224.

——. "City Replanning and Rebuilding." *Journal of Land and Public Utility Economics* 18 (August 1942): 284–92.

——. "The Future of Urban Real Estate," *Mortgage Bankers Association of America* (1943): 1–2.

——. "Getting Ready for Federal Aid in Urban Redevelopment: The Hansen-Greer Plan." *American City* 58 (May 1943): 47–49.

——. "Layman to Architect – a Sermon." *Journal of the American Institute of Architects* 7 (June 1947): 260–63.

——. "Must Our Cities Continue to Decay?" In *Proceedings of Annual Meetings,* National Association of Housing Officials, 66–70. 1942.

——. "New Start for the Cities." *Fortune* 30 (September 1944): 152–55.

——. "A Plan for Post-War Urban Rebuilding." *Real Estate Record and Builders Guide,* July 11, 1942, 2–3.

——. "A Plan for Post-War Urban Rebuilding." *Real Estate Record and Builders Guide,* July 18, 1942, 6–7, 19.

——. "So You're Going to Plan a City." *Fortune* 29 (January 1944): 122–25.

——, ed. *The Problem of the Cities and Towns. Report of the Conference on Urbanism, Harvard University, March 5–6, 1942.* Cambridge, Mass., 1942.

——. *The Ruhr-Lorraine Industrial Problem: A Study of the Economic Inter-Dependence of the Two Regions and Their Relation to the Reparation Question.* New York: Macmillan, 1925.

——. *Your City Tomorrow.* New York: Macmillan, 1947.

Greer, Guy, and Alvin Harvey Hansen. *Urban Redevelopment and Housing. Planning Pamphlets No. 10.* Washington: National Planning Association, 1941.

Griffith, Robert. "The Selling of America: The Advertising Council and American Politics, 1942–1960." *Business History Review* 57 (Autumn 1983): 388–412.

Gropius, Walter. *Rebuilding Our Communities.* Chicago: P. Theobald, 1945.

Gropius, Walter, and Martin Wagner. "The New City Pattern for the People and by the People." In *The Problem of the Cities and Towns. Report of the Conference on Urbanism, Harvard University, March 5–6, 1942,* edited by Guy Greer, 95–116. Cambridge, Mass., 1942.

——. "A Program for City Reconstruction." *Architectural Forum* 79 (July 1943): 75–86.

Gruen, Victor. *The Heart of Our Cities: The Urban Crisis: Diagnosis and Cure.* New York: Simon & Schuster, 1964.

Guilbaut, Serge. *How New York Stole the Idea of Modern Art: Abstract Expressionism, Freedom, and the Cold War.* Chicago: University of Chicago Press, 1983.

"Gypsum Men Discredit 'Dream House.' " *Bulletin of the Michigan Society of Architects* 4 (August 22, 1945).

Hamby, William. "More Labor-Saving Devices Predicted for Future Homes." *New York Times,* March 29, 1942, RE1.

Hamlin, Talbot. "Can We Plan Action in Crisis, or Are We Doomed to Muddle Through?" *Pencil Points* 22 (December 1941): 747–50.

——. "A Public Opinion for Planning." *The Antioch Review* 3 (June 1943): 182–90.

Hansen, Alvin Harvey. *Fiscal Policy and Business Cycles.* New York: W.W. Norton, 1941.

——. Foreword to *The Problem of Cities and Towns: Report of the Conference on Urbanism, March 5–6, 1942,* ix–xi. Cambridge, Mass., 1942.

——. "Mr. Keynes on Underemployment Equilibrium." *The Journal of Political Economy* 44, no. 5 (October 1936): 667–86.

——. "Social Planning for Tomorrow." In *The United States after the War, The Cornell University Summer Session Lectures,* 32–33. Ithaca, N.Y.: Cornell University Press, 1945.

——. "Some Notes on Terborgh's 'The Bogey of Economic Maturity.' " *The Review of Economic Statistics* 28 (February 1946): 13–17.

Hansen, Alvin Harvey, and Guy Greer. "Toward Full Use of Our Resources." *Fortune* 26 (November 1942): 130–33.

——. "The Federal Debt and the Future." *Harper's Magazine* 184 (April 1942): 489–500.

Hanten, Edward W., Mark J. Kasoff, and F. Stevens Redburn. *New Directions for the Mature Metropolis: Policies and Strategies for Change.* Cambridge, Mass.: Schenkman, 1980.

Harris, Jonathan Gil. *Foreign Bodies and the Body Politic: Discourses of Social Pathology in Early Modern England.* Cambridge Studies in Renaissance Literature and Culture, 25. Cambridge, United Kingdom: Cambridge University Press, 1998.

Hartman, George E., and Jan Cigliano, eds. *Pencil Points Reader: A Journal for the Drafting Room, 1920–1943.* New York: Princeton Architectural Press, 2004.

Hartmann, Susan M. *The Home Front and Beyond: American Women in the 1940s.* Boston: Twayne Publishers, 1982.

Haskell, Thomas L., ed. *The Authority of Experts: Studies in History and Theory.* Bloomington: Indiana University Press, 1984.

Hayek, Friedrich A. von. *The Road to Serfdom.* Chicago: University of Chicago Press, 1944.

"Hearings before the Temporary Economic Committee." *Savings and Investment, Part 9* (1939): 3503.

Henry, George W. *Sex Variants: A Study of Homosexual Patterns.* New York: P.B. Hoeber, 1941.

Herrey, Erna M. J., Hermann Herrey, and Constantin Pertzoff. "An Organic Theory of City Planning." *Architectural Forum* 80 (April 1944): 133–40.

Hines, Thomas S. "Housing, Baseball, and Creeping Socialism: The Battle of Chavez Ravine, Los Angeles, 1949–1959" *Journal of Urban History* 8, no. 2 (February 1982): 123–43.

——. *Richard Neutra and the Search for Modern Architecture: A Biography and History.* New York: Oxford University Press, 1982.

Holden, Thomas S. *The Great Illusion: An Inexhaustible Public Purse.* Economic Policy Division Series. New York: National Association of Manufacturers, 1949.

——. "Who's Afraid of Prosperity?" *Architectural Record* 95 (April 1944): 82–83.

Honey, Maureen. *Creating Rosie the Riveter: Class, Gender, and Propaganda during World War II.* Amherst: University of Massachusetts Press, 1984.

"House Omnibus." *Architectural Forum* 82 (April 1945): 89–145.

"The House Planned for Peace." *Ladies' Home Journal* 61 (1944): 54–55.

"Housing Problem Confronts Detroit." *New York Times,* February 7, 1942, 30.

Hudnut, Joseph. "Architecture after the Peace." *Magazine of Art* 36 (April 1943): 122–27.

——. "The Political Art of Planning." *Architectural Record* 94 (October 1943): 44–48. Reprinted in *Architecture and the Spirit of Man* (Cambridge: Harvard University Press, 1949), 185–95.

Huizinga, Johan. *Homo Ludens: A Study of the Play Element in Culture.* New York: Roy Publishers, 1950. Originally published in Dutch in 1938.

Israeli, N. "Originality in Planning." *Psychiatry: Journal of the Study of Interpersonal Processes* 8 (1945): 139–45.

——. "The Psychology of Planning." *Psychological Record* 4 (1941): 254–56.

Jacobs, Jane. *The Death and Life of Great American Cities.* New York: Random House, 1961.

Justement, Louis. *New Cities for Old: City Building in Terms of Space, Time, and Money.* New York: McGraw-Hill, 1946.

Kennedy, David M. *Freedom from Fear: The American People in Depression and War, 1929–1945.* New York: Oxford University Press, 1999.

Keyserling, Leon H. "Deficiencies of Past Programs and Nature of New Needs." In *Saving American Capitalism: A Liberal Economic Program,* edited by Seymour Edwin Harris, 81–94. New York,: A.A. Knopf, 1948.

Kinnard, William N., ed. *The New England Region: Problems of a Mature Economy. Papers and Proceedings of a Conference Held at the University of Connecticut, November 18, 1967.* Storrs, Conn.: Center for Real Estate and Urban Economic Studies, 1968.

Klein, Kerwin Lee. *Frontiers of Historical Imagination: Narrating the European Conquest of Native America, 1890–1990.* Berkeley: University of California Press, 1997.

Koppes, Clayton R., and Gregory D. Black. *Hollywood Goes to War: How Politics, Profits, and Propaganda Shaped World War II Movies.* Berkeley: University of California Press, 1990.

Krueckeberg, Donald A., ed. *The American Planner: Biographies and Recollections.* New York: Methuen, 1983.

La France, Ernest. "Rebirth of an Avenue." *New York Times Magazine* (March 19, 1939): 11, 19.

Lakoff, George, and Mark Johnson. *Metaphors We Live By.* Chicago: University of Chicago Press, 1980.

Le Corbusier. *The City of Tomorrow and Its Planning.* Translated by Frederick Etchells. New York: Payson & Clarke, 1929.

——. *Towards a New Architecture.* New York: Dover Publications, 1986.

Le Corbusier and H. Allen Brooks. *Le Corbusier Archive.* New York; Paris: Garland Publishing, 1982.

Le Duc, Carlos. "Proposed Building." *Architectural Record* 83 (February 1938): 46–47.

Lears, T. J. Jackson. *Fables of Abundance: A Cultural History of Advertising in America.* New York: Basic Books, 1994.

Ledoux, Claude Nicolas. *L'architecture considérée sous le rapport de l'art des Moeurs et de la Législation.* Paris: L'imprimerie de H.-L. Perroneau, 1804. Reprinted by Princeton Architectural Press, 1983.

Lee, Antoinette J. *Architects to the Nation: The Rise and Decline of the Supervising Architect's Office.* New York: Oxford University Press, 2000.

Leipziger-Pearce, Hugo. *The Architectonic City in the Americas: Significant Forms, Origins, and Prospects.* Austin: University of Texas Press, 1944.

Lekachman, Robert. *The Age of Keynes: A Biographical Study.* London: Pelican Books, 1969.

Lescaze, William. *A Citizens Country Club or Leisure Center.* New York: Revere Copper and Brass, 1943.

——. *Uplifting the Downtrodden.* New York: Revere Copper and Brass, 1943.

Leuchtenburg, William Edward. "The New Deal and the Analogue of War." In *The FDR Years: On Roosevelt and His Legacy,* 35–75. New York: Columbia University Press, 1995.

Leven, Charles L., ed. *The Mature Metropolis.* Lexington, Mass.: Lexington Books, 1978.

Longstreth, Richard W. *City Center to Regional Mall: Architecture, the Automobile, and Retailing in Los Angeles, 1920–1950.* Cambridge, Mass.: MIT Press, 1997.

"Magazine Advertising." *Printers' Ink* (July 25, 1941): 68–72.

Maginnis, Charles D. "Musings on the Morrow." *Journal of the American Institute of Architects* 1 (January 1944): 10–13.

Mamiya, Christin J. *Pop Art and Consumer Culture: American Super Market.* 1st ed. American Studies Series. Austin: University of Texas Press, 1992.

Marberry, R. M. "Leg Art?" [Letter to the Editor]. *Architectural Forum* 79 (October 1943): 33.

Marchand, Roland. *Advertising the American Dream: Making Way for Modernity, 1920–1940.* Berkeley: University of California Press, 1985.

Mayer, Albert, and Julian Whittlesey. "Horse Sense Planning (Part I)." *Architectural Forum* 79 (November 1943): 58–63.

——. "Horse Sense Planning (Part II)." *Architectural Forum* 80 (January 1944): 69–80.

McGovern, Charles. "Sold American: Inventing the Consumer, 1890–1940." PhD diss., Harvard University, 1993.

McLaughlin, Glenn E., and Ralph J. Watkins. "The Problem of Industrial Growth in a Mature Economy." *The American Economic Review* 29, no. 1, Supplement, Papers and Proceedings of the 51st Annual Meeting of the American Economic Association (March 1939): 1–14.

Mennel, Timothy. "'Miracle House Hoop-La': Corporate Rhetoric and the Construction of the Postwar American House." *Journal of the Society of Architectural Historians* 64, no. 3 (September 2005): 340–61.

Merriam, Charles. "Book Review and Notices." *The American Political Science Review* 40 (February 1946): 133–36.

Merrifield, C. "Morale and the Planning Society." *Journal of Educational Sociology* 15 (1942): 421–29.

Mershon, Sherie R. "Corporate Social Responsibility and Urban Revitalization: The Allegheny Conference on Community Development, 1943–1968." PhD diss., Carnegie Mellon University, 2000.

Meyer, Agnes Elizabeth Ernst. *Journey through Chaos.* New York: Harcourt, Brace & Co., 1944.

Modley, Rudolf. "Pictographs Today and Tomorrow." *Public Opinion Quarterly* 2 (October 1938): 659–64.

"More Daydreams." *American Builder and Building Age* 66 (February 1944): 26.

Moreno, J. L., and Helen H. Jennings. *Who Shall Survive? A New Approach to the Problem of Human Inter-relations, Nervous and Mental Disease Monograph Series, No. 58.* Washington, D.C.: Nervous and Mental Disease Publishing Co., 1934.

Moses, Robert. "Mr. Moses Dissects the 'Long-Haired Planners.'" *New York Times Magazine* (June 25, 1944): 16–17, 38–39.

Mumford, Eric Paul. *The CIAM Discourse on Urbanism, 1928–1960.* Cambridge, Mass.: MIT Press, 2000.

Mumford, Lewis. *City Development: Studies in Disintegration and Renewal.* New York: Harcourt, Brace & Co., 1945.

———. "Mass-Production and the Modern House." *Architectural Record* 67 (January 1930): 13–20.

———. "The Neotechnic Phase." In *Technics and Civilization,* 212–67. New York: Harcourt, Brace & Co., 1934.

———. "The Sky Line: Cloud over Sixth Avenue: Home on the Park." *New Yorker* 78 (December 21, 1940): 78–80.

———. *The Social Foundations of Post-War Building.* London: Faber & Faber, 1943.

Musselman, G. Paul. *The Church on the Urban Frontier.* Greenwich, Conn.: Seabury Press, 1960.

"Must Our Cities Continue to Decay?" In *Proceedings of Annual Meetings,* 66–70. National Association of Housing Officials, 1942.

Myers, Howard. "Was the Architect of Tomorrow Here Yesterday?" *Journal of the American Institute of Architects* 2 (July 1944): 13–17.

Nast, Heidi J., and Steve Pile, eds. *Places through the Body.* London: Routledge, 1998.

National Planning Board. *Final Report, 1933–34.* Washington, D.C.: U.S. Government Printing Office, 1934.

National Resources Planning Board. *National Resources Development Report for 1943, Part 1, Post-War Plan and Program.* Washington D.C.: U.S. Government Printing Office, 1943.

Neider, Charles. "Advertise for Victory." *The Nation* 156 (May 29, 1943): 770–72.

Nelson, George. *Your Children Could Romp Here While You Shop.* New York: Revere Copper and Brass, 1943.

Nelson, Paul. "Home Owner of the Future Held Likely to Give More Study to Interior Plan." *New York Times* (April 5, 1942): X, 1: 5.

———. *Researching for a New Standard of Living.* New York: Revere Copper and Brass, 1942.

Nettels, Curtis. "Frederick Jackson Turner and the New Deal." *Wisconsin Magazine of History* 17, no. 3 (March 1934): 257–65.

Neurath, Otto. "Visual Representation of Architectural Problems." *Architectural Record* 82 (July 1937): 56–61.

Neutra, Richard Joseph. *Survival through Design.* New York: Oxford University Press, 1954.

"New Building for 194X." *Architectural Forum* 78 (May 1943): entire issue.

A New Era of Building Is Only Marking Time. Erie, Pa.: J.A. Zurn Mfg. Co., 1943.

New York State Financial Control Board. *The Mature City Model: An Econometric Model for New York City in the 1980s.* New York: The Board, 1981.

Noble, David. "The Reconstruction of Progress: Charles Beard, Richard Hofstadter, and Postwar Historical Thought." In *Recasting America: Culture and Politics in the Age of Cold War,* edited by Lary May, 61–75. Chicago: University of Chicago Press, 1989.

"Organization of the City: From Corpus Christi Newspapers." *Pencil Points* 24 (August 1943): 34–50.

Pai, Hyungmin. *The Portfolio and the Diagram: Architecture, Discourse, and Modernity in America.* Cambridge, Mass.: MIT Press, 2002.

Park, Robert E. "Human Ecology." *American Journal of Sociology* 42 (July 1936): 1–15.

Pei, I. M. "Standardized Propaganda Units for the Chinese Government." *Task* 1, no. 2 (1942): 13–16.

Perkins, Lawrence B. *After Total War Can Come Total Living.* New York: Revere Copper and Brass, 1942.

"A Personal Invitation to Every Reader of the Architectural Forum." *Architectural Forum* 79 (August 1943): 63.

Peterson, Jon A. *The Birth of City Planning in the United States, 1840–1917, Creating the North American Landscape.* Baltimore: Johns Hopkins University Press, 2003.

"A Plan for Harlem's Redevelopment," *Architectural Forum* 80 (April 1944): 145–52.

Planned Parenthood Federation of America. *Planned Parenthood: Its Contribution to Family, Community, and Nation.* New York: Planned Parenthood Federation of America, 1944.

"Planning with You." *Architectural Forum* 81 (August 1944): 79–81.

Plunz, Richard. *A History of Housing in New York City: Dwelling Type and Social Change in the American Metropolis.* New York: Columbia University Press, 1989.

Polanyi, Karl. *The Great Transformation.* New York: Farrar & Rinehart, 1944.

Polenberg, Richard. *America at War: The Home Front, 1941–1945.* Englewood Cliffs, N.J.,: Prentice-Hall, 1968.

———. *War and Society: The United States, 1941–1945.* Philadelphia: Lippincott, 1972.

"A Portfolio of Work by Edward D. Stone." *Architectural Forum* 75 (July 1941): 13–30.

"Post-War Delusions." *American Builder and Building Age* 65 (April 1943): 18.

"The Prefabricated House." *Architectural Forum* 78 (January 1943): 53–64.

Rand, Ayn. *The Fountainhead.* Indianapolis: Bobbs-Merrill, 1943.

Ranis, Gustav, ed. *Taiwan: From Developing to Mature Economy.* Boulder, Colo.: Westview Press, 1992.

Raskin, Eugene. "Out on a Limb: Horoscope for Architects after the War." *Pencil Points* 22 (December 1941): 759.

Reagan, Patrick D. *Designing a New America: The Origins of New Deal Planning, 1890–1943, Political Development of the American Nation.* Amherst: University of Massachusetts Press, 1999.

Reed, Peter Shedd. "Toward Form: Louis I. Kahn's Urban Designs for Philadelphia, 1939–1962." PhD diss., University of Pennsylvania, 1989.

Reid, Kenneth. "Here, There, This and That." *Pencil Points* 22 (January 1941): 17.

———. "New Beginnings." *Pencil Points* 23 (May 1942): 242.

———. "Plan." *Pencil Points* 24 (January 1943): facing 18.

"Report of a Conference on Germany after the War." *American Journal of Mental Deficiency* 50 (1945): 149–200.

Repplier, Theodore S. "Advertising Dons Long Pants." *Public Opinion Quarterly* 9, no. 3 (Fall 1945): 269–78.

Riley, Terence, and Joseph Abram, eds. *The Filter of Reason: Work of Paul Nelson.* New York: Rizzoli, 1990.

Rodgers, Daniel T. *Atlantic Crossings: Social Politics in a Progressive Age.* Cambridge, Mass.: Belknap Press of Harvard University Press, 1998.

Roll, Eric. Review of *The Road to Serfdom. The American Economic Review* 35, no. 1 (March 1945): 176–80.

Rosenfield, Isadore. "Planning for Shock Treatment." *Progressive Architecture* (November 1946): 88.

Rosenman, Dorothy Reuben. *A Million Homes a Year.* New York: Harcourt, Brace & Co., 1945.

Rosenof, Theodore. *Economics in the Long Run: New Deal Theorists and Their Legacies, 1933–1993.* Chapel Hill: University of North Carolina Press, 1997.

Rovira i Gimeno, Josep M., ed. *Sert: Half a Century of Architecture: 1928–1979, A Complete Work.* Barcelona: Fundació Joan Miró, 2005.

Saarinen, Eliel. *The City, Its Growth, Its Decay, Its Future.* New York: Reinhold, 1943. Reprint, Cambridge, Mass: MIT Press, 1965.

Salant, Walter S. "Alvin Hansen and the Fiscal Policy Seminar." *Quarterly Journal of Economics* 90, no. 1 (February 1976): 14–23.

Sanders, Walter B. *Apartment Homes for Tomorrow's Better Living.* New York: Revere Copper and Brass, 1942.

"A Satellite Town for the Detroit Area." *Architectural Forum* 79 (October 1943): 91–99.

Schaffer, Marvin R. "Tacoma Looks Forward." *American City* 58 (September 1943): 53–55.

Schapiro, Meyer. "Nature of Abstract Art." *Marxist Quarterly* 1 (January–March 1931): 77–98.

Schildt, Gèoran. *Alvar Aalto, the Mature Years.* New York: Rizzoli, 1991.

Schindler, R. M. "The Architect – Postwar-Post Everybody." *Pencil Points* 25 (October 1944): 16, 18.

———. "The Architect – Postwar-Post Everybody." *Pencil Points* 25 (November 1944): 12, 14, 16.

Schumpeter, Joseph A. Review of *The Road to Serfdom. The Journal of Political Economy* 54, no. 3 (June 1946): 269–70.

Sert, José Luis. *Can Our Cities Survive? An ABC of Urban Problems, Their Analysis, Their Solutions.* Cambridge: Harvard University Press, 1942.

Seward, Georgene J. "Sex Roles in Postwar Planning." *Journal of Social Psychology* 19 (1944): 163–85.

Shanken, Andrew M. "Architectural Competitions and Bureaucracy, 1934–1945." *Architectural Research Quarterly* 3, no. 1 (1999): 43–55.

——. "Better Living: Toward a Cultural History of a Business Slogan." *Enterprise and Society* 7, no. 3 (2006): 485–519.

——. "Between Brotherhood and Bureaucracy: Joseph Hudnut, Louis I. Kahn and the American Society of Planners and Architects." *Planning Perspectives* 20, no. 2 (April 2005): 147–75.

——. "From the Gospel of Efficiency to Modernism: A History of Sweet's Catalog, 1906–1947." *Design Issues* 21, no. 2 (Spring 2005): 28–47.

——. "Planning Memory: Living Memorials in the United States during World War II." *Art Bulletin* 84, no. 1 (March 2002): 130–47.

——. "The Uncharted Kahn: The Visuality of Planning and Promotion in the 1930s and 1940s." *Art Bulletin* 88 (June 2006): 310–27.

Shreve, R. H. "The Outlook of the Profession." *Octagon* 14 (January 1942): 3–4.

Sitte, Camillo. *The Art of Building Cities: City Building According to Its Artistic Fundamentals.* Translated by Charles T. Stewart. New York: Reinhold, 1945.

"Sixth Avenue to Help Hemisphere Trade." *New York Times,* June 12, 1941, 19:5.

Slotkin, Richard. *Gunfighter Nation: The Myth of the Frontier in Twentieth-Century America.* New York: Atheneum, 1992.

"Slum Surgery in St. Louis." *Architectural Forum* 94 (April 1951): 128–36.

Sontag, Susan. *Illness as Metaphor.* New York: Farrar, Straus & Giroux, 1978.

Soule, George Henry. *A Planned Society.* New York: Macmillan, 1932.

Stein, Clarence S. "Dinosaur Cities." *Survey Graphic* 54 (May 1, 1925): 134–38.

——. *The Writings of Clarence S. Stein: Architect of the Planned Community.* Edited by Kermit C. Parsons. Baltimore: Johns Hopkins University Press, 1998.

Stern, Robert A. M., Gregory Gilmartin, and Thomas Mellins. *New York 1930: Architecture and Urbanism between the Two World Wars.* New York: Rizzoli, 1987.

Stonorov, Oscar G., and Louis I. Kahn. *Why City Planning Is Your Responsibility.* New York: Revere Copper & Brass, 1943.

——. *You and Your Neighborhood: A Primer for Neighborhood Planning.* New York: Revere Copper and Brass, 1944.

"Store Designers Don't Suffer from Traditional Fixations, Thank God." *Pencil Points* 25 (August 1944): 40–41.

"Storm over New Housing in Detroit." *New York Times,* March 15, 1942, E7.

Strasser, Susan, Charles McGovern, and Matthias Judt, eds. *Getting and Spending: European and American Consumer Societies in the Twentieth Century.* Publications of the German Historical Institute. Cambridge, England: Cambridge University Press, 1998.

Swanson, Ernst Werner, and Emerson Peter Schmidt. *Economic Stagnation or Progress: A Critique of Recent Doctrines on the Mature Economy, Oversavings, and Deficit Spending.* 1st ed. New York: McGraw-Hill, 1946.

"Syracuse Tackles Its Future." *Fortune* 27 (May 1943): 120–23.

Teague, Walter Dorwin. *New Homes for Better Living.* New York: Revere Copper and Brass, 1942.

Terborgh, George Willard. *The Bogey of Economic Maturity.* Chicago: Machinery and Allied Products Institute, 1945.

"These Advertisers, Now Great, Began in 1915–1918." *Printers' Ink* 197 (August 22, 1941): 97–103.

Tobey, Ronald C. *Technology as Freedom: The New Deal and the Electrical Modernization of the American Home.* Berkeley: University of California Press, 1996.

"The Tragedy of Pruitt-Igoe." *Time* (December 27, 1971): 38.

Turner, Frederick Jackson. "The Significance of the Frontier in American History." State Historical Society of Wisconsin, Proceedings, 1893. Reprinted in *The Early Writings of Frederick Jackson Turner,* ed. Fulmer Mood (Madison: University of Wisconsin Press, 1938), 183–232.

United States Gypsum Company. *Let's Be Sensible about Post-War Building: A Practical Forecast of Residential Building Immediately Following the End of the War.* Chicago: United States Gypsum Company, 1944 (unpaginated).

———. *Pak of Ideas.* Chicago: U.S. Gypsum Company, 1944.

———. *Popular Home's Ideas Galore: How to Build . . . Buy . . . Modernize and Decorate.* Chicago: United States Gypsum Company, 1946.

U.S. Bureau of the Census. Sixteenth Census of the United States: 1940. Washington, D.C.: U.S. Government Printing Office, 1940.

U.S. Housing Authority. *What the Housing Act Can Do for Your City.* Washington, D.C.: U.S. Government Printing Office, 1938.

Walker, A. C., and R. S. Colley. *Sketch Plan for the Development of Metropolitan Corpus Christi.* Corpus Christi: Clyde Rainey Printing Co., 1943.

Walker, Ralph. "Planning for Peace." *New Pencil Points* 23 (June 1942): 40–43.

Wallace, Henry Agard. *New Frontiers.* New York: Reynal & Hitchcock, 1934.

Walsh, J. Raymond. "Action for Postwar Planning." *The Antioch Review* 3 (June 1943): 153–61.

Westbrook, Robert B. "Fighting for the American Family." In *The Power of Culture: Critical Essays in American History,* edited by Richard Wightman Fox and T. J. Jackson Lears, 195–222. Chicago: University of Chicago Press, 1993.

"What's in a Name?" *Pencil Points* 23 (October 1942): 32.

Williams-Ellis, Clough. *England and the Octopus.* New ed. Great Britain: Robert MacLehose & Co., 1975.

Wills, Royal Barry. Cartoon of "Architectural Man." *Pencil Points* 23 (June 1942): 8.

Winkler, Allan M. *Home Front U.S.A.: America During World War II.* Arlington Heights, Ill.: H. Davidson, 1986.

———. *The Politics of Propaganda: The Office of War Information, 1942–1945.* New Haven, Conn.: Yale University Press, 1978.

Wolman, S. "Sociometric Planning for a New Community." *Sociometry* 1 (1937): 220–54.

Woods, Mary N. *From Craft to Profession: The Practice of Architecture in Nineteenth-Century America.* Berkeley: University of California Press, 1999.

Wright, Frank Lloyd. "The New Frontier: Broadacre City." *Frank Lloyd Wright Collected Writings. Vol. 4. 1939–1949,* edited by Bruce Brooks Pfeiffer, pp. 45–66. New York: Rizzoli, 1994.

———. *Frank Lloyd Wright Collected Writings. Vol. 4. 1939–1949,* edited by Bruce Brooks Pfeiffer, New York: Rizzoli, 1994.

Wright, Henry N. "Bathrooms for the Future." *Parents Magazine* 18 (November 1943): 48–49, 99–101.

Wurster, Catherine Bauer. "Planning Is Politics . . . But Are Planners Politicians?" *Pencil Points* 25 (March 1944): 66–70.

Zucker, Paul, ed. *New Architecture and City Planning: A Symposium.* New York: Philosophical Library, 1944.

———. "The Role of Architecture in Future Civilization." *Journal of Aesthetics and Art Criticism* 3, no. 9/10 (1944): 30–38.

Archives

Alexander, Robert, Papers. Cornell University.

Archives of the American Institute of Architects.

Ferriss, Hugh, Collection. Avery Drawings and Archives. Columbia University.

Hansen, Alvin Harvey, Papers. Harvard University Archives.

Haskell, Douglas Putnam, Papers. Avery Drawings and Archives. Columbia University.

Isaacs, Reginald, Papers. Archives of American Art. Smithsonian Institution.

Kahn, Louis I., Archives. University of Pennsylvania.

Lescaze, William, Papers. Syracuse University Archives.

Maginnis, Charles D., Papers. Archives of American Art. Smithsonian Institution.

Mumford, Lewis, Papers. University of Pennsylvania.

Neutra, Richard, Papers. Syracuse University Archives.

Papadaki, Stamo, Papers. Princeton University.

Smith, Sophia, Collection. Smith College.

Stephen, J. Davidson, Papers. Archives of American Art. Smithsonian Institution.

Warshaw Collection of the Archives Center, Advertising Industry. Smithsonian Institution.

Index

Created by Eileen Quam

Andrew M. Shanken is assistant professor of architectural history at the University of California, Berkeley. His work has appeared in numerous publications, including *Art Bulletin, Design Issues, Landscape, Places,* and *Planning Perspectives.*